CRITICAL A
ENCOUNTERS WITH

"Each of the more than two-dozen well-written tales in this dazzling collection is a brightly colored stone in a mosaic revealing, warts and all, a Middle East that is often charming and always complex. For those Americans who see a Middle East inhabited exclusively by terrorists and fundamentalists, these stories bring to life ordinary Middle Easterners (Arabs, Turks, Iranians, Israelis, and Cypriots) and help us understand our shared humanity."

—*David Dunford, former U.S. Ambassador*
to the Sultanate of Oman

"There are as many impressions of the Middle East as there are visitors fortunate enough to travel there, and this book earnestly and engagingly samples a wide swathe of them."

—*Alan Weisman, author of* The World Without Us

"Free from any hint of political correctness or academic pretense, this highly readable collection presents tableau after tableau of travelers' encounters with the colorful and sometimes confusing intensity of the Middle East. Over and over we see Westerners' fear and ignorance give way to flashes of insight and real appreciation of the shared humanity, the generosity, the humor, and the serendipity of the life and people of this misunderstood region. This book will provide background, reassurance, and interpretive guidance for the increasing number of North Americans and Europeans traveling to the Middle East."

—*Leila Hudson, Assistant Professor of Near Eastern Studies,*
University of Arizona

"*Encounters with the Middle East* provides a beautiful collage of snapshots from many corners of the Middle East, adding up to a picture that's not often seen in the violence-obsessed coverage of the Middle East. It's a sensitive, insightful, and engaging account."

—*Shibley Telhami, Anwar Sadat Professor for Peace*
and Development, University of Maryland,
and Senior Fellow at the Brookings Institution

"It's refreshing to find a place (the most headlined in our time) described and interpreted not by experts and academics but by writers and poets. The ones gathered here all approach their subject with curiosity, compassion, and a desire to comprehend—to the benefit of both the reader and the region."

—*Thomas Swick, Travel Editor, South Florida* Sun-Sentinel
and author of Roads Not Taken

ABOUT SOLAS HOUSE

Solas House, and its imprint Travelers' Tales, publishes the best in travel, humor, and spiritual writing from world-famous authors and emerging writers. Celebrating fourteen years in publishing, the series has won many awards for excellence, including five Lowell Thomas Awards for Best Travel Book, and multiple best book awards from the Independent Publishers Association, *ForeWord Magazine*, and the Benjamin Franklin Awards.

Encounters
with the
Middle East

TRUE STORIES OF PEOPLE
AND CULTURE THAT HELP YOU
UNDERSTAND THE REGION

Encounters

with the

Middle East

TRUE STORIES OF PEOPLE
AND CULTURE THAT HELP YOU
UNDERSTAND THE REGION

Edited by

NESREEN KHASHAN

AND JIM BOWMAN

SOLAS HOUSE

PALO ALTO

Art Direction: Stefan Gutermuth
Cover Photograph: Franz Aberham/Getty Images. Khazneh, Petra, Jordon
Map: Mike List
Page Layout: Patty Holden using the font Bembo

Encounters with the Middle East : true stories of people and culture that help you understand the region / edited by Nesreen Khashan and Jim Bowman. — 1st ed.
    p. cm.
  Includes bibliographical references and index.
  ISBN 1-932361-48-0 (pbk.)
1. Middle East—Description and travel. 2. Middle East—Social life and customs.
I. Khashan, Nesreen. II. Bowman, Jim, 1968-

DS49.7.E53 2007
956.04—dc22

                      2007012477

First Edition
Printed in the United States
10 9 8 7 6 5 4 3 2 1

To our parents

Where are the favors?
Where are the wise men?
Where are the open doors?
Where is the Revealer of Secrets?—
The answer is: "Right here!"
They are here, from the beginning to the end.
So it says,
"You are what you seek."

—RUMI

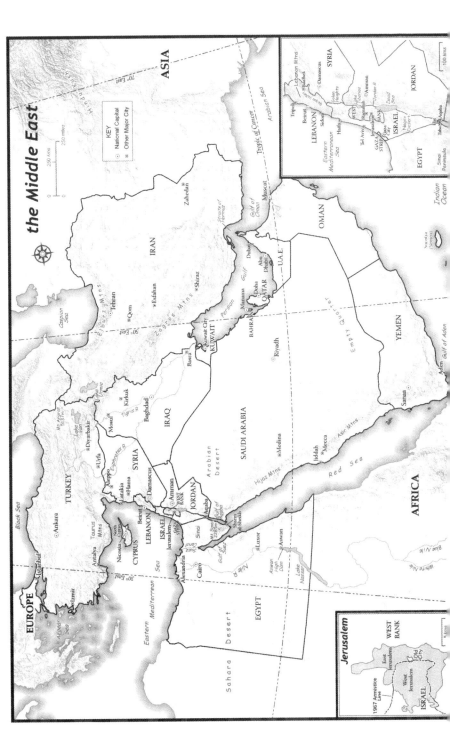

the Middle East

ASIA

KEY
⊛ National Capital
✱ Other Major City

0 250 miles
0 250 kms

Jerusalem
ISRAEL
WEST BANK
East Jerusalem
Old City
West Jerusalem
1967 Armistice Line

EUROPE

AFRICA

Table of Contents

Preface

The sun was setting in the West Bank village, casting shadows
on the terraced hillsides lined with olive trees. As evening
brought coolness, villagers emerged from their homes to walk
along the dirt paths. Young and old walked, women linked
arms while men held salty watermelon seeds in their palms
that they then cracked between their teeth, letting the shells
return to the dusty ground. In the distance, calls to prayer
echoed in the twilight sky, overlapping one another like waves.
It felt as though the exhortations came from the heavens
themselves. Talk was about what uncle was doing, what
cousins were studying, who had asked whom for a hand in
marriage, which relatives were visiting the homeland at present.
It was here that someone from the outside could learn to let
life pass slowly. Here in this land so holy, yet so unassuming,
that the traveler can practice, perhaps even learn, patience.

It was not as though she set out to learn patience, this outsider who longed to belong to the club. She had really come
for another purpose: to discover that kindness and innocence
that she had come to associate with her parents. So it was that
she returned to the West Bank village that her mother last took
her to during infancy, when relatives clutched her chubby
arms before memories could take hold...

It is a portrait so unimaginable these days. It may even seem
absurd that such a calm exists on land associated with tumult

and strife, that someone can tell of something so serene where others know only of unrest. The scene is unlikely because a din obscures daily life in this region, and rarely do the voices of the everyday—sublime and mundane—get to be heard.

The land that most people imagine as the Middle East has become engulfed in a kind of madness transmitted via the twenty-four-hour media circuit, the front pages of newspapers, the images transmitted on the evening news, crammed hastily between commercials for twitching legs, bad hearts, and weakening sexual prowess.

Yet amidst the cacophony called perception that supplants the ordinary, people in the Middle East still go about their lives. They do so through a cultural and existential prism that is unfamiliar to most Westerners. They do so whether roadside bombs, menacing fighter jets, political assassinations, or other forms of violence occur around them. They do so as we all would because at the end of the day, all human beings are remarkable for their ability to adapt and to reveal their resilience and strength, no matter what they face outside their front doors.

In fact, they exist much as people anywhere would when forced to endure hardships. Losing sight of this link and failing to recognize our potential connection with the lives behind the headlines can have devastating consequences. When we don't connect people to the greater global scheme that includes us, we consign ourselves to the images presented on television. In that way, we become myopic and abandon all the moments that represent the complexity of lives in the Middle East. While those experiences remain hidden from our view, we remain deficient by failing to see them. When we are unaware of other possibilities, how then can we imagine solutions to the global challenges that face us? We are a single community bound to share the same planet. Plowing ahead without forging coexistence is a dangerous plunge. Whether people live in war zones or hundreds of miles from them, there is still something akin to normalcy in this region: places where instability remains something delivered by a television set, places where homes are kept intact with spirit rather than mortar.

This collection offers a snapshot of moments worth preserving. It works because many of the narrators are Westerners who come to places like Jordan, Iran, Israel and Palestine, Syria, Egypt, and Turkey, in search of a particular type of knowledge about the region; invariably, they end up leaving with something unexpected. This is true whether the traveler is a first-time visitor like Pat Walker, who leaves shattered when she discovers a Bethlehem so different from the one she clung to from childhood, or Yasmine Bahrani, a native Iraqi who finds optimism amidst the turmoil upon a return to the land of her youth.

Like all great moments of travel, the delight in these stories comes not so much from discovering when the narrators, as Nicholas Seeley put it, "finally, finally, get it." It comes from the process of untangling that revelation, from owning up to the misconceptions that we carry into a situation, and the relief of leaving without them, bundles we are no longer burdened with.

There is no smoke screen here, no quixotic gloss presenting an undisturbed Middle East. There are plenty of portrayals of awkwardness and discomfort to remind the reader of the culturally unfamiliar terrain so many of these narrators have travailed. Attrition will happen, as when Erika Trafton bemoans the unfolding of yet another sleepless night in the boiling intensity of Jerusalem's Old City, or when Mal Karman recalls the details of his trip to Iran while detained at gunpoint by a sentry in Tehran.

Some realities are coarser than others. Karman's predicament is unenviable, but the stoicism and dark humor he displays in the face of a mini-crisis leave us with a memorable story and an enlightening picture of a terribly misunderstood country. Joel Carillet's portrait of animosity among Palestinians and Israelis is tempered by descriptions of individuals from these backgrounds working together to build something enduring that promotes peace.

The emotional range of the collection spans a wide spectrum, including stories that are bittersweet, exuberant, poignant. Each in its own way contributes to our understanding of the complex mosaic that is the Middle East, "warts and all," as one reviewer writes. The rest we leave for the reader to discover.

—NESREEN KHASHAN AND JIM BOWMAN

Introduction: The Wonders of the World

BRUCE FEILER

Not long ago, I was invited to join a panel that would select the Seven New Wonders of the World. Seven of us, convened by a major television network and leading newspaper, were locked into a room for the better part of a day. Among us were the Asia Guy, the Astronomy Guy, the Naturalist, and the Archaeologist. I was the Middle East Guy. I scoured the region for places that I thought might make the final list. Places that were magical, transcendent, and meaningful. Places that were timeless, but also contained a message that was important for today.

I ultimately chose three sites for consideration. All three had roots in antiquity, had deep spiritual connections, and were symbols of inter-religious coexistence.

The first was the Old City of Jerusalem. As Jeff Greenwald notes in his piece, "In Jerusalem," one of thirty essays contained in this book, "Walled cities are worlds unto themselves." But Jerusalem is a world that still influences the rest of the world. Half the globe's believers consider it holy. While Jerusalem is often in the news for the tension on its streets, the defining fact of the city is that any panorama, any camera angle, any genuflection that incorporates one of its holy sites will necessarily include one of the others. For all its conflict, Jerusalem is a living laboratory of different cultures.

The second place I chose was Persepolis. As Peter Jon Lindberg explains in his essay, "To Hamadan," Persepolis was conceived by Persian king Darius the Great in the sixth century B.C. It honored Cyrus the Great, who, among other things, destroyed Babylon, ended the exile of the Israelites, and paid for the Israelites to rebuild their temple in Jerusalem. Darius's commitment to respecting other faiths is on view in Persepolis, one of the great sites in the ancient world. The highlight of the place is a giant wall with carvings of men from twenty-three different countries bringing tribute to the king. They're smiling, holding hands. Happiness was a virtue here. And the king promoted that happiness by telling believers in all those different countries that they could worship their own god. Pluralism was pioneered in Ancient Persia.

The final site, St. Catherine's Monastery, is not included in this collection, though the opening essay, "Bread," takes place on a boat to the Sinai peninsula and puts the traveler in the mood. Located in the red granite hills in the southern quarter of the Sinai, St. Catherine's was built 1500 years ago by monks who said that one particular bush at the base of one particular mountain is the actual burning bush where Moses heard the voice of God. The bush is still there today, and is guarded by a fire extinguisher. When I first visited, I thought the fire extinguisher was an eyesore, then I realized the unintended humor: Is it there in case the bush catches on fire? And if it does catch on fire, should I put it out or look for the face of God?

Like so many of the places discussed in this fascinating compendium, St. Catherine's blends religions and cultures into a mesmerizing mélange. The monastery contains the oldest operating church in the world, where they still conduct services five times a day in Byzantine Greek, but it also has a mosque, which was built to appease local Muslims. The

Bedouin come weekly to receive handouts from the Greek monks, including bread and soap.

Reading this book, I stumbled onto many similar scenes, both familiar and fresh. The first breath of tobacco from a water pipe in Egypt, the smell of incense at an all-female gathering in Yemen, fresh mustard greens sautéed in olive oil served in Cyprus. Some are funny, like Chris Kipiniak's account of a wearying rug negotiation in Cairo. "It was love," he says when he finally succumbs and makes a purchase, "in a medieval, arranged, political, marriage-of-necessity sort of way. The rug was everything I wanted; it was red, I got it in Egypt, it wasn't ugly."

Some are blunt. Murad Kalam writes in his piece, "If It Doesn't Kill You First" about the hundreds of people sometimes killed during the Haj, "In one twenty-four-hour period during my pilgrimage, eighty-two hajjis will die. People perish in many ways, from natural causes like heart attacks to unnatural ones like dehydration and trampling."

A surprising number involve blood. Rolf Potts opens his piece, "I arrived at the Jordanian customs stations in Aqaba with the bloodstains still on my pants." He's referring to blood from the annual Festival of the Sacrifice. Shannon O'Grady witnesses human blood at the Shia festival of Ashura. "The drumming was loud and sounded as if it was building to a crescendo when, suddenly, I began to smell the blood. I looked toward the square and saw droves of young men beating their backs with razor blades attached to the ends of chains."

Any traveler to the Middle East will find scenes in here that are reminiscent of earlier trips. Any traveler will discover new places to visit. As for our panel charged with picking the Seven Wonders, Jerusalem was the only place that received a unanimous vote. My other two recommendations lost out. Reading

Encounters with the Middle East made me long for the original list, where all seven came from the same, wondrous region.

Bruce Feiler is The New York Times-*bestselling author of seven books, including* Walking the Bible, Abraham, *and* Where God Was Born, *an award-wining journalist, and the host of the series* Walking the Bible with Bruce Feiler *on PBS. A frequent commentator on NPR, CNN, and others, he is a contributing editor at* Gourmet *and* Parade. *He blogs about religion, travel, and the Middle East at www.feilerfaster.com.*

NICHOLAS SEELEY

✶ ✶ ✶

Bread

Aboard a cargo boat on the Red Sea,
a traveler sees no gulf between cultures.

IT'S THE LAST NIGHT OF RAMADAN, AND I'M ON A FERRY crossing the Red Sea to the Sinai. Now, I seldom pay much attention to holidays, and as a non-Muslim in the Middle East I do my best not to get involved with Ramadan. It's an interesting display of devotion to God, but it's not mine. For the first few days it's a curiosity, an intriguing departure from the familiar. Later, it's an annoyance: the Jordanian government closes down all but the swankiest tourist restaurants during fasting hours, and many shops and grocery stores close out of solidarity. You can get ticketed or harassed by cops for eating, drinking, or smoking in public. It's not a big deal for most foreigners, who try to be respectful, but it's a lousy break if, say, you happen to be diabetic or pregnant or on vacation with small children. By the end of the month of fasting, Ramadan is simply a fact of life, an event one tries to be respectful of but need not comment on.

This particular year, I happen to be traveling with friends to the Egyptian beach-party town of Dahab for Eid al-Fitr, the

1

feast that follows the end of the holy month. The overland passage is closed, or as good as, since it would require crossing the Palestinian territories, so the alternative is a three-hour bus trip to the south of Jordan, followed by a boat ride across to Egypt. Two types of boats make the crossing. The "fast boat" is a slick and fairly expensive commuter service. The "slow boat" is a cargo freighter that happens to take passengers. Our bus had arrived too late for the fast boat, and so, with some trepidation, we bought tickets for the freighter.

Now that we're here, we don't quite know what to expect. I've ridden enough cargo-and-passenger ferries in other countries to know that they are seldom particularly comfortable or fun, but nothing prepares me for the boat to Egypt.

The boarding dock is crowded with Egyptian migrant workers waiting for jobs, or perhaps coming off them. Some squat on the hot pavement while others shout at each other or at the dock workers, or else sit in silence, squeezing themselves into the tiny corners of shade etched out by the noonday sun.

Stepping aboard the boat feels like stepping onto a plague ship. There are no seats or benches, and every inch of the oil-slicked black deck is covered with sprawled human figures. Barefoot old women sit slumped on blankets against the rails and crowded into the narrow walkways like so many bundles of rags, while men with yellow nails and tired faces try to sleep or brush the swarming flies away with dirty fingers.

Crowds of eyes—vacant, disinterested eyes, bleary with exhaustion or sickness—follow us as we pick our way over the bodies. I think of *Heart of Darkness* or *The Fever* or the nightly news images of African famines. I think I am going to vomit.

So we find ourselves in a corner on the second level from the top, wedged against the side of a large engine shaft that belches gasoline fumes across the deck; it's a lot more carcinogenic, but a bit less crowded. Across from us, an ancient woman with tattooed hands sits cradling her scabbed and swollen feet. My friends and I don't talk much. If we do, it's about the heat or the flies or where we should go that's private to drink from the bottles of water in our packs without offending those who are fasting. No one mentions the eyes that turn to stare at us. I do my best to bury myself in a book.

Nothing moves. The only activity on the deck is a barber a few meters down who sits with his tools spread out before him on a blanket. I find myself staring at him as he changes the blade in his razor between clients. He takes a full three or four minutes just to lather each new face, first with the brush, then with his fingers, brushing the shaving cream to a thick foam. He shaves with short, deft strokes, effortlessly paring away days of stubble and dirt, even as the ferry churns its way out into the Red Sea. He looks like one heck of a barber. One of our group tries to convince me to get him to shave my head, but I can't stand the thought of the attention it would gather—all those glazed eyes, all turned on me.

"I'm a little scared of what's going to happen when the call to prayer sounds," another friend says to me as evening draws near. "This whole boat's going to light up like a Christmas tree." I look around, suddenly worried: When the sunset call to prayer signals the end to the day's fast, it is a mathematical certainty that everyone on the boat is going to immediately light a cigarette. I shudder, sniffing at the gasoline fumes billowing out of the grate behind me. If the boat hasn't blown up on any other day of the year, I rationalize, it probably won't today either.

After another hour dusk is gathering, and a couple of us get up and walk to the railing to watch the red ember of the sun settle behind the mountains of the Sinai. Instead I'm distracted; I find myself looking down at the sea of packed bodies on the deck below. One of our friends in Amman likes to refer to

Egypt as a mother with too many children, who can't feed all of them, and looking down from this high deck the metaphor seems vividly real.

The sun is beautiful as it sinks into its cradle of rust-colored stone.

And then I smell something. The faint, tantalizing scent of...roasting garlic? And vegetables? And bread?

And in a moment that seems to last an hour, I suddenly realize how many things I have just gotten wrong. The deck below us has come alive with people, human figures suddenly animated, like marionettes whose strings have been pulled taut. They are sitting up on their blankets, chatting, laughing, eagerly fingering bottles of water and packs of cigarettes. The shapeless bundles they had carried have been unrolled into picnic blankets piled high with food. From nowhere, old Bedouin women are producing boxes of figs and dates, whole wheels of cheese, bags heavy with thick bread; men push by each other in the tight passages carrying plates piled with fresh vegetables, beans, hummus, and *foule.*

Across the deck, families are cooking over tiny fires, while below us mothers divide up portions for those gathered around, and children's fingers tear eagerly at their bread, anticipating the droning sound of the call to prayer that means they can begin their *iftar* meal.

And so I finally, finally get it. Many of the people on this boat are poor, yes—but they are not hopeless or helpless or lost in an abyss of poverty and despair. They're just tired. They've been traveling all day and haven't eaten or taken a drink or smoked a cigarette in twenty hours. Because it's Ramadan, that thing that I'd forgotten.

"Hey there!" a man calls up from the deck below. "Where are you from?"

"We're Americans," I say, fearing the worst, but feeling trapped.

"Very good," he shouts back. "Welcome to our country! Welcome to Egypt! I wish you pleasure!"

"Oh God," mutters one of our party, who has lived a long time in the Arab world, "run!"

"What, are they gonna stone us now?" I ask.

"No," she says, "but if we keep talking to them, they're going to invite us to dinner with them, and they can't afford it."

Smiling and waving back at the man below, we turn away from the railing and retreat to where our friends are sitting by the engine, gratefully swigging water as the call finally sounds. But it's too late: here's the barber, leaning over us with a smile, holding out a huge tub of dates, passing it around and gesturing for us each to take some, then smiling and passing it around again.

We had packed food for the trip, but it spoiled, stowed in the hot luggage compartment of our bus, and we have nothing to offer in return. So, suddenly, we are the ones being looked at pityingly by the feasting Egyptians, who offer us olives and water and sugared dates. One old woman hands us an entire round of cheese.

And then the barber is back, with his friends, smiling as he presents us with a bag stuffed with thick, crusty bread, which he shoves into our hands with a smile. He doesn't speak a word of English, and my Arabic is meager, but he repeats over and over the phrase "*Ahlan wa sahlan*"—Arabic for welcome.

We thank him as best we can, in broken sentences, and he goes back to his family. There is nothing more to say. My friends and I sit in silence on the freighter's grease-stained iron deck and share our dinner. It's one of those nights.

Nicholas Seeley is a features writer and sections editor for JO, *an English-language magazine in Amman, Jordan, that covers social issues, art, and culture. He moved to the Middle East in 2004, after studying journalism at Northwestern's Medill School of Journalism in Chicago and theater at Cornell University. He joined the staff at JO in September 2005. In his spare time he writes fiction and manages a theater company in Amman.*

MICHAEL McGEE

* * *

The Promise Coffee

*A traveler finds tenderness in
an Anatolian love story.*

FOR TWO WEEKS I LIVED IN FETHIYE, A TINY PIECE OF PARADISE
on Turkey's Mediterranean coast where ancient ruins dot the
cliffsides, and *gulets* (Turkish yachts) line the marina, just
itching for the turquoise sea beyond. While wandering through
an alleyway brimming with shops selling leather coats and
jewelry, I fell prey to yet another Turkish carpet salesman.
Correction: Turkish *kilim* salesman. The two products are
notably different. The approach by the salesman was notably
different as well—far more hands-off than I'd come to expect.
The fellow simply said hello to me and asked where I was
from, a greeting typical of any Turk, salesman or otherwise. His
name was Mustafa, and in his untucked shirt and worn sandals
he bore a slight resemblance to a young and pudgy Peter Lorre.
He was originally from Kayseri, a conservative city in central
Turkey, and he and his wife, Huriye (pronounced Hooreeyeh),
along with their five-year-old son, Ibrahim, ran their kilim
shop in Fethiye eight months a year. They worked every day
without a break from 8 A.M. until 2 in the morning so they

could return in winter to Kayseri and their sorely missed families. Like so many in Turkey they were struggling to survive, clinging to the dream of one day actually owning a car which could transport their goods.

Huriye herself was a delight. If she were back in the U.S., with her English just good enough to be dangerous, I could see her being one of my closest friends. She was charming, funny, and even beneath all the conservative clothing accessories— the headscarf, red waist-length overcoat, and dowdy skirt—her loveliness showed through. And just from watching her and Mustafa interact, I could tell that even after ten years of marriage, they were very much in love. This made the discovery that theirs was actually an arranged marriage all the more surprising. Curiosity and American chutzpa getting the better of me as usual, I couldn't help but ask how it all happened. Just how are marriages arranged? After all, to me the idea of a contract of this sort always seemed so archaic, the type of thing where the chances of real love developing between husband and wife seemed as remote as the moon—yet here was *Fiddler on the Roof* in the twenty-first century. Even stranger, by the time they finished explaining how they'd been brought together, and all the lovely traditions involved, for the life of me I couldn't find much fault with it. It was impressive in its logic, and yet—oddly enough—terribly romantic, too.

Their story began (as with the stories of most arranged marriages in their hometown) when Mustafa left for his military service, something which occupies a mandatory year and a half in the life of almost every male citizen of Turkey. During that time, Mustafa's family scoured the town, asking if anyone knew a nice girl of marrying age. Connection led to connection and they eventually heard of Huriye.

After contacting her parents and making their intentions clear, the "surprise visit" was made. This consisted of an impromptu call on Huriye early in the morning by Mustafa's family, around 8 or 9 A.M., to get a better idea of her habits. Was her room messy or clean? Was she still sleeping lazily (I'd soundly flunk given my 2 and 3 A.M. bedtimes), or was she already up helping her family? Huriye, of course, received a passing grade, which prompted more inquiries around town by Mustafa's parents—as well as Huriye's. Even their friends became an important part of the network. Huriye's girlfriends, for instance, acted as investigative reporters, getting the scoop on Mustafa as they interrogated friends and coworkers. Was he good-natured or hot-tempered? Did he drink a lot? Did he gamble? Was he a philanderer? Was he nice? Mustafa's friends made similar inquiries about Huriye, until gradually pictures of both emerged.

Mustafa and Huriye, to this point, had still never laid eyes on each other, but having won the approval of their peers, it was time the two families met formally at "the promise coffee." The process would prove a nail-biter—mostly for Mustafa— primarily because the focus of the families' get-together would be a tiny secluded room where, on a small table, sat the key to their entire meeting: an empty vase.

Though Mustafa and Huriye would see each other for the first time at the promise coffee, they could still only glance across the gathering at their intended. There would be no words allowed between them. No approach. That was what the room was for. When all was ready, the two would be ushered inside—together for the first time, and alone. Mustafa's eyes would be fixed on the vase as he entered. He knew Huriye would have already told her mother whether she was interested or not. If she liked him, the vase would contain red roses. If she didn't… it would remain empty.

Then, upon a great hush, the door to the room was opened and the two young people were coaxed in. Mustafa held his breath. Already, having only seen Huriye across the room, his heart had been deeply affected. So as he walked in, his eyes immediately fell upon the table. To his delight, the vase over-flowed with flowers.

And so the two talked for the first time—ten minutes, perhaps fifteen, no more. First meetings rarely last more than that; it's done merely to test the waters, to see how their personalities mesh. They spoke about mundane things, asked questions, giggled nervously.

When they'd finished, Mustafa and Huriye, both blushing, joined their families for a drink of thick Turkish coffee, all of them raising their cups as the two families pledged their hearts and minds to the proposed match.

Around this time, too, the two families hired a "dream woman."

When called to help with matches, the dream woman recites particular *surahs* (chapters) from the Koran repeatedly, as if in a trance. Preparing special mixtures and drinks before bed, she then dreams for three nights. Each night it's the same dream, but by the third night, the dream is clearest, and she interprets this gift from Allah, which tells her whether the marriage will be happy or unhappy. If it's an unhappy dream, the whole match may be called off.

Lucky enough to be blessed with a good dream, Mustafa and Huriye's courtship officially began. Their dates resembled our own in the West—dinner, a movie, a picnic perhaps—except that a chaperone always accompanied them. Sometimes it was Huriye's mother; other times, it was Mustafa's five-year-old nephew. During their dates they could hold hands, but they could not kiss. Not until they were married. After a few months came engagement, and finally wedding plans, the courtship lasting a year in total.

As they told their story, Huriye brought me another round of apple tea. Wherever you go in Turkey, tea is served to guests, bottomless pots of it. The tradition is ages old, but apple tea (or *elma chai*) only came into being a few years back, an invention for the tourists, with whom it's been a huge hit. I let it cool a moment, as steam dithered across its surface, blown by tiny winds invisible to me.

Mustafa was just about to start into how he and Huriye were married when he got distracted and began looking through some of the kilims created by girls in the more remote eastern villages. Since most young women in these circumstances aren't allowed to show off their figures or use makeup to accent their beauty, they spend months creating individualized kilims to show interested families that they would be good wives for their sons. The kilims are of various colors and are used as floor mats and tent coverings—a roof essentially—having patterned holes in them that let light in like woven constellations. Each kilim tells a story, revealing the girl's soul—her passions, fears, sometimes her outright defiance of family and tradition. Unlike Turkish carpets, which today are often mass-produced in factories, each handmade kilim is a unique dramatic story, littered with symbolism. Mustafa lifted one kilim, looking for some secretive "S" marks on its backside. This is a common symbol in the kilims, being it's the first letter of the Turkish word for love, *sevmek*. He spotted two tiny ones near the bottom of the kilim, placed irregularly. They were nestled in the design as if hiding within the kilim's colored strips like secret wishes, things dared not spoken—in this case perhaps, a girl's longing for love, when faced with the possibility of a marriage she would have no choice in. As Mustafa explained, arranged marriages in eastern Turkey were much different than his own. A girl may be forced to marry a man twice her age or older; the fellow might be cruel, selfish. The choice depended on her father and the dowry offered.

"A couple in eastern Turkey may be together for sixty

years," he said, sighing, "and not once may the man ever tell the woman 'I love you.'"

With this Huriye burst into laughter and said something to Mustafa in Turkish. His face turned pink, and he looked down suddenly, his words drying up on him.

This was too perfect to pass up, and playing devil's advocate, or rather Huriye's, I smiled and said, "Mustafa, how many times in the last ten years have *you* told Huriye you love her?"

He got shy again and Huriye laughed even harder, again saying something in Turkish.

I raised my eyebrows, letting him know I was still waiting for an answer.

"Not once!" Huriye finally burst in.

"I cannot," Mustafa pleaded, hands out. "It is our culture. She knows I love her. I just cannot say it. A man is not supposed to say things like this to his wife."

This produced more giggling and Turkish from Huriye. "I *need*," she said, leaning forward and pointing to herself.

Mustafa sighed, then tried to deflect this a different way, saying they'd been together a long time, and that their early sparkling love was past, that it's no longer like girlfriend and boyfriend, but like family: husband and wife and child. Huriye didn't buy it, and, frankly, I can't say I did either. I told him that in America there are many jokes about men who can't say "I love you" to their wives and girlfriends—in fact, whole movies and books devoted to the notion.

"No, no," Mustafa said. "It's like when you give a child everything it wants, it just wants more and more. What is that called?"

"You mean you will 'spoil' Huriye if you tell her you love her?" I said, smiling.

"Yes, that's it."

Huriye was rocking with laughter now, and Mustafa,

knowing he'd not handled it well, grew even shyer, looking more at the kilims on the floor than either of us.

Huriye finally came over and stood beside him, leaning back against the stacks of kilims behind her. As he sat on the ground, she gently brushed his hair back with her hand. It was a light touch, and warm—more the kind you'd expect from newlyweds.

Just like little Ibrahim himself, here was simply more evidence of how well their particular system had managed to preserve both love and family using a method that, to me, seemed so antiquated. Its greatest charm was that it was able to take something like love—something so often fickle and flighty—and temper its failings through both logic and the caring efforts of friends and family. And in a world full of dating horror stories, the kind so many of us have endured for so much of our lives, where too often the opportunities for meeting our significant other have relied upon less-than-ideal environments like the bar scene or the internet, it was a type of arrangement that I, for one, could very well welcome.

Michael McGee is a writer and book editor living part-time in San Francisco. He spends half the year traveling the globe, settling down in various cities or countries for a month or more at a time, making new friends, and learning about the local culture while still working full-time for companies in the U.S. thanks to the internet. His stories and articles have appeared in newspapers and magazines such as the San Francisco Chronicle, San Jose Mercury News, *and* Amelia Magazine.

* * *

Key to the City

Sometimes, travel hands you a second chance.

IF THE KEY HAD BEEN PRETTY, I COULD HAVE WORN IT AROUND my neck like jewelry for the last forty years, but it's utterly plain—bronze-colored, round-headed, the kind the Yale company stamps out by the millions every year.

I have kept it anyway, not for its looks, but for what it meant. It was the key to my first apartment, and it opened much more than a front door. It opened a whole city to me. It opened my eyes. It opened my life.

This is the address the key belonged to: No. 1, Makdisi Building, Rue Jeanne d'Arc, Beirut, Lebanon.

I lived there in the summer of 1963, when I was nineteen. Grew up there, is more like it. I fell in love that summer, got—not my first kiss—but the first I wanted, learned to smoke, drank too much Lebanese beer, worked at being sophisticated.

That summer also turned my future upside down. Now I would just say I changed careers, but back then I didn't have one to change. Back then, I just felt lost. Beirut became my comfort.

I had loved it from the start. When my college group stepped out of the plane on our first evening there and started down the shuddering aluminum ladder to the tarmac, the warm, scented air of the city rose up around my bare legs—ankles, knees, thighs, as if I were wading into bathwater. It was the most sensuous thing I had ever known.

No. 1, Makdisi was the address that got us our mail—a mild flood of flimsy blue envelopes from our families in the Middle West to their exchange-student offspring in the Middle East.

There were ten of us, five men, five women, all Minnesota undergraduates working on projects we'd proposed the previous year. I remember only three: Jim investigated the politics of student groups; Kirsten focused on the rights of women, and I studied archaeology, something I'd dreamed of since I was old enough to read.

The men lived in a dorm on the pine-shaded, sea-side campus of the American University of Beirut, always referred to simply as the A.U.B. The women rented an apartment nearby, and the men came over all the time to use the phone.

I was assigned to a small A.U.B. dig in the Bekaa, Lebanon's long central valley, and went down to Beirut whenever I could. As the summer wore on, that was more and more often.

I had arrived in Lebanon believing that archaeology would be what my favorite books had promised me all my life—an endless stream of rich discoveries and richer adventures, Egypt one year, Yucatan the next, and so on and on, all over the globe. But the real thing wasn't like that. All the days were the same, and there was no treasure.

The archaeologists took long midday siestas, to avoid the worst of the sun. I read a lot and practiced smoking. Soon, the best things in my life were listening to jackals howl around the dig house at night—and planning what I'd do next weekend, back in Beirut.

Beirut always wore summer colors—newer buildings in blazing white, older ones in the warm weathered yellows of provincial France, the country's former colonial master. Our apartment was on the ground floor of one of the old yellow buildings. It belonged to a woman whose family owned a jam and jelly factory and who was going to Europe for the summer; her son let us have the place cheap.

The apartment had floors of inlaid tile, a dining-room table that could accommodate all of us, a decent kitchen (we learned to enter it slowly and loudly at night, to give the cockroaches a chance to hide) and a living room furnished with comfortable old club chairs and a gray daybed. The other women claimed the bedrooms, and I camped on the daybed when I wasn't at the dig.

I was helping to excavate the kind of hill that Arabic labels a *tell*—a flat-topped, man-made hill, as opposed to a *jebel*—a natural, roundish, God-made hill. Tells look like layer cakes when you slice into them, each layer a mud-brick town—they get older the farther down you dig.

For a few hours each morning and fewer in the afternoon, I stood with the director on top of the tell and watched a line of women—farmers' wives and daughters dressed, despite the heat, in heavy skirts and long-sleeved sweaters—filing down into a wide pit and filing back out again. They were hauling dirt.

Each carried a black rubber basket made out of an old tire. One by one, at the bottom of the pit, they went up to the local men who were doing the actual digging, held out their baskets and received a shovelful of earth.

Then they hoisted the black baskets onto their heads and swayed up and out of the pit and over to a refuse tip, dumped out the dirt and started back down again. It was stately—classic, even. And very, very slow.

It had taken ten years of digging to get down to where the Iron Age met the Bronze. The director figured it would take another ten before he got through the last of the villages below.

"Give me a dozen American graduate students," I muttered patriotically into my journal, "and I could knock this thing off in a couple of summers."

Occasionally, I was allowed to jump down into the pit and dig too. Somewhere in an A.U.B. storeroom, there is a clay oven in a cardboard box that my hands lifted free from its grave.

And somewhere, I suppose, is the time-fractured pot I was assigned to glue back together, shard by shard. Gradually, its shape emerged, and I realized it was an amphora, a tapered jar that would have stood about four feet tall. All I had managed to reassemble was its rounded shoulder and part of the neck. It had taken me a month.

"I cannot do this," I finally admitted to my journal. "I cannot spend my life doing this."

The problem was, I didn't know what else to spend it on, and I felt bereft and scared. Years would pass before I realized that the summer hadn't been a failure—before I saw that it had done exactly what it should have, turning me away from archaeology and onto a path that was a better fit.

These were the summer's real lessons: That no path is permanent. That roads, however chosen, always lead somewhere. That sometimes the hardest lessons stick the best. And that sometimes—if you live—you get a second chance. By the time I understood all that, Beirut would need those lessons too.

When work ended on Friday afternoons, I flagged down one of the old Blue Bird school buses that were Lebanon's Greyhounds and rode south through the Bekaa, up over the coastal mountains and down into Beirut.

If I got a seat on the left side of the bus, there was always a moment when the road curved around a last shoulder, and I could see the hazy city, with the blue Mediterranean beyond, flowing out into the distance like a land of dreams.

The bus took me to the Bourj, the heart of downtown. Trams, buses, taxis, people—everything in the city started or ended there. The streets were a permanent State Fair, and the busiest were the awning-shaded souks, Beirut's equivalent of Istanbul's Grand Bazaar.

You could get anything in the souks, from baklava to brassieres. I was drawn to the Arabian Nights stuff: Daggers, curved and jeweled and harmlessly dull. Gaudy, gilded sandals, glittering with rhinestones. Hammered brass trays and thimble-sized coffee cups. Tables and chairs inlaid with mother-of-pearl. And Lebanon's trademark silverware, its black handles carved in the shape of resting nightingales.

The crowds were just as varied. On any afternoon, I'd encounter peasant women in jet-black robes that left only their hands and faces bare; old farmers with long moustaches and baggy Ottoman-style breeches; impeccable businessmen in French-cut suits, striding between office buildings, and city women as elegantly dressed and coifed as any on the Champs-Elysées.

There were other differences, of course—dangerous ones that didn't meet the eye. More than a dozen religions were afoot in those crowds, and the tensions between them had already triggered conflicts. But on summer afternoons in the human whirlpool of the Bourj, real war seemed unimaginable.

From downtown, I caught the little tram that ran west along Rue Bliss—named for a person, not my state of mind—to the Moorish arch of A.U.B.'s main gate. Then I walked a few blocks along Jeanne d'Arc to a candy store called Chantilly, ducked around it into a dead-end alley, stepped into our tiny front garden, put the key in the lock and let myself in. It always felt like coming home.

As archaeology faded, my summer took on an end-of-the-world recklessness, something Beirut knew how to cater to. What I liked best were the evenings at our apartment—long salon-like evenings when it seemed as if every person we'd met in Lebanon would drop by for beer and Chantilly chocolate, cigarettes and conversation.

We attracted American expatriates and teachers from the international schools, A.U.B. medical students, people we'd interviewed and a lot of young Lebanese guys irresistibly drawn to this nest of Minnesota girls.

We were only college kids in wash-and-wear dresses, but those evenings made me feel glamorous and sought-after. They allowed me to think I knew Beirut, and that Beirut had nothing better to do that summer than shine its spotlight right on us.

All this sounds silly now: Beirut was a big city, more than a million even then, and we knew only a tiny corner of it. But that corner felt open and free and safe. It was my first real taste of adult life. I felt intensely alive, and something different happened every day.

One day it was simply a cloud in the sky—an event so rare in a Beirut summer that one of our new friends came over to make sure we didn't miss it.

Another day it was the U.S. Navy's entire Sixth Fleet, stopping by on a training mission. The embassy sent out messages to all the young American women in town, encouraging us to date sailors and help keep them out of trouble.

There were so many uniforms ashore that the streets near the port looked like rivers of white. We dated them in groups. By the end of fleet week, one of my roommates had been out with twenty-three sailors; I'd been out with eighteen. But—in the classic phrase of the time—nothing happened. It was 1963, after all, and the sexual revolution hadn't arrived. None of us slept with anybody.

My most intimate moment, in fact, came when one sailor showed me the last letter he'd gotten from his girlfriend. I had not known until then that nations are defended—and torn apart—by armies of homesick boys. I learned it earlier in Beirut than I would have at home: The Six-Day War would not happen for another four years; Vietnam was lurking in the future, and Beirut's long self-destruction would not begin until the Vietnam War was over.

The guy I fell in love with that summer wasn't among the sailors. Bob was a student from Northwestern, making up a chemistry class at A.U.B. He had black hair and hazel eyes so light that they shone like gold when the sun hit them.

He had grown up in Saudi Arabia, in the sheltered enclaves of Aramco, the Arab-American Oil Company—exactly the kind of ex-pat upbringing I envied. Every time I saw him, my heart turned over. I never knew if his did, but Bob took to dropping by the apartment too, and I spent my weekends trying to be fascinating.

My journal devotes an embarrassing amount of space to the details of this romance—going to downtown discos together, sharing hamburgers at an A.U.B. hangout called Uncle Sam's, our failed attempt to smuggle Marlboros out of the free port, sunbathing on the stony campus beach. One night we skipped through the marble halls of the grand Phoenicia Hotel, holding hands. And once, by our apartment's front door, he kissed me goodnight.

Bob left Beirut before I did, and I went down to the airport with a farewell bottle of champagne and talked a Middle East Airlines flight attendant into taking it to him on board. Just before the passenger door closed for take-off, Bob leaned out and waved goodbye; I never saw him again.

When the rest of us scattered for home, I took my Beirut house-key with me, more as talisman than souvenir. Someday, I promised myself, someday when I had my life figured out, I'd go back, find my old apartment, unlock the door as if I still lived there, hand the key to the startled residents and say thanks.

For years afterward, when the Minnesota winter finally broke and real spring warmed the air at home, there would be a night when I stepped outside and felt the soft, sweet air of Beirut swirl around me again, and I would grieve for the city, missing it, unable to find a way back.

By the time I'd finished a degree in journalism, gotten a job at a newspaper and could afford to return, Lebanon was in the middle of its civil war. When the fighting finally stopped, fifteen years later, the heart of the city had been devastated, and it seemed too late.

Then, early in 2003, some of my old student group got serious about an anniversary reunion in Lebanon. It still seemed dangerous, but we were running out of time. "The way I see it," one man said, making the clinching argument, "it's never going to be safe."

We went back that June. As I'd always intended, I retrieved the apartment key from my jewel box and took it with me.

Amazingly, our old neighborhood hadn't changed much, and the ruined downtown was being resurrected. The old souks were gone, but many of the beautiful yellow buildings had been restored, the sidewalk cafes were back and booming, the crowds were as cosmopolitan as I remembered, and I was just as happy.

Being in the city again gave me such intense déjà vu that I kept forgetting my real age. I remembered it fast enough when I went looking for my apartment: I couldn't find anyone old enough to ask.

I looked for it anyway, but I'd never known more than a few words of Arabic, and while neighborhood residents tried to help, I got nowhere. The next time I tried, I asked an A.U.B. staffer to come along and translate.

Khaled and I walked down Jeanne d'Arc to a cross street called Makdisi, and he pointed to a tall, white building on the corner, its facade a mix of shop signs and modern balconies. He thought it must be that one.

It can't be, I said. It's too new. Too big. It didn't look like that. And it wasn't on a corner.

Khaled asked a shopkeeper. "He says that's the Makdisi building," Khaled said. No, I insisted, it isn't.

We walked up a narrow lane beside it. Midblock, tucked behind the modern building so it was invisible from Jeanne d'Arc, there was a lower building, worn yellow stucco with old green shutters.

Ours was like THAT, I told Khaled. But it wasn't this far back, and it faced the other way. If you took this building and turned it around...

A balding, middle-aged man in a navy turtleneck had come out onto a little terrace on the ground floor and was standing quietly, watching me pantomime turning his building around in the air. He asked in Arabic what I was up to. Khaled told him.

And then the man did something that the Lebanese always used to do: He simply opened the terrace gate and, with a huge smile, welcomed us into his home.

"Come in," he said in English, and we stepped into his living room. It was very plain, with an old tile floor (the pattern looked familiar), divans along two sides, a treadle sewing machine serving as an end table, a few kitchen chairs scattered around and a large TV mounted high on the wall.

Our host, along with his younger sister, her husband, their

four-year-old son and a frail elderly lady—"my auntie," our host said—had been watching an Arabic news report about the war in Iraq. He turned it down a little so we could talk.

No, he said, he didn't remember any building like the one I described. Neither did his auntie, who had moved over to sit beside me.

She had been a teacher, she confided, in a delicate blend of French and English. As the evening went on, more and more words came back to her. She practiced them, moving her lips silently, before she shyly whispered them to me. It was like listening to lace.

Another wraith-like old auntie drifted in and perched on one of the divans. She said she didn't know about the apartment either and drifted back out.

"My mother will know," our host assured us: She ran a dressmaking shop around the corner and knew everyone in the neighborhood.

By the time his mother appeared, we'd learned how to pronounce each other's names; I'd told everyone about our study group and its reunion trip; we'd all agreed that the Iraq war was a bad thing; they'd offered coffee and tea, Khaled and I had accepted, and the English-speaking auntie had gone into the kitchen and fetched a plate of homemade stuffed grape leaves.

"Eat," she commanded. Plump with lamb and rice, they were the best I'd ever tasted.

Eventually the mother came in, a woman with dyed-black hair, wearing a kerchief and a loose flowered housecoat. She didn't look much older than her son.

But he was right: She knew. And she knew instantly.

Before he'd said anything, she froze, stared hard at my face and rattled off something in fast, excited Arabic. "My mother say she know you directly!" the son translated, and lots of talk broke out.

Khaled translated more precisely. This is what the mother had said about me: "She rented the apartment behind our house forty years ago!"

I was so shocked that my skin tingled. I'm still shocked. I think she was actually remembering one of the other women, but I didn't mind. The important thing was, she remembered US. And she remembered the apartment.

Which wasn't there any more. She said the owners—yes, the very same ones who'd owned a jam factory—had torn it down in 1975, just before the civil war started, and put that big white building in its place. The dead-end alley beside our old building had been made into a lane, which was how the replacement ended up on a corner.

I'd been afraid of something like this, but the family's unexpected hospitality took the sting out of the loss. At least it hadn't been war damage.

I dug the old apartment key out of my purse and held it up for them to see. "I was going to open the door and walk in and give it back," I said, and Khaled translated.

Everyone collapsed in laughter. "Now I guess I can keep it," I said. More laughter.

The elderly auntie worked out another of her gossamer English sentences and offered it to me. "You found the key," she said gently, "and you lost the house."

I slipped the key back in my purse and zipped it shut. Yes, I said, and smiled at her. Yes, the house is gone.

But by then it didn't matter. The key had done its old familiar work, as surely as if I'd turned it again in the front door of No. 1, Makdisi Building, all these years later.

It had let me back into a city I loved and permitted me, in that Lebanese family's plain, friendly living room, once again to feel at home.

Catherine Watson was an exchange student twice—in high school with American Field Service to Germany and in college with the Minnesota SPAN program to Lebanon. She has been fascinated ever since by the relationship between "home" and "away." She was the award-winning travel editor of the Minneapolis Star Tribune *from 1978 to 2004 and is the author of* Roads Less Traveled: Dispatches from the Ends of the Earth *and* Home on the Road: Further Dispatches from the Ends of the Earth.

ROLF POTTS

✶ ✶ ✶

Dancing at the Blood Festival

*A search for meaning in a Muslim celebration takes
an unlikely twist atop an Aqaba hotel.*

SINCE I HADN'T HAD TIME TO CHANGE MY CLOTHES THAT
morning, I arrived at the Jordanian customs station in Aqaba
with the bloodstains still on my pants. The blood had dried to
the point where I didn't look like a fresh mass murderer,
but no doubt I appeared a bit odd walking through the ferry
station with scallop-edged black droplets on my boots and
crusty brown blotches soaked into the cuffs of my khakis.

The blood was from the streets of Cairo, which at the time
had been in the midst of celebrations marking the Islamic Feast
of the Sacrifice, known locally as the Eid al-Adha.

As with everything in Cairo, the Eid al-Adha was an inadvertent exercise in chaos. For the entire week leading up to
the holiday, the alleys and rooftops of the city began to fill up
with noisy, nervous knots of livestock brought in for the feast.
Cairenes paid little mind as cattle munched clover outside coffee shops, goats gnawed on empty Marlboro packs in alleyways,
and skittish sheep rained down poop from apartment building
balconies. For Egyptians, this preponderance of urban livestock

was part of the excitement of the feast—and it was certainly no stranger for them than putting a decorated tree inside one's house in anticipation of the winter holidays.

In Islamic societies, the Eid al-Adha is a four-day feast that commemorates Abraham's near murder of his son, Ishmael, to prove his obedience to God. Since tradition tells us that Allah intervened at the last minute and substituted a ram for Ishmael, Muslim families celebrate the Eid by slaughtering their own animal for the feast.

Consequently, on the first morning of the Eid, all of the thousands of sheep, cows, and goats that have been accumulating in Cairo during the week are butchered within the span of a few bloody hours. In keeping with tradition, devout Islamic families are instructed to keep a third of the butchered meat for themselves, give a third to friends and family, and distribute the final third to the poor. For Muslims, it is an honorable ritual.

For infidel visitors to Cairo, however, the Feast of the Sacrifice seems much more like a Monty Python vision of pagan mayhem. This has less to do with the intent of the holiday than with the fact that Cairo is a very crowded city where almost nothing goes as planned. Thus, on the first morning of this year's Eid, the lobby of my hotel resonated with vivid secondhand reports of gore: the lamb that panicked on the balcony at the last minute and avoided the knife by tumbling five stories to the alley below, the cow that broke free from its restraints with its throat half-slit and lumbered through the streets spraying blood for ten minutes before collapsing, the crowd of little girls who started puking as they watched the death spasms of their neighbor's sheep.

Regardless of how accurate these stories were, there was no disputing that free-flowing blood was as common as Christmas mistletoe on the first morning of the Eid. By the middle of that afternoon in Cairo, puddles of blood stood like rainwater around drainpipes, and doorjambs and minivans alike were smeared with clotted red-brown handprints.

I'll admit that there is much more to the Muslim Feast of the Sacrifice than public displays of carnage. Unfortunately, Cairo has a way of drawing one's attention away from nuance and subtlety. By the end of the day, I was so accustomed to seeing blood that I didn't even realize that my pants and boots had been stained until I boarded an overnight bus headed for the Gulf of Aqaba.

For most Westerners, Islam is a religion that doesn't quite make sense. No doubt this is largely the result of the Western press, which tends to portray Islam only in terms of its most extreme and violent factions.

When I first traveled to the Islamic world earlier this year, I'd hoped that the Arabs' legendary hospitality would break down such barriers to religious understanding in a direct and personal way.

After ten weeks of traveling through Egypt, I'd found that Islamic hospitality more than lived up to its reputation: Most of the Muslims I'd talked to were amiable, kindhearted people who practiced their faith with natural sincerity. By the same token, however, none of the Muslims I'd met seemed to know why they were Muslims; they just instinctively knew that their faith allowed them to live with a special sense of peace. Whenever I tried to qualify this faith in objective terms, people became defensive and impatient with me.

Reading the Koran didn't help. Perhaps when studied in its classical Arabic form, the Koran is a heart-pounding page turner. My English translation, however, has all the narrative appeal of a real estate contract.

After reading it for a while, my mind wandered about aimlessly. I ultimately found that my reflections on Allah were being offset in equal portion by thoughts of breakfast, girls I should have kissed in high school but didn't, and the lyrics to "Rhymin' and Stealin'" by the Beastie Boys. I gave up on the Koran less than a tenth of the way through.

Thus, I considered my trip to Jordan on the second day of the Eid to be my most immediate and realistic chance of knowing the intimate ways of Islam. Just as a person can't know Christmas by interrogating shopping-mall Santas, I figured my understanding of the Eid al-Adha lay outside the bloody distractions of Cairo. In Aqaba, I hoped, I stood a better chance of experiencing the Feast of the Sacrifice as an insider.

Aqaba, Jordan, owes much of its fate to the rather arbitrary international borders drawn up in Versailles, France, and London in the wake of World War I. Though the city had been used as a trading post since the days of the Edomites and Nabateans, its port and beaches never found much permanent distinction. This all changed in 1921, when Winston Churchill (who was the British colonial secretary at the time) oversaw the creation of a Trans-Jordanian state that featured a mere eleven miles of coast on the Gulf of Aqaba. Nearly eighty years later, Jordan's only seaport has inevitably blossomed into a dusty, yet functional resort town. Jet skis and glass-bottomed boats ply its waters, weekend revelers from Amman, Jordan's capital, crowd its beaches, and drab concrete buildings dominate its shore.

Upon arriving in Aqaba, I hiked into the city center in search of a hotel where I could change out of my blood-stained clothes. Because most hotels in Aqaba were full of Jordanians spending their Eid holiday on the beach, my only option was to rent a foam pad and sleep on the roof of a six-floor budget complex called the Petra Hotel.

I shared the roof with four other travelers, from Denmark and Canada. When I told them about my plans to celebrate the Feast of the Sacrifice in Aqaba, I got two completely different reactions. The Danes, Anna and Kat, were horrified by the thought that I would intentionally seek out Arab companionship. Both of them had just spent a week at the Egyptian beach resorts in Sharm al-Sheikh and Dahab, where the aggressive local Casanovas had worn them both to a frazzle. The two spoke in wistful terms of getting back to the peace and predictability of their kibbutz in Israel.

Amber and Judith, on the other hand, stopped just short of calling me a wuss. The two Canadians had just returned from spending a couple of weeks with Bedouins in the desert near Wadi Rum. Not only did they celebrate the Eid as part of their farewell party, but they personally helped butcher the goats. To experience the Feast of the Sacrifice any other way, they reasoned, would seem a tad artificial.

"And besides," Amber told me as I changed into clean clothes and prepared to hit the streets, "Aqaba is a tourist town. The only people you'll find here are college kids and paper pushers on vacation from Amman. You'd have better luck getting invited to the Eid in Toronto."

Amber had a point, but she was wrong: I was invited to celebrate the Eid before I reached the ground floor of the Petra Hotel.

My would-be host was Mohammed, a bespectacled sixteen-year-old who stopped me in the second-floor stairwell. "Where are you going?" he asked as I walked by.

"Well, I'm hoping to go out and celebrate the Eid al-Adha," I said.

"The Eid!" he exclaimed. "Please come and celebrate with us!"

It was that simple. Such is the gregariousness of the Arab world. Unfortunately for my notions of authenticity, however,

Mohammed's "Eid" consisted of him and two other goofy-looking sixteen-year-olds drinking canned beer in a tiny room on the second floor of the Petra. Mohammed introduced his two friends as Sayeed and Ali. Neither of them looked very natural as they grinned up at me, clutching their cans of beer.

I noticed there were only two beds. "Are you all sleeping in here?" I asked.

"Just Sayeed and Ali," he said. "I sleep at my uncle's house in Aqaba. My family always comes here for the Eid al-Adha."

Mohammed poured some of his beer into a glass for me and put an Arabic pop tape into his friends' boom box. The four of us sat in the room chatting, drinking, and listening to the music. After about fifteen or so minutes of this, I began to wonder what any of this had to do with the Feast of the Sacrifice. "Aren't we going to celebrate the Eid?" I asked finally.

"Of course," Mohammed said. "This is the Eid."

"Yes, this is the Eid," I said, "but won't you be doing something special at your uncle's house?"

"It's not interesting at my uncle's house. That's why I came here."

I looked skeptically at my three companions. "But isn't there something traditional that you do when you celebrate the Eid?"

Mohammed thought for a moment. "We spend time with our family."

"But you just said that you didn't want to be with your family."

"Yes."

"So you aren't really celebrating the Eid, are you?"

"No. This is the Eid!"

"How?" I asked, gesturing around the tiny room. "How is this the Eid?"

"We're drinking beer. Many people drink during the Eid."

Ignorant as I was about Islam, I was positive that a true Muslim holiday would have very little to do with swilling beer.

"I'm sorry guys," I announced, "but I think I'm gonna have to go now."

Mohammed looked hurt. "But you said you came here for the Eid!"

"Yes," I said, "but I could drink beer and listen to music back home in America. I want to do something different."

"Maybe you want to dance?"

"Maybe," I said. "Where can we dance?"

Mohammed reached over to the boom box and turned up the music. The three Jordanian teens leapt up and started to shake their hips to the music. There was no room to move, so they stood in place and waved their arms around. The Arabic music was as stereotypical as it could get: a snake-charming, harem-inspiring swirl of strings and drums and flutes. Mohammed took me by the arm; I stood and tried to mimic his dance moves.

"Is this an Eid dance?" I yelled over the din of the music.

"No!"

"Is this Eid music?"

Mohammed laughed. "Of course not!"

"Then why are we doing this?"

"Because it's the Eid! It's fun, yes?"

I told Mohammed that it was indeed fun, but that was a lie. As with freeze tag, heavy petting, and bingo, many exercises in human joy are best appreciated at a very specific age. To truly understand the appeal of drinking beer and dancing with your buddies in a bland resort-town hotel room, I suspect you have to be sixteen years old. I danced halfheartedly to the music, politely waiting for it to stop.

When I sat down after the first song, Mohammed happily yanked me to my feet. Twenty minutes later, the young Jordanians had moved on to the Side B songs without any sign of fatigue. I weakly shuffled in place, desperate for an excuse to leave. It occurred to me that, technically, I could just sprint out of the room and never have to talk to these guys again.

Then the inspiration hit. Leaning across the bed, I shut off the boom box and unplugged it from the wall. Mohammed and his friends looked at me in confusion.

"Let's go," I said to them. Carrying the boom box with an air of authority, I led the Jordanian boys up the stairwell to the roof of the Petra Hotel. There, I introduced them to Anna, Kat, Amber, and Judith.

Serendipity is a rare thing, so it must be appreciated even in its humbler forms. As Mohammed, Sayeed, and Ali exchanged formal handshakes with the Danes and the Canadians, I saw that their faces were frozen into expressions of rapturous terror; they had probably never been that intimate with Western women in their lives. Perhaps charmed by the boys' awkwardness, the girls regarded the young Jordanians with sisterly affection.

I plugged in the boom box and announced that it was time to dance.

I'm not sure if that evening on the roof of the Petra Hotel meant much to any of the other parties involved, but I like to think that it was an all-around triumph: Anna and Kat were able to interact with Arabs in a light, unthreatening setting; Amber and Judith got to boss the boys around in colloquial Arabic and showcase their Bedouin dance steps; Mohammed, Sayeed, and Ali—in their goofy, reverent, sixteen-year-old way—got to dance with angels on the heights of Aqaba.

For me, however, the night was a technical failure: I'd come to Jordan to experience the Islamic soul of the Eid al-Adha, and I'd ended up spearheading a secular sock hop on the roof of my hotel.

But, at a very basic level, even this was a bona fide extension of the Feast of the Sacrifice. After all, any holiday—when stripped of its identifying traditions and theologies—is simply an intentional break from the drab routines of life: a chance to eat or drink heartily with family and friends, an opportunity to give thanks to God or fate or randomly converging odds, a date to anticipate with optimism or recall with satisfaction.

With this in mind, I reckon that the ritual intricacies of feasts and festivals anywhere are mere decoration for a notion we're usually too busy to address: that, at the heart of things, being alive is a pretty good thing.

Six stories above Aqaba, the eight of us talked and joked and danced to the Arabic tunes, improvising our moves when we weren't sure what else to do.

Rolf Potts is the author of Vagabonding: An Uncommon Guide to the Art of Long-Term World Travel, *and his adventures have taken him to over sixty countries on five continents. His writing has appeared in venues such as* National Geographic Traveler, Slate, Outside, *public radio, and several Travelers' Tales anthologies. Though he keeps no permanent residence, Potts feels somewhat at home in Bangkok, Cairo, Pusan, New Orleans, and north-central Kansas, where he keeps a small farmhouse on thirty acres near his family. His virtual home is http://rolfpotts.com.*

ERIKA TRAFTON

* * *

The Way of Suffering

*In Jerusalem, the sacred and profane live
in nervous coexistence.*

FRIDAY, SPECIFICALLY: 3:30 A.M., STATION THREE. TWO thousand years ago Christ fell here, bowed under the weight of the cross he carried to his crucifixion. I am awakened by the Muslim call to prayer, the melancholy, droning chant that begins with a speaker crackle and the wail, "*Allaaahhhuakbar!*" Other muezzins join in, one by one, a tapestry of prayer broadcast across the Muslim Quarter of the Old City, Jerusalem. It is the Muslim holy day, so shops will not open until much later. Friday mornings are not for sleep, not for commerce; Friday mornings are for God.

I am not Muslim. Or Jewish. Or Christian. But I sleep at the intersection of all three religions. Or, rather, I yearn for sleep. Kids ride bikes through the narrow, cobblestoned streets honking horns that make beeping noises like mini-ambulances. Tractors pulling garbage wagons clatter past. Church bells peal across the rooftops, the same rooftops where Muslim women hang laundry; where Israeli flags fly, dirty and limp at this hour, to mark the territory of encroaching settlers; where sweaty backpackers sleep on bunks jammed between sheets of fiber-glass and scrap metal. ("Refugee camps," the hotel owner called them.) Across the street from our hostel, at the immaculate Austrian Hospice with its palm trees, flowers, and scrubbed white steps, guards with large guns pace the roof like snipers. We occupy a deluxe room, a bargain at $18. It smells of sewage. I share the space with mosquitoes and spiders and ants so small they hide in the tread of my sandals so I can't kill them. We stay for one reason alone: for the balcony and a bird's-eye view of The Way of Suffering.

The sun assaults the Holy City on this June day just as it has for thousands of years. The crush of humanity begins: Palestinian vendors squeezing through Damascus Gate, tour groups piling off buses, holy men and women hurrying into the dark caverns of their churches, mosques, and synagogues. A black monk in a brown robe tied with a white rope fails to conceal the cuffs of his blue jeans or his brand new Birkenstocks. Two white nuns swaddled in stiff, all-white garb look straight ahead. Africans in flowing green-and-orange cotton walk single file past Armenian priests in dark robes with pointy hoods. Christian groups traipse solemnly down the Via Dolorosa, taking turns carrying the replica of Christ's burden. Even though the cross is only big enough to crucify a pygmy, they carry it in pairs as the priest intones scripture. Jewish tour groups sporting yarmulkes and clutching digital cameras look nervous as soldiers and police armed with Uzis and M-16s herd them through enemy territory. Techno music blares from a car, clashing with the hymn-singing and the subsequent muezzin calls. Fifteen soldiers lead a bedraggled Palestinian prisoner in handcuffs through the streets. (Humiliation is a punishment older than the one Christ suffered.) A young boy and girl throw stones at a crippled beggar with twisted legs and laugh when he covers his face and cries. This continues until a shop owner chases them away. The tour groups step over him all day without seeing him or even videotaping him.

In the afternoon, we descend from our stinking perch to get tea at a sidewalk café next door.

"Jesus ate pizza here!" the owner yells. He says this only to scantily-clad girls. Beside me sits a French girl, anorexic, with shrink-wrapped skin, protruding teeth, and a weird fur sprouting from her chin. She sits with her back to the tourists hauling their baby crosses.

Also sitting near us is Derrick, a black, thirty-something EMT from the U.S. He says to the café owner, "You don't look Jewish."

"I'm not."

"But you work here, man!"

"This is the Muslim Quarter."

"See, in the States, we're so far away, everything just gets mixed together."

The Arab launches into an explanation of politics, religion, settlers, ignorance.

"I heard about that, dude—when they wreck your buildings down without asking you first—that really sucks."

Finally, both the American and the Palestinian can agree on one thing: Israeli girls are "really hot." While they rate the bare midriffs and boob jobs walking by, I notice the French girl's hair. It is so thin I can see her scalp, and it looks blue, like something trapped underwater.

Celine Dion wails from an apartment now. She is promising Leonardo DiCaprio that her heart will go on, even though he has sunk to the bottom of the sea. We buy crumbly falafel from a vendor near the hotel. As we make our way through the crowds, I notice campaign posters for Benjamin Netanyahu pasted to the walls. In every one of them, someone has blacked out his eyes with spray paint so he looks like an alien.

The sound of drums approaching drowns out the love theme from *Titanic*. Crowds part for a Palestinian marching band, complete with green military uniforms, black and white-checked kaffiyehs, and bagpipes—yes, bagpipes. Police with blue flak jackets and soldiers in army green guard them. All is calm until yeshiva students on a rooftop begin taunting the band members. They wave flags with the royal blue Star of David and shout epithets. Locals try to calm the younger marchers who want to fight back. The police tell the Jewish kids to go inside as they try to stop the Muslim kids from kicking in the door to the yeshiva school. The soldiers are practically kids themselves. They do not flinch when the Arabs begin chanting "*Allah u Akbar!*" ("God is great" being a war cry as well as a prayer of thanks.) I hide behind a soldier because I am trapped, and while it is the yeshiva students on the roof the Palestinians are angry with, it is me on the ground, feeling suddenly very unarmed, very female, and very white. When the marchers scream in this soldier's face, I can see hatred in their young eyes. The police club the unruliest marchers with their big sticks, and for a moment I fear someone will fire a gun, although for some reason I am too curious to dive into a doorway. When I study the soldiers and the locals to gauge the danger, I can see this is a familiar scene—*too* familiar. But this time the soldiers defuse the riot before anyone can get hurt. This is a time of unprecedented peace.

I am still reeling from the incident when an Arab merchant thrusts a menorah in my face.

"Very nice, eh? For you—very cheap!"

Dusk: the Dome of the Rock glitters golden in a pink sky, and rats outnumber people in the streets of the Muslim Quarter. *Don't walk alone at night here*, people say. *It's dangerous.* Headscarved women scurry inside to cook dinner. Children play on rooftops. Young Orthodox Jews, with their black coats and swinging earlocks, stride defiantly past, their Sabbath beginning just as the Muslim one ends. The Jewish Sabbath, in turn, will finish just before the Christian one begins. It's quite practical: the Sabbath in shifts.

All day there are at least two soldiers in front of our hotel. After the locals have gone to bed, after the neighborhood has grown remarkably quiet, a truck drops off more soldiers. Police, too. Some wear khaki yarmulkes, some wear Nike baseball caps. They belch and yell and sing and laugh.

I can't sleep. I creep to the rickety balcony again to survey nighttime on the Via Dolorosa. I crouch low, afraid of inviting more abuse. There are eight of them, lining up bottles where Christ supposedly stumbled. They kick the bottles soccer-style, and the sound of smashing glass echoes off the stone canyons. Two female backpackers in sandals and sarongs hurry past. A soldier calls out in a heavy accent, "Hello! Where you going? You want to party?" The travelers do not answer. Cheered on by his pals, the boy chases after them, his M-16 banging against his butt as he runs. Meanwhile, his buddies bash the butts of their guns against walls and doorways and revel in the noise. I start to cry because I have been here for eight nights and for eight nights this has gone on and I am so tired I no longer have any perspective and I want to call the authorities but they *are* the authorities and when I ask the hotel owner about it he pretends he never heard anything and says perhaps I am imagining things.

"But I *watch* them from the balcony."

"No, madam. I'm afraid you are mistaken."

Around 3 A.M., the soldiers grow tired of making constant noise. I fall asleep, briefly, until the crackle of speakers sounds at 3:30, and the muezzin cries out in Arabic for the lazy to rouse themselves and offer their thanks to God.

Erika Trafton is a San Francisco Bay Area writer who has traveled in thirty-seven countries. Her piece, "Wood Nymphs and Viagra," was published in Adventures in Wine.

* * *

Kidnapped by Syrian Hospitality

*The most rewarding journeys lie beyond
the borders of suspicion.*

"MOM?"

The voice at the other end of the phone was silent. Either that or the line had gone dead.

Finally, a nervous cough. My mother's breathing seemed heavy, rushed. I could almost see her closing her eyes and rubbing her temples, all in an attempt to figure out what her son was going to do this time.

"You're going…where?" she said.

"The Middle East," I repeated. "Turkey, Egypt, Jordan, Lebanon…"

A long pause. As usual, I was reciting the countries in ascending order of impropriety. And I was saving the best for last.

"…and Syria."

I could feel her wincing.

"Why don't you go to Europe or something?" she said.

The reaction was predictable. My wife Charlotte and I had told approximately ten people about our trip thus far. Everyone reacted this way.

Why would my mom, of all people, be any different?

"Well," she began. "I can't stop you. But be careful. You never know when you might find yourself in…trouble."

Exactly what kind of trouble? No one seemed to have a precise answer for that. It was always a vague suggestion of sinister possibilities, as if danger would surround me at every turn. One day, it might be a riotous mob or a car bomb. The next, I might spontaneously combust. You never knew with the Middle East. Even the falafel seemed suspect.

It was absurd, of course. When we first started planning this trip I laughed off any suggestion of danger. Yes, this was the post-9/11 world, and the 3/11 terrorist bombings in Spain still dominated the headlines. But what were the chances that we'd be caught up in something like that? Shouldn't we be worried about the U.S. highway fatality rate, or all those murders in Los Angeles? These people were just paranoid, and that was their loss. They'd never see the ruins of Palmyra, the splendid façades of Petra, or the Pyramids.

But as our departure date drew closer, and as more people registered their concerns, a funny thing happened: the propaganda began seeping into our subconscious. I began to notice subtle changes in the way Charlotte and I anticipated the trip. Rather than losing ourselves in an orgy of excited planning, we were becoming more and more concerned with what we *shouldn't* do.

Our itinerary for Egypt was thin because ever-changing safety situations meant we might have to travel in armed caravans. The eastern part of Syria looked off-limits—too close to Iraq. And what about southern Lebanon? Were the ruins of Tyre safe from Hezbollah-Israeli clashes?

By the time we left for Istanbul, our seven-week fantasy getaway was looking more like an excruciatingly difficult obstacle course. Then, less than a week into our trip, a series of bombs exploded in three Istanbul hotels. That settled it: we had made a mistake.

We didn't give up, of course. We'd blown too much money on airfare for that. But we did retreat into our shells. Every passerby was a suspect, and each gesture of kindness became a carefully plotted trap.

Avoiding the locals might sound like a simple task, but in the Middle East, where kindness to travelers is practically the Sixth Pillar of Islam, withdrawal requires the utmost vigilance. It also makes you feel like a deviant, if only because hospitality flows so freely. How to be simultaneously gracious and guarded?

When a merchant in Aleppo refused to let me pay for a pound of olives, I was sure they were poisoned. When a random man in Syria offered to walk a half mile in order to show us to the bus station, I was certain that we'd end up in a secret terrorist den. And when a glass cutter invited us into his shop for coffee after we asked him for directions, well, let's just say I took note of each mirror shard within reach.

But after a week of such defensive posturing—and no negative incidents—I began to wonder: Could it be that these people really were just generous? It took an episode in Latakia, Syria, to finally set us straight.

The day of our epiphany didn't start in a particularly auspicious fashion. We woke at 6 A.M. in Aleppo, bleary-eyed and cranky, and caught an early train to Latakia. Upon finding our seats, we were promptly befriended by Haddi, a pudgy nineteen-year-old college student looking for a chance to hone his stilted English and share his eccentric opinions.

Haddi's conversation was consistently bizarre. He jumped haphazardly from history to politics to amateur anthropology, and everything he said seemed vaguely insulting. Upon learning Charlotte was French, for example, he replied: "French men are very girlish, no? Why are they so girlish?"

And upon learning I was American: "Americans know so little about the world. So much ignorance."

An example? He said I probably had no idea that the United States was engaged in a conspiracy to keep the world's Arab nations from achieving their ultimate destiny: a pan-Arab state.

"We are all the same people," he exclaimed. "It is natural that we must become one superpower. But your country will not allow this."

"The same people?" I asked. "Are you saying that Syrians are the same as Moroccans?"

"Of course not!"

He didn't explain any further, and I didn't push him. I think I was afraid of what he might say. It was still early in our trip and Haddi was the first Syrian I'd talked to in any depth. But after talking for an hour, his doctrinaire rants had me doubting the sincerity of a week of Syrian hospitality. Were they all this wacky?

The conversation put me in a cranky mood, and upon our arrival in Latakia, the outlook didn't improve: we were greeted by 100-degree heat and 98 percent humidity. Not exactly sightseeing weather.

We raced to our hotel, tossed our bags aside, and walked a mile in the late morning heat to the bus station. An hour later, we were touring the ruins of Qala'at Salahidin, the remains of an outrageously picturesque castle built by the Crusaders. After spending an hour hiking around the ruins, we were back in Latakia, exhausted, sweaty, and hot. It was only 3 P.M., but we couldn't imagine doing anything productive in the muggy heat. Resigned to call it a day, we retreated to a small sidewalk café near our hotel.

The idea was to order a *sheesha*, drink coffee, play some cards, and avoid any more Haddis. The last part was wishful thinking. After thirty minutes we were interrupted by a call that had become familiar over the last week:

"Where are you from?"

I turned to see a disheveled man in his thirties, sitting alone at the table behind us. Surely a terrorist. Or perhaps another Haddi. With some trepidation, I told him I was American.

His eyes gleamed with curiosity, but his expression wasn't quite like Haddi's. This guy didn't seem to be fishing for English lessons or looking for a foreigner to scold. Instead, my American nationality seemed to be a positive.

"Governments and people are not the same thing," he later told us.

Our new friend's name was Sammir. He was a Latakia native and possessed a New Yorker's certainty that his city was simply unbeatable.

"Where should we go in Syria?" I asked him.

"Latakia," he said, without thinking twice.

"But we're already in Latakia."

"I know. You must stay. Latakia is the best!"

We talked for more than an hour, with our conversation interrupted frequently by Sammir's random gestures of hospitality. When a vendor passed by selling *sous*, a cold licorice drink, he insisted that he treat us to some. When we wanted more coffee, he hailed the waiter. And when our bill came he didn't even let us see it. Our tab was paid before I could pull out my wallet.

Even for Syria—home to perhaps the most hospitable people in the Middle East—his kindness was extreme. Although it all seemed so genuine, I couldn't help but wonder: where was all this going?

We got our answer as we rose to leave.

"Would you like to come to my house for dinner? You can meet my wife."

The casual setting of the past hour had forced me to let my guard down. But this invitation, which from our cultural standpoint seemed unusual, catapulted us back to paranoid mode. Charlotte and I exchanged alarmed looks. Meet his wife? He barely knew us. We couldn't go. Yet how could we refuse?

After some waffling, we settled on a compromise. We agreed to meet Sammir at the same café at 8 P.M. That way, Charlotte and I could think it over—and possibly skip out.

We spent the remainder of the afternoon debating how to proceed. Our first instinct was to not show up. But even in our paranoid state this seemed inexcusably rude. It'd be better to show up and directly tell him that we didn't feel well—or some other white lie.

"But what if he insists?" Charlotte said. "It'll be hard to refuse if we're already there."

"True," I said. "And then he might just kidnap us."

I was kidding, of course, but only slightly.

Ultimately, we came up with a hybrid plan: we'd show up a few minutes early, stake out a safe spot, and spy on Sammir. If he was wearing a black bandana and carrying an AK-47, we'd leave. If he wasn't, well, then we'd go to Plan B, which at that point was still undetermined.

We arrived at 7:50 P.M. and took our positions about one hundred feet from the café. We spotted Sammir within five minutes. He was in the café, sitting at a table with four other men—suspicious, each one.

We watched nervously as Sammir chatted with the men. They appeared to be talking business, perhaps discussing where they would take us once we were bound and gagged. The thought of leaving crossed my mind again, but it barely had time to percolate before Sammir spotted us. He rose from his seat.

"Friends!" he called out as he approached. "I am glad you

made it. Please let me finish my business and then we will go."

"This is our last chance to leave," I told Charlotte after Sammir left.

"Yeah, but he would see us go," she said.

"And he might chase us," I concluded.

So we waited. Soon, Sammir had wrapped up his business and approached us again. We followed him to a taxi, which proceeded to snake its way to the city's fringes. As we drove, the streets became darker, pedestrians were less common, and the taxi seemed to pick up speed.

After fifteen harrowing minutes, we pulled up before a large apartment building. I assumed we'd be headed inside, but Sammir turned in the other direction, heading for a small building next door.

This was the first sign that something might be amiss. The second? The building appeared to house a dress shop.

I fell a step behind and called out to Sammir.

"Where are we going?"

"To see my wife," he said. "She works here."

He opened the door and signaled for us to follow. Inside we found three women, unveiled and clad in tight jeans and flowing blouses, puffing away at cigarettes and drinking tea. Their appearance was a stark contrast from the clusters of *burka*-clad women we'd seen roaming the streets of Aleppo. They looked like any group of chatty thirty-something women back home.

"My wife!" Sammir announced.

The youngest of the women rose from her seat abruptly. She looked startled and barked something in Arabic.

"Heh," Sammir chuckled nervously. "She is a bit surprised."

"He didn't tell her?" I whispered to Charlotte.

It appeared not. Sammir and his wife talked for perhaps three minutes, exchanging increasingly impatient words while the other women laughed.

"I am sorry," Sammir finally said. "I think we will have to go to a restaurant tonight. Alone! My wife has plans."

"No problem," I said. "Let's go."

"Actually, I would like you to wait here for a moment," Sammir continued. "My wife says I must change my clothes because I am dirty from work. Would you please wait?"

So much for the stereotype of timid Syrian women.

While Sammir changed, we stayed behind with the women. The trio didn't speak a word of English, but that didn't stop them from playing charades and teaching us a bit of Arabic. Despite the language barrier, the three managed to communicate an endless series of questions—they wanted to know our religion, how my wife and I met, how many kids we were planning to have, what we thought of Syria. Our paranoia had now officially been revealed as absurd.

Finally, Sammir returned. We hopped in his car and drove to a sprawling seaside restaurant, where we feasted on grilled meats, a dozen *mezze*, and endless cups of *arak*, a potent aniseed-flavored liquor.

"It's O.K. for you to drink alcohol?" I asked Sammir when he requested a bottle and three glasses.

His demeanor turned serious; he knew what I was getting at.

"Yes," he confessed, before adding: "The rule about alcohol is only for good Muslims."

There was an uncomfortable pause.

"Yes," he finally said, "only good Muslims drink!"

The line was classic Sammir—always defying conventions and challenging my expectations. I couldn't help but think of the words of warning we had received from friends and family back home. I tried to reconcile them with the reality I was experiencing. My hostility was met with hospitality. Fear was met with friendliness. We were welcomed even when we tried to withdraw.

Dinner stretched to the wee hours of the night. When it was over, Sammir paid, drove us to our hotel, thanked us for our company, and wished us luck. That was it.

"Wasn't he supposed to kidnap us or something?" I joked as we walked back to our room. Charlotte laughed. "I suppose that's what everyone back home might have thought," she said.

She was right, of course. In the U.S., we seem to have but a handful of terms to describe Syria: police state, terrorist, backward, brainwashed. The sweeping and definitive nature of these words can lead us to think they tell the whole story, but usually they say very little. More often, they distort.

Yes, Syria is a police state. It is poor. There are terrorists and there are people who think like Haddi.

But a police state also produces a person as hospitable and kind as Sammir. And a "haven for terrorists" is home to someone willing to walk a half mile to show a stranger to the bus station. And merchants of modest means will give a pound of olives to wealthy foreign customers without thinking twice.

Our black-and-white descriptive terms lack the subtlety to capture such contradictions. There is, of course, a way to remedy this problem: Go.

Jeff Vize is a writer who lives in Los Angeles. He is currently at work on a travel memoir, Pigs in the Toilet (And Other Discoveries on the Road from Tokyo to Paris).

✦ ✦ ✦

Just Under Your Feet

An artist recreates Byzantium out of forgotten ruins.

MONA AND I WERE JUST WANDERING AROUND SULTANAHMET—
Istanbul's district of imperial ruins and splendors—the day I
first heard of the Magnaura Palace. We'd been walking over it
for weeks and never realized it was there.

That entrancing Istanbul autumn would stay with us. "All
the leaves were glistening and golden and the moon was big,"
she would say years later on the phone from New York, "and
the air was crisp but still forgiving…"

"I remember you spending all day in the tea garden, writing poetry."

"I remember cappuccinos and hanging out with you drawing
all the time, and Jake in his embroidered cap." We'd met at Jake's
Hotel in Sultanahmet and been friends ever since. Sultanahmet,
the holy center of the city that was once Constantinople,
inspired the best drawing I'd ever done. Two millennia of history made visible in violent counterpoint: square turreted towers
marching down the sycamore hillsides to the sea, domes with
minarets spearing up next to buildings like filing cabinets, traf-

fic surging through the arches of a Roman aqueduct, forgotten stone doorways leading into the blackened, trash-strewn foundations of Western civilization. Having to dodge the relentlessly grinning carpet hustlers was a small price to pay for such visual opulence. I grew up in Los Angeles, where nothing is over fifty. Turning fifty myself had driven me overseas in search of something grand that wasn't a movie set; years of poring over art history books had sent me to Istanbul. To me it was Oz.

"What's amazing about those days," I would say to Mona on my cell phone years later, driving up the L.A. freeway, "is that we *knew* they were wonderful *at the time.*"

On that Istanbul day back in 1999, we saw a hillside construction site, closed for the weekend. Through a crack in the padlocked gate I saw a long barrel-vault of Byzantine brickwork. To the left of the site and on the street below was the elegant saffron façade of the Four Seasons Hotel, flanked by another closed construction site. "Boy, I'd love to get in there and draw whatever it is," I said to Mona. We were just turning away when two guys came bustling down the street. The taller one had shoulder-length hair and a blazer.

"May I help you?" he said.

"Yes," I said. "I'm an artist, I draw Istanbul and put it on my website, I work with Turkish Tourism, and I'm trying to get into that site." I proffered my card.

"But Madam," he said, very urbane, "I am the engineer for that site." He said something in Turkish to his companion, a short burly fellow in dirty jeans. Magically, the gate was unlocked and we were ushered inside.

"I can't miss this," I said to Mona. "How long can I stay?" I asked the engineer.

"How long do you need?"

"Let's say two hours," I said, looking at Mona. "Jake's at four?" She left.

The engineer and I went down into the site. Wheelbarrows and shovels were everywhere, covered with brick dust, dirt, and frozen drips of plaster. He led me carefully down a steep flight of steps and over a catwalk to a terrace under huge arches. The distinctive Byzantine style was all around, horizontal stripes of thin red bricks alternating with rows of thicker cut stones. The openings in the walls were all arched with intricate brickwork. A brick lay at my feet, about an inch thick and five inches wide, ten inches long. It looked very old. "What is this place?" I said.

"This is part of the Magnaura Palace," he said. He pronounced it "Manora." A huge Byzantine palace, he told me, honeycombed all through the hill, built in the fourth century and abandoned in the ninth; myriad rooms and passages and even tunnels lead to the Hagia Sophia and down to the sea. "Now this is owned by the richest man in Turkey. He is renovating this part of the palace for a hotel." Renovating. So this antiquity would never be seen.

"Can I take a picture in here?" I asked.

"Cameras are not allowed," he said. "The palace stables, they were over there,"—he pointed at the saffron wall across the street. "They were, for a time, used as a prison, was very famous."

"The one in *Midnight Express*?"

"That movie was filmed in Malta, but right there was prison. Now is Four Seasons."

Midnight Express, the 1975 tale of an American drug dealer's escape from a Turkish prison exaggerated into epic horror for the movies, put a hole in Turkish tourism that has lasted to this day. In 2005 the movie's director and screenwriter came to Istanbul to publicly apologize. They stayed at this very Four Seasons and held press conferences, which put a respectably colorful spin on the hotel's past. But back in 1999, the hotel staff was still tight-lipped about their location on the site of the infamous prison at the top of the hill. Below it the historic neighborhood—now a forest of cement and red tile, lumpy old stonework, splintery wooden houses, and the occasional minaret—canted steeply downward to the Marmara Sea. I looked back across the catwalk to the arches of the massive multi-level structure just being fortified by new brickwork. The ground was cut away, showing a cross-section. The lowest arches showed dark underneath. Just above the highest of them was a layer of dirt and rocks about two feet thick. On top of that was grass, with the ubiquitous strolling cat. The bones of a whole forgotten civilization, just under your feet. "How far down does it go?" I asked.

"Many levels," he said, "All through the hill here." I realized the source of various chunks of old masonry sticking up through the pavement, and a lot of the old arches and tunnels around town.

I sat down in a dirty plastic chair and went right to work, turning the sketchbook sideways and laying out the perspectives. There was no time to think. I had to just plow right in and get it all down somehow. Remembering my friends back home too busy, sick, old, or poor to see this for themselves, I forgot about style, wanting only to capture the most information in the least time, and the style developed of itself.

Every now and then, just to keep me hooked, the gods hand me a day like that one. I never know when my life is going to hit such a high. Once was when I read an article about myself, and the interviewer wrote about my art with such intelligence that I actually wept with happiness. Once was when, after fifteen years in a tiny apartment, I moved into a house. And once was in the ruins that day, drawing things that had been underground for 1,200 years. As I worked, part of my mind thought about the hands that placed those bricks, hands long since dust. Were there glittering mosaics, lush brocades, fabulous murals? I wondered who had walked through that arch, under that dome, and what they looked like in so many centuries of comings and goings under the old red bricks.

The burly blue-jeaned workman and another guy came down the catwalk. One carried a table and the other a samovar on a tray. Behind them came the engineer. I was volubly grateful but didn't stop drawing. They set up the table and poured *chai*, stirred in my sugar, set it at my elbow, and left. I drew for two hours straight, until the engineer came back to tell me it was time to go. "It would be my pleasure to show you some of the sights of Old Istanbul," he said. I agreed to go to dinner with him.

"It's business," I told my boyfriend Kazim, "like your carpet customers." That night the engineer and his buddy took me to dinner. It seemed a bit strange that the Old Istanbul the engineer wanted to show me was the worst food at the schlockiest tourist restaurant in the neighborhood, but I was too tired to care. Afterwards we went dancing at a huge disco in Taksim, the trendy district across the Golden Horn. Then we came back across the bridge and visited the buddy's carpet shop around the corner from my hotel. Somehow everything in Sultanahmet seems to be about buying a carpet.

"What were you *doing?! Worst gigolo in Sultanahmet!*" screamed Kazim the next day. His friends always told him everything.

"Who?" I said, "What are you talking about?"

"*Long Hair*, is *gigolo!*"

"He's an *engineer!*"

"Oh, Sweet, why you never *listen* to me?" Why indeed! When I went back the next day, the gate was locked, strange workmen were there and no amount of wheedling would induce them to let me in to draw. "See? He fools you!" said Kazim angrily.

"What do I care?" I said, "They didn't get any money, and

I got to draw the Magnaura Palace." Wanting more, I called my contact in Tourism. He tried mightily but couldn't get permission from the Four Seasons for me to draw either construction site. It made me crazy. They were irrevocably altering the antiquity with renovation before I could document it with a drawing. I walked all around the Four Seasons with my sketchbook, a pen clenched between my teeth, growling. Across the street was a carpet shop with huge windows. In front of it stood a young guy drinking *chai*. He watched me peer through the fence and get shooed away by a workman. "What's up?" he said. I told him. "But we have the Magnaura Palace in our basement!" he said.

"Oh my G—may I draw it?"

"Come back this afternoon and ask my uncle."

I charged back to Jake's Hotel. Jake was there with Mona. "We almost bought that shop," he said. "That family bought it because of the ruins in the basement. They almost went bust trying to turn it into a wine-tasting room."

"So it's just sitting there?"

"Yes. Tell the old man you're a friend of ours. He's proud of his ruin. Six hundred truckloads of dirt came out of that hill."

That afternoon, my pal the nephew led me to a courtyard behind the carpet showroom. A handsome old man sat imperially at a table. He was just cutting into his fish when I was announced. He set down his knife and invited me to join him. Several *chais* later I had convinced them that I would not allow a brick to fall on my head in the event of an earthquake.

"My uncle says you may draw as long as you like," said the nephew. "Now I must walk with you." Suddenly the tranquil garden exploded with deafening roars. Ahead of us was a cement area with a little roofed hole in the middle. Chained there was the biggest dog I had ever seen, a fanged yellow behemoth, barking like thunder. "Skylight," shouted the nephew, pointing at the hole. The dog roared and flung itself at us, chain rattling against the cement. We edged past, down a steep flight of cement stairs, and crossed a wooden platform. The racket above grew muffled and stopped. Another set of steps led down into a stone room, barely lit from the small skylight above, floored with plywood and full of dusty chairs. The nephew went over and began flipping switches on an electrical box on the wall. Many cords came out of it and went every which way. As lights came on I began to see dim walls of huge pitted stone blocks. At the bottom of the wall to my left was a low arch. One of the cords traveled along the wall and into this black hole. It lit up suddenly. I stuck the sketch-book under my arm, bent over, put my hands on my knees, and looked in. The wall was so thick that it was almost a tunnel. I bent double and went in.

It was a little irregular room with a tall, vaulted ceiling. Amid the stones of one wall was a broken terracotta pipe. A bathroom? Across from the entrance was another archway. I crowded through it into a narrow passage, rough stone walls going up into shadows, iron prongs sticking out from the stones above my head, hammered into them in some forgotten necessity a thousand years ago. To the left, the passage was sealed with a solid wall of cement, shovels, and empty sacks piled at the bottom. Way down to the right, the passage ended with a wall of very old pitted brick. I walked down there on warped wooden planks. The orange electrical cord looped along ahead of me, buzzing, strung here and there with glow-ing yellow bulbs. At the end of the passage it disappeared through a tall square opening in the stone wall. I followed the cord through this portal. I smelled damp earth and age. The yellow lights made aureoles in the dusk.

I was in a big dim space, looking down the wooden catwalk at a brick archway about fifteen feet high, plugged almost to the top with rubble. Between the rubble and the arch was a black hole going back forever. The walls on either side were stone. At the bottom were cement sacks and a shovel. Above was a small dome made of worn red bricks in a spiral pattern. To the left and right of the central arch were more pitted brick archways, at right angles to the one in the center. Each led to another spiral brick dome over another archway, each full of rocks and dirt that went off into the shadows. In the center arch, next to the black hole, was a bright square yellow lamp. The electrical cord swooped along to this and stopped. End of the line. I was in Byzantium.

Below the walkway were rough rocks and muddy pooled water. A broken column tilted out of the mud next to a wall of massive stone blocks. Through the arch at the end of the wall, to my surprise, was daylight. I went slowly down the catwalk. It made a right-angle turn and stopped. A ragged opening in tumbled stone gaped to the sky. Bushes and flowers lined the enormous hole. I could see the remains of an arched window. "Chai?" said a voice behind me. I had forgotten the nephew.

I followed him back to the room of dusty chairs, grabbed one, and bumped it back through all the tunnels and passages into that last chamber. Everywhere I looked was a drawing. I didn't know where to start. I plunked the chair down on the boards, sat down, and began to draw the center archway with the lamp, which reminded me of an *Indiana Jones* movie. I didn't get up for three hours. The damp cool silence settled in all around me. A cat came around the far corner, saw me, and stopped dead, its eyes saying, "What are you doing here?" as it became part of the drawing. At some point someone came with chai and silently left again. I remembered to thank her and to drink it before it was cold. I kept drawing.

The Magnaura Palace is still there in the waiting silence

under the carpet shop. It doesn't appear in any guidebook. Asia Minor Carpets spent hundreds of thousands of dollars putting in a metal stairway and glass skylights. Outside, in the summertime, obtuse tourists walk by the sign that says, "See a Byzantine Palace for FREE!" I've taken archeologists and engineers and historians there and watched their jaws drop open in shock and recognition. They tell me that one of the stone arches is pre-Christian Roman, that the blocks of stone in what I have come to call the Indiana Jones Arch are the biggest ever discovered in Sultanahmet. One said, "I knew everything about this palace except that it had been discovered." Another, a Turk, told me that this was where the palace guards were, and that it has a dig number, nothing more. The Magnaura Palace with its hydraulic throne housed a university in its day and many imperial households. Justinian and Theodora walked in its halls. These lumpy old walls were indeed plastered and covered with glittering mosaics, fabulous murals, and tapestries. There's a tunnel adjacent to the first room, a hole going down into the dark. An old lady from the neighborhood told us that when she was a child, they used to go into that tunnel and come out on the Marmara. Some historians faint when told about the 600 truckloads of dirt. In another country it might be carefully sifted for years for tiny clues to life in days gone by. But other countries don't have so many ruins to choose from. The handsome old man flings out his hands. "It was a dump for 1,000 years," he says. "Whenever they built an apartment house, they threw the dirt in here."

In a city so rich with antiquities, this little chunk of palace doesn't get much attention. I don't care. The more I learn, the more I love it. Enduring, it gives me perspective. I think of all the worried or frightened people who have walked here, the problems they had all lost and forgotten now, but the bones of their creation are still here and still beautiful. This encourages me to concentrate on what is important. Art endures. Kazim is long gone, Mona the poet is a big New York marketing executive now, and my life has completely changed. I would spot that fake engineer for a gigolo from a mile away now after living for years in Istanbul. Old friends have died and new ones have moved into my life. A new war has begun, all is in upheaval in this part of the world, but the Magnaura Palace is still there. I've mapped and photographed and drawn it many times. If it fills up again, at least there will be a record, starting from that first day. My hands were stiff, my fingers were aching where they clamped the pen, and I was sore from the hard chair. I'd never been happier in my life.

Californian Trici Venola is a Los Angeles visual artist with a background in digital art. She fell in love with Turkey when it reawakened her talent after a bad case of computer burnout creating art for a slew of video games, such as the Super Mario Brothers. Drawing from life in pen and ink, she has completed an illustrated memoir of her experiences in and about Turkey over the past five years. Her tale is adapted from that memoir, Drawing on Istanbul. *She lives in Istanbul's Sultanahmet neighborhood.*

CAROLYN A. THÈRIAULT

✳ ✳ ✳

Confessions of a
Water Pipe Smoker

*Local culture travels well through the
chambers of the* sheesha *glass.*

I AM A DR. FRANKENSTEIN, A CREATOR OF SORTS; I HAVE harvested liberally from the defunct bodies of my less fortunate water pipes in order to generate, or perpetuate, the life of one. I look upon my sole remaining progeny and confess that it has a face only a mother can love. In spite of, or rather because of its spurious legitimacy, I dote on my gaudy green water pipe, made (so its faded label tells me) of the finest Bohemian crystal, its chipped body stained and sticky from overuse and inadequate cleaning, its now tarnished stem and valves pathetically bereft of a tin of Brasso. I have plugged its many airholes with bits of cellophane and cardboard in an effort to facilitate airflow. Its faded leather hose has become dangerously brittle and its many resultant cracks repaired with duct tape. The dapple-gray plastic mouthpiece has broken twice but is still serviceable when used backwards. It is truly a thing of beauty, but then again, love is blind.

When my water pipe was but a twinkle in my eye, I secured a position as an archaeological site supervisor in Upper Egypt for several months. I flew into Alexandria, believing that it would be a logical transitional point between East and West, mitigating the inevitable culture shock awaiting me in Cairo. Within hours of my early evening arrival and imbued with a heady cocktail of jetlag, adventurousness, and naïveté, I veered off the beaten path and found myself lost among myriad alleys which split from the main thoroughfare like the legs of a centipede, half-heartedly illumined with sallow neon lights and bare bulbs suspended by lone wires.

Like so many alleyways in Egypt, this one was also a makeshift tea stand where wobbly chairs (no two of which shared a common ancestor) stood precariously along each wall and where men in suits or *galabiyyas* came to discuss the events of the day over a glass of tea and a *sheesha* (for such is the water pipe called in Egypt). Behind me I could hear "Alex," as many locals and expats refer to this city, freshly awakened from its siesta, traffic and promenading youth shaking off the fug of the afternoon heat, gathering momentum and volume. Before me, men sat in huddles, gesticulating with the mouthpieces of their water pipes, voices raised in mock rage or laughter, while boys ran up and down the length of the alley, deftly bearing trays of glasses, foodstuffs fetched from other shops, or shavings of live embers to refresh a pipe.

The alley was filled with the din of conversation, the clinking of glassware, and the sound of a lone lovelorn woman, her recorded voice rendered warbled and tinny by the archaic cassette player that stood in an open doorway, doubling as a doorjamb. I stood at the mouth of this Aladdin's cave and gaped like an idiot.

I wanted in. But I was an *agnabeeya,* a female foreigner, and before me were none of my kind, neither female nor foreigner. Would I be allowed to sit? Would I be offering offense, sowing discord by my very presence? Would I be transgressing some age-old code of male solidarity?

Gathering what little resolve I had, I passed over the outstretched legs of a number of men who, startled, shifted awkwardly to make way for me until I found a vacant chair. Immediately a young man in track pants and a t-shirt appeared with a small table and a glass of water. I asked for a glass of tea, looked about me, and then paused. He paused. I pointed to my neighbor's pipe and attempted to win him over with my pidgin Arabic.

"*Mumkin sheesha?*" I asked feebly. Can I have a *sheesha*?

"*Aiwa! Aiwa!*" he cried. Yes! Yes!

My neighbors, who had been watching me covertly up until that point, made no attempts to hide their interest and apparent delight as my waiter told everyone in earshot that I had asked for a *sheesha*. Chairs scraped as they were repositioned in my direction. All eyes were on me as my waiter carried the *sheesha* over. I was the stage show. God, I was the headliner! From a brass dish he deftly removed the sizzling embers breathing fire into the quickening night, positioned them on the clay cone that was filled with the treacle-sticky tobacco, and stood back a few paces. The cone sputtered and hissed from the marriage of cool, moist tobacco and glowing charcoal; within seconds a sweet perfume of smoke serpentined before my eyes. I took my first drag. I heard the intake of many breaths. Heads were cocked to watch me closer. I closed my eyes. I inhaled; I exhaled.

I neither coughed nor hacked up a lung; instead, I experienced The Rapture as the first rich hit of unadulterated molasses-flavored tobacco began to undulate within my body. I felt myself billowing, if not swaying, in an ineffable awareness of bewildering peacefulness: two days' worth of traveling stress was suddenly washed from my body. I opened my eyes and smiled.

"Good?" my nearest neighbor asked me in thick English, with a co-conspiratorial look in his eye.

"Kwayyis," I answered in Arabic, "Good!" The men about me broke into peals of approving laughter. My neighbor slapped me on the back with a bear paw, which nearly sent me reeling onto the pavement.

"Tamaam!" I added, "Excellent!" and I was a hit.

I spent another hour or so drinking tea and chatting in the patois of travel: bits of whatever tongue worked, be it Indo-European, Semitic, or body language. Fresh tea was served, more embers added to my pipe. When I eventually got up to leave, I realized that I had somehow lost my land legs so that the act of standing and balancing was not as simple a task as I had remembered it to be. Nobody seemed terribly concerned about my condition and I did manage to stagger out of the alley without falling. As I rounded the corner, I lurched against a wall and retched uncontrollably; remarkably nonchalant, I kicked dust on my roadside offerings and went on my way.

From Alexandria to Aswan I whiled away many the hour in swank coffee houses, impromptu tea stands, hotel patios— wherever a *sheesha* glowed and the kettle was clanking on the fire. Men unquestioningly shared their water pipes. With the exception of that first *sheesha* in Alex (you always remember your first), none were sweeter than the *sheeshas* I shared with the site caretakers and staff at our excavation site. In their gracious company, we talked and laughed, and smoked languidly at the door of the dighouse after their evening prayers. In the lengthening shadows of the Temple of Karnak, we would watch desert fox course the outer mudbrick walls, watch nighthawks and owls careen through the tall grasses, and listen as donkeys laden with fodder appeared out of the charred night, their drivers offering up a litany of greetings to us all. Sometimes they would sit and join us; more often than not they continued on, their donkeys' little hooves never missing a beat.

On the penultimate day of my Egyptian sojourn, with only a hundred or so last-minute errands to run, I ventured into the Khan el-Khalili market, once the largest caravansary of the Islamic world and now Cairo's largest tourist mecca (second only to the pyramids at Giza). I had neither the time nor the inclination to comparison shop or negotiate for my "best price." Nevertheless, thirty minutes later, after a considerable amount of haggling, I left the medieval-era district with three *sheeshas* (one to use and two for parts), and a goodly supply of tobacco which, when wrapped up and placed side by side in my suitcase, looked suspiciously like bricks of hashish.

My *sheeshas* are still with me in spirit although only one survives, a hopeful monster, an amalgam of my original three. My furniture is irrevocably permeated with the smell of Egyptian tobacco. I unabashedly enlist anyone I know traveling to Egypt to bring me back tobacco, which is, unfortunately, the weak link in this narrative. Shops here in Canada that do carry *sheesha* tobacco tend to sell the newer blends (apple, banana, strawberry, mint and, horror of horrors, cappuccino and licorice), tantamount to offering Juan Valdez a cup of butter pecan coffee. I am a purist: it is *maasel*—tobacco sweetened with molasses—or nothing. I sourced out Egyptian merchants in Montreal who will occasionally sell me a few packages of the unadulterated stuff clandestinely in their backrooms, and every once in a while I am able to track down a rogue shipment to a local Lebanese food store. It is all so sordid, yet so worth the effort.

I fear that my sources will eventually go up in smoke—I know that I must return to Egypt with a couple of empty suitcases for the mother-of-all tobacco runs. If successful, I could follow the trend of larger cities and open up a *sheesha* bar—but how would this jibe, I wonder, with our smoke-free sensibilities? Perhaps I would qualify for some level of government funding as long as I didn't use tobacco in my advertising. I'll have to look into that a bit deeper. In the meantime, a new Egyptian restaurant has opened in town. I should pay a visit to the owner.

Holding a questionably practical graduate degree in Egyptology, Carolyn A. Thèriault has worked and traveled throughout North Africa, Europe, and her native Canada in an effort to avoid debt and responsibility. She currently resides in Morocco whose sheeshas, she is sad to report, pale in comparison to their Egyptian counterparts. She has been most recently published in Travelers' Tales The Best Travel Writing 2007, Gastronomica, Glimpse Quarterly, Transitions Abroad, *and* The Square Table, *and is also co-founder of Urban Caravan Photography, a web site that features her travel photography (www.urbancaravan.com).*

PETER JON LINDBERG

⋆ ⋆ ⋆

To Hamadan

Unexpected joys lie just behind the curtains.

I FELL FOR IRAN BY PROXY, FROM AFAR, LONG BEFORE ARRIVING there myself. My wife, Leila, was born in Tehran in 1971. Just after Leila's ninth birthday she and her family boarded an oversold flight to New York, taking along nine Louis Vuitton suitcases. They didn't return to Iran for fifteen years.

The Mahmoudis left before staying became intolerable. In early 1980 Leila's international school had closed. At her parents' dinner parties, the customary dancing after dessert had turned to somber talk of war with Iraq. Rumors suggested a draft. Eighteen months in, the chaos of Khomeini's revolution was replaced by dread over what might come next.

Spending her formative years in New York, Leila became outwardly Americanized; unlike that of her older siblings, her English has no trace of inflection, and her demeanor is more Manhattan than, well, mine. Yet Leila proudly identifies herself as Iranian — even if the homeland she claims as her own no longer exists.

Or does it? In 1995, encouraged by reports from relatives

back home, Leila's parents returned to Tehran, first dipping their toes in with a brief foray, then paying more frequent visits. During this time many fellow émigrés were repatriating, with the tacit approval of a regime hoping to reverse the brain drain and investment shortfalls of the eighties. By the time I met Leila, her parents were living half the year in Tehran.

For the other six months they were back in New York, in a house filled with Esfahani carpets and Qajar tapestries. I came to know them inside this microcosmic Iran they'd re-created, and I became fascinated by all things Persian. The languorous cadences of Farsi, which the Mahmoudis still spoke at the kitchen table. The bewitching poetry of Hafez, which Leila and I wove into our marriage vows. The sinuous Persian music we danced to at our wedding—arms raised high, fingertips stirring the air. I learned to accept their insistent generosity (I once complimented my brother-in-law on his tie; three days later an identical one arrived in the mail). I joined in their dramatic affirmations ("*Chash'm,*" one expression goes, or "on my eyes") and flourishes of affection (Iranians append the endearment *jahn* to a loved one's name, so I became "Peter Jon-*jahn*"). I grew accustomed to double-cheek kissing, the scratch of my father-in-law's whiskers, the smell of his Armani cologne. And I fell hard for Persian cooking, great silver platters of which greeted us on every visit to Westchester: the saffron rice with its sunset-orange crust, or *tahdig*; the fall-apart eggplant in my mother-in-law's *khoresh bademjan*; the bowls of melon spritzed with rose water; the feta and cucumbers laid out for a family breakfast.

None of these things had I associated with Iranians back in 1980, when, as fifth-graders, my friends and I sang along to the hostage-era radio hit "Bomb Iran," set to the tune of "Barbara Ann." ("Bomb Iraa-a-aan! Let's take a staa-a-aand!") Our local station played the song every afternoon for months.

My in-laws' Iran seemed nothing like the one I'd grown up with. (Even the name: Americans insist on "eye-*ran*," Persians call it "ee-*rahn*.") Still, I was perplexed by the Mahmoudis' decision to return. How enjoyable could life there be? Western music and movies, satellite television, alcohol, and dancing are officially banned. Even in private, one endures a constant buzz of anxiety. When my in-laws call from Tehran, we avoid talk of politics, since we never know who might be listening.

And yet, and yet, three years ago, Leila's brother and sister moved back to Iran as well, trading careers in New York finance and medicine for similar work in their lost-and-new-found homeland. They were, by all accounts, happier there. Farhad and Maryam's vivid descriptions convinced me: I had to see Iran for myself. My wife had visited six years earlier and was eager to return. So in November 2004, Leila and I landed in Tehran.

Our timing is unusually canny: we have arrived just after the twenty-fifth anniversary of the hostage-taking. Driving into town, we pass by the former U.S. embassy, whose crumbling walls are now emblazoned with government-sanctioned graffiti reading *MARG BAR AMRIKA* ("Death to America"). Today a modest crowd is commemorating the "triumph" of 1979. Rumors about U.S. intentions in Iran have clearly fueled the demonstrators' ire. But besides the defiant remarks in state-run papers, this is the only anti-American sentiment we encounter on our trip.

In a reversal of souvenir-buying protocol, we have carried three extra suitcases stuffed with gifts from New York. To live in Iran is to do without a great many things, some of them consequential, some of them not so much. Trade embargoes and isolation have taken their toll. We bring screwdrivers, steel wool, Kiehl's shaving cream, DVD-Rs, Duracell batteries, perforated notebooks, Claritin, magazines, and electric tooth-brushes for our extended family. It's as if we're traveling to a space station. We've also brought a leather jacket for Leila's teenage cousin Reza, who spends hours browsing European fashion web sites even though he can't buy anything. (Credit cards are nonexistent in Iran, and few retailers will ship there anyway.) Reza is dumbstruck. He doesn't take the jacket off for three weeks.

Leila, for her part, has packed a dozen silk scarves to use as head coverings, and a rain jacket to serve as her manteau, the overcoat worn by women who forgo the traditional black cloak, or chador. (Both the head scarf and coat are required in public for all women, including foreigners.) Like the chador—literally, "tent"—the manteau was intended to drape loosely and conceal the feminine form. But daring young women now buy jackets a size too small and lash them taut at the waist, accentuating the very curves a manteau is meant to hide. The headscarf, too, has gradually migrated back from the brow to reveal provocative bouffants and dangling locks. Nervous first-time visitors, by contrast, pull their scarves tight over the forehead, like do-rags.

On a quiet Friday morning—Iran's one-day weekend—Leila and her siblings take me on a nostalgic drive through their old neighborhoods. It is a rare smogless day in Tehran, and to the north, the snowy Elburz peaks glisten in the sun. We pass the dilapidated remains of the Ice Palace, a grand indoor rink where seven-year-old Leila would go skating on Thursday nights. Farhad points out the former site of his beloved Toyland, a five-story shop full of European imports. Maryam recalls the pâtisserie on Seventh Street where her mother stopped every Friday to buy napoleons. As we cross Vanak Square, Leila remembers afternoons spent horseback riding in the nearby meadows.

Children today experience a Tehran that's different in every respect, a soot-gray sea of concrete and asphalt punctuated by idle cranes. Rows of dispirited housing blocks stretch to the horizon. The bridle paths of Vanak have given way to traffic-choked roundabouts. Tehran's population has quadrupled to 16 million since the revolution, overwhelming the city's infra-structure to a shocking degree: during the evening rush it can take hours to drive two miles across town. On bad days, the pollution stings the lungs; after a rainfall, sidewalks are coated with sticky residue from the oil in the air.

But Tehran does hold pockets of tranquility. Leila and I spend a morning in Darakeh, in the foothills of north Tehran, where a rushing brook cuts through a ravine crisscrossed by hiking trails. Along the path we're joined by dozens of young couples holding hands—up here there are no authorities to keep watch, and several women have even removed their head-scarves. We spot one couple pitching a tent in the woods while tea brews on a Coleman stove and a portable stereo quietly plays Dylan. An old man and his donkey appear on the path, hauling a snack cart of dried fruit. As the sun crests the ridge we stop at a trailside *chaykhuneh* (teahouse) for wood oven-baked eggs and *lavash* bread.

From Darakeh's hills the grime of Tehran seems light-years away. The brook runs clear as a Colorado stream. In fact, this same water is funneled into the city by a series of underground channels. (The manipulation of water, one of Iran's most precious resources, is a testament to Persian ingenuity.) The streams reemerge as canals, or *jub,* that run beside major boule-vards. The water produces a cooling effect in summer and nourishes the plane trees alongside it. On rainy days the canals turn the color of chocolate milk, like a Willy Wonka fantasy. But when the water runs clear, the *jub* and rows of trees bestow a grace on the avenues of north Tehran.

Despite the exodus of so many wealthy Tehranis after 1979, there is still a visible upper class here, and a palpable divide between the moneyed and the working poor. The latter—deeply religious and reliably pro-regime—dominate Tehran's south side. The more affluent and secular north side might as well be a separate nation. Here one sees traces of the sophisticated, Europeanized city that was envisioned in the 1930s by Shah Reza Pahlavi. The northern reaches of Val-ye-Asr Avenue are lined with jewelry shops and clothing stores. At the popular north Tehran restaurant Nayeb, customers are greeted by a white-gloved doorman and serenaded by a pianist. One evening, Farhad and Maryam take us to a California-style shopping plaza, replete with (counterfeit) Esprit and Levi's boutiques, a mahogany-walled "pub" serving smoothies in lieu of beer, and a trendy sushi bar. Over spicy tuna rolls, Leila and I survey the room and count seven women with plastered noses—in Tehran, rhinoplasty bandages are proudly exhibited as status symbols.

The real nexus of Tehran's wealth, however, is not in the north but in the sprawling Tehran Bazaar, on the south side. Billions of rials pass through the bazaar's humble stalls, representing a third of all commercial and retail trade in Iran. (The conservative *bazari* hold great political power and were a driving force behind the Islamic revolution.) On a busy Saturday we plunge head-long into the bazaar, led by my mother-in-law, who seems to have every nook hardwired into her brain. It's like watching a kid dominate a Nintendo game. Expertly dodging mule carts and speeding wheelbarrows, Monir guides us to her favorite spice dealers, haberdashers, and goldsmiths. Leila ogles a necklace.

"That's Italian," the jeweler says in Farsi. "Funny, it doesn't look Italian," Leila says. "No, not *from* Italy," he explains. "*Italian* means 'best quality.'" Monir, unblinking, wangles a 50 percent discount. (It's then that I realize how fortunate I am to be shopping with my in-laws; without such help, an outsider could be hopelessly fleeced.)

A chai vendor trudges past, carrying two buckets roped to a stick, one containing a samovar, the other full of cups and sugar cubes. (Iranians like to hold a cube between their teeth while sipping tea.) At the rear of the bazaar is the famous carpet showroom, where a fine cloud of dust is kicked up by the clap of unfurling rugs. Most patterns are traditional and stunningly beautiful. Alongside those are woven illustrations—designed for European tourists—depicting the Last Supper, Napoleon on his horse, and Kate and Leo on the prow of the *Titanic*.

Westerners are conditioned to imagine Iran as a joyless place. "Isn't it illegal to laugh in public there?" an acquaintance in New York had asked. Before Leila corrected him—"No, you idiot"—I caught myself wondering if it were true. How could we know better? News reports paint a grim picture: stern-faced women in mourning-black chadors, wild-eyed men howling for their martyr Hossein. From that distance, one would believe Iranians are a gloomy and severe lot.

How reaffirming, then, to visit the tomb of the fourteenth-century poet Hafez, in Shiraz, Iran's most soulful city. The tomb is surrounded by rose gardens and pomegranate groves; on this moonlit evening a jubilant crowd has gathered to hear recitations of Hafez's lusty verse about wine, dancing, and nightingales. And if two of those three are currently against the law, that hardly diminishes the mood. The audience hoots at the bawdiest double entendres and joins in unison at the most exuberant lines. As preschoolers dart among the rosebushes and old men laugh over a backgammon game, I watch one couple exchange a swoon-worthy kiss.

Leila and I get delightfully lost in the jumble of Old Shiraz. Along dusty back lanes we come upon a dilapidated mansion, its timbered roof caved in, century-old frescoes peeling off the walls. Several families of Afghani refugees have taken up residence on the sagging upper floors. Above us, the women wash clothes in a vast, cracked iron cauldron while their children play soccer in the courtyard.

On a sweltering morning we drive across the red-clay desert outside Shiraz to the ruins of Persepolis, the magnificent palace complex conceived by Darius the Great in 518 B.C. Persepolis is renowned not just for its grandeur—sweeping staircases, towering sculptures of winged lions and bulls— but for its graceful synthesis of foreign elements. The Achaemenids of ancient Persia were a remarkably catholic people, noted for their tolerance of other cultures. An endless stream of foreign guests were received at Persepolis, including Egyptians, Syrians, Babylonians, Ethiopians, and Cappadocians. These and other peoples were respectfully depicted in evocative bas-reliefs—clad in their native dress, astride camels, goats, and stallions, bearing gifts of elephant tusks, honeycombs, and lion skins from their distant homelands. The tableau is a stirring reminder of an age when Iran was literally at the center of the world.

In 1971, the Shah staged an extravagant celebration at Persepolis in honor of its 2,500th "anniversary." He invited scores of world leaders to pay tribute, just as Darius had done in his day. Untold millions were spent on the party, at which (in accordance with the Shah's tastes) guests ate food flown in from Paris and sipped champagne in Baccarat flutes. As a bid to shore up the Pahlavis' legitimacy and to rally "Persian pride," the party was a bust, and only further alienated the people from the monarchy. Within a decade the Shah would be deposed, and the glories of imperial Persia would be rejected by many as symbols of corruption. The more ardent revolutionaries hoped to purge Iran not only of Western influences but of its

Persian (i.e., pre-Islamic) past; hardliners even proposed bull-dozing the ruins at Persepolis.

As we travel through Iran, I find myself recognizing quirks I'd thought were unique to my in-laws. Their preference for using tissues instead of napkins at the dinner table. (Turns out every restaurant in Iran sets out boxes of them.) Their habit of sheathing leftovers in plastic wrap pulled tighter than a drum. And, especially, the curious etiquette of *ta'arof.*

To understand Iranians, it is essential to comprehend *ta'arof,* which mandates self-effacement in social interactions. Stepping aside at a doorway to let your companion through first is *ta'arof.* Declining an offer of tea is *ta'arof,* even if the host, per custom, repeats the offer three times. (A fourth try means the offer is probably genuine, and it's O.K. to accept.) In Iran, even taxi drivers and shopkeepers practice *ta'arof,* to the bewilderment of foreign visitors. At a newsstand I try to buy some gum. "Paying is not worthy of you," the cashier says, pushing my money away. "But I insist," I say. "Please, *agha,* no charge," he replies. This goes on for a full minute—there are customers waiting—before he takes any money. Sometimes *ta'arof* reaches absurd heights, as when, after dinner at a restaurant in Tehran, our waiter presents the bill. My father-in-law reaches for his wallet, whereupon the waiter launches into florid protest: "Your money is too good for me!... On my eyes, I am your humble servant!"

Manners are everything in Iran. Attending a dinner party, you can't show up with just a dainty box of pastries; you have to bring a whole kilo of pastries—even if the dinner is for only four people. Anything else would look cheap. At restaurants, if you ask for lemon for your tea, the waiter won't dish out a few slices; he'll bring an entire bushel. Visit someone's apartment at four in the afternoon and you'll be greeted by a massive Dutch still life of fruit, nuts, and candies—and you'd damn well better eat some. Back in Tehran, Leila and I stagger among countless parties, dinners, and "casual" family get-togethers. (Never trust an Iranian who promises a "casual" get-together; you'll still be fêted like a king.) By our second week, we have consumed more tea, baklava, kebabs, and rice than seems sensible, and been offered five times that.

To the disappointment of many visitors, much of Iranian life lies hidden behind closed doors. The reasons for this are partly pragmatic—the regime has essentially forced socializing into the home—but also cultural. For all their effusiveness, Iranians are a very private people. This was true long before Khomeini. There's a phrase in Farsi that describes this schism between public and private life: *posht-e pardeh*, or "behind the curtain."

Step inside one of north Tehran's concrete housing towers, ride the elevator up twelve floors, and open an apartment door: behind the curtain lies a whole other Iran. Guests are welcomed by the aroma of freshly cut flowers, heaping bowls of pomegranates, whiskey and vodka smuggled in from Turkey, and black-market caviar just a day out of the Caspian. A flurry of cheek kissing begins. The women remove their scarves and overcoats to unveil low-cut blouses, high-cut skirts, and impeccably coiffed hairdos. Soon the apartment fills with swirling Persian dance rhythms. The sofas are pushed aside and guests take to the parlor floor and sway to the sultry music—yes, arms raised, fingertips stirring the air, just as it was at our wedding, just as so many Iranians did back when dancing was allowed.

As the music grows louder, I'm pulled onto the floor, and suddenly it dawns on me: I am in Iran. This is where my wife grew up. This is where our children will someday visit their grandparents. And from this spot, as I dance across the candlelit parlor, Iran feels strangely like home.

For all the undeniable challenges, many returned émigrés have carved out an agreeable life in Iran, albeit largely *posht-e pardeh*. Being surrounded by Farsi-speaking friends and family helps: the majority enjoy far richer social lives here than they had in Europe or America. At one party I meet Mehrdad, a Tehran native who grew up in Wisconsin. Six years ago he returned to Tehran, where he now has a consulting business, a broad circle of friends, and an apartment with a roof deck and a Weber grill. Mehrdad is especially excited because he has just hooked up an illegal satellite-radio dish. So he can get news from Voice of America? No, Mehrdad wants to tune in to *A Prairie Home Companion* live from St. Paul. "Man, I love Garrison Keillor," he says. "There are two things I miss about America—Lake Wobegon stories and Brewers games." A sports fanatic, Mehrdad plays shortstop for a pickup hardball club in Tehran, mostly made up of fellow returnees. Official name: The Imam Khomeini Memorial Baseball Team.

Mehrdad seems remarkably happy in Tehran and has no regrets about moving back home. "Of course, it can be stressful and frustrating," he admits. "But at the end of the day you can still come home to NPR, a bottle of Maker's Mark, and a barbecue with your friends. Little victories, but you do what you can, you know?" A baseball league, top-shelf whiskey, a pirated DVD of *Ocean's Twelve,* mascaraed girls in miniskirts, *Everybody Loves Raymond* via satellite from Dubai…those "little victories" can make a half life somehow feel whole.

But what of the real things? What of then-President Khatami's reform efforts, the student protests, the upcoming election? I gently press for answers, yet most Tehranis I talk to—especially the young—are curiously disengaged from politics. Those who do speak openly express disenchantment with the stalled reform movement and hold a cynical view of Khatami. They voted for reform in 1997 and 2001, and will likely do so again at some point, but they no longer believe much will come of it. Instead, many have turned inward.

Everyone I meet is on a self-improvement kick. One architect is reading Jung and embarking on night journeys; a banker friend is learning Reiki. A female lawyer studies feng shui, and her sister takes courses in homeopathy. Yoga and meditation classes are all the rage. The logic is clear: If you can't change your reality, at least you can change your outlook.

During our visit, the state-sponsored papers are full of articles about the government's latest campaign against blasphemy. The crackdown has led to the detainment of several Iranian journalists accused of "disturbing the public mind and insulting sanctities." The arrests are acknowledged and even celebrated in the official media. Meanwhile, dozens of domestic web sites are being shut down, and more overseas sites have been blocked. (Try to log on to the *The New York Times* home page from Iran and you'll get nothing but a message in Farsi saying STOP!) Still, the regime's efforts are tantamount to sweeping a beach. After twenty-five years, many Iranians have learned to negotiate the vast gray zone between "unauthorized" and "unlawful."

Consider the scene at Jaam-e-Jam. I've been curious to see how the younger half lives, so one night we accompany Leila's cousin Reza—and his new leather jacket—to his favorite haunt, the Jaam-e-Jam mall. Upstairs is a food court proffering pizza and burritos. This, it turns out, is north Tehran's hottest nightspot, drawing huge crowds of thirteen- to thirty-year-olds to socialize in one of the few public spaces available to them.

Reza strides into the food court like Tony Manero—I swear there's a disco soundtrack inside that jacket—pops open a Red Bull, and exchanges high fives with a tableful of buddies. A flock of girls nearby shoot coy looks at the boys. Unless you're married or otherwise related, it's forbidden to consort with the opposite sex; to discourage this, two sullen guards patrol the area like 1950s schoolmarms, armed not with rulers but with truncheons. No matter: the kids have cell phones. The boys simply beam the girls their numbers, and all commence to flirt telephonically while sitting fifteen regulation feet apart.

We never made it to Hamadan. The *bagh* would have to wait.

Leila has spoken rapturously of her family's ancestral home, in the western city of Hamadan. She spent childhood summers at her grandfather's orchard, which the Mahmoudis refer to simply as the *bagh,* or garden. It was an idyllic time. Leila and Maryam would perch themselves in a sour-cherry tree and eat the fruit straight off the dewy branches; when they'd had their fill, they would fashion sour-cherry earrings to match their crimson-stained lips. On the grass below, their parents laid out Persian carpets and a bountiful picnic, chilling drinks in the stream that snaked through the orchard. (As in Tehran, an ingenious network of subterranean wells steered water down from the mountains.)

You could walk for hours across the *bagh* and never leave its confines. The air was rich with the humic tang of the soil. "It smelled like life," Farhad recalls. Water flowed magically from underground, replenishing peaches, persimmons, and apricots. On late-summer nights the skies would fill with thunderclouds, pouring nourishment down from above.

We'd hoped to visit the *bagh* ourselves, but time got away from us. Instead, on our final night in Tehran, we gather at Farhad's apartment, open a leather-bound album, and pore over the yellowing images within: Leila laughing in her tree, her parents lounging on a carpet below, Maryam filling teacups from a samovar by the brook. Most of the photos were taken in the spring of 1980.

It strikes me that in the spring of 1980, nightly newscasts in America led off with "Day 109," "Day 110," "Day 111," counting the days since the hostages had been taken. In small-town New Hampshire, a boy who didn't know better sang along to "Bomb Iran." In the spring of 1980 Tehran was a madhouse of street thugs and burning flags. And in a stone-walled orchard 250 miles away, a girl sat in a cherry tree—shielded, for the moment, from the chaos unfolding beyond the *bagh.*

Gazing over the skyline of Tehran, we reflect on what has changed—and what has not. We peer into the windows of a highrise across the street. A party is under way on the fifteenth floor. Inside, the women can take off their scarves and breathe. An ingenious network of underground channels—black-market boys, friends of friends—has brought liquor, wine, caviar, and other nourishment, all flowing in magically from who knows where. The night above Tehran is cloudless, but the skies are surely filled with satellite signals, pouring the world down from above.

Leila flips through more old photos: the horse carts used to gather fruit, the pond at the center of the orchard, her father's favorite walnut tree. "Next time," she promises.

Maryam raises her teacup. "To Hamadan," she says.

"To Hamadan, to Hamadan," we reply, hoisting our cups to the west, toward the *bagh,* back to the garden.

Peter Jon Lindberg is an editor-at-large for Travel and Leisure. *He lives in Brooklyn, New York.*

* * *

If It Doesn't Kill You First

Making the hajj tries a pilgrim's soul.
But then something else happens.

I WANDER BAREFOOT OUT OF THE GRAND MOSQUE THROUGH a cruel blanket of Saudi heat, floating in a sea of strangers from almost every country on earth. It's my third day in the city of Mecca, where I've come to take part in the hajj, the annual five-day pilgrimage to some of Islam's holiest places. This trek is required once in the lifetime of every able-bodied Muslim, and I'm one of 2 million people, part of the largest mass movement of humans on the planet.

The birthplace of Muhammad, the prophet of Islam, born in the sixth century, Mecca sits at the base of the Hejaz Mountains in western Saudi Arabia, forty-six miles east of the Red Sea port of Jidda. To someone watching from atop the thousand-foot peaks that surround the city, we must look like countless insects as we spill out of the high, arching gates of the 3.8-million-square-foot Grand Mosque, the most important religious site in the Islamic world.

Mecca is home to 800,000 gracious people, any of whom will tell you not to worry about your well-being when you're here. "This is Mecca," they say. "No one will harm you." Maybe not, but the less devout might steal from you—I'm barefoot because somebody ran off with my sandals this morning when I removed them, as required, before entering the Grand Mosque to pray.

Meanwhile, it's a fact of hajj life that people die all around. Earlier, I watched the Saudi religious police—the *mutawaeen*, stoic, hard-faced men with henna-dyed beards—carry green-shrouded gurneys holding the bodies of five pilgrims who died today, setting them on the marble floor of the Grand Mosque for funeral prayers. In one twenty-four-hour period during my pilgrimage, eighty-two hajjis will die. People perish in many ways, from natural causes like heart attacks to unnatural ones like dehydration and trampling.

Trampling is what I'm concerned about at the moment, and with each frantic step I become more worried about my safety. The problem is the hajj's sheer numbers. Despite many improvements, the hajj facilities and infrastructure—which are managed by the House of Saud, the iron-fisted royal family that has ruled Saudi Arabia since 1932—haven't expanded to meet the fourfold increase in attendance that has occurred over the past thirty-five years. The result is that people too often wind up in death traps.

In 1990, a stampede in the pedestrian tunnel leading from Mecca to Arafat, a rocky, arid plain twelve miles southeast of Mecca and one of the final way stations of the hajj, killed 1,426 pilgrims. Another 270 were trampled to death four years later at Jamarat, a site just east of Mecca where a ritual called the Stoning of the Devil takes place, and the most crowded of all hajj settings. In 1997, 343 pilgrims burned to death and another 1,500 were injured in a giant fire started by a gas cooker in the tent city of Mina, an encampment a few miles east of Mecca where all pilgrims gather near the end of the hajj.

It's a bizarre sensation, but I keep imagining my own

demise, visualizing my shrouded body being carried into the Grand Mosque above the wheeling masses. Every Muslim knows that a believer who dies on this journey is guaranteed a place in paradise. Personally, though, I'd much rather live to tell about it.

Why take this risk? The answer starts with my spiritual beliefs. I've been a Sunni Muslim for nine years. (The Sunnis make up 90 percent of all Muslims but are the minority in Shiite-dominated nations like Iran and Iraq. Sunnis and Shiites differ on major theological matters—like who should have succeeded Muhammad after his death, in A.D. 632.) I was born in Seattle in 1973 to a Jamaican father and an American mother, grew up a lapsed Baptist-turned-agnostic in Phoenix, and started college in Boston, at Harvard, in 1994.

As an undergrad, I happened upon an English translation of the Koran, the written version of Muhammad's revelations from Allah. I was so floored by its persuasive power that I converted to Islam, stopped drinking, and adopted an Islamic name, Murad Kalam. Like many new converts, I was zealous and naive at first. I bought the fundamentalist line that the cause of all the Muslim world's problems—poverty, corruption, and repression—boiled down to a simple failure to apply the tenets of the religion, and nothing more.

Like every American Muslim, I've had a lot to think about in the past few years. When Al Qaeda launched its attack on September 11, 2001, I was a third-year law student at Harvard and an aspiring novelist. I had not yet traveled to Muslim countries, but I had made friends from Egypt, Saudi Arabia, and Jordan, and they'd schooled me in the complex realities of Muslim life. While Islam is dear to the majority of Muslims, they said, Koranic law should not be taken as the cure-all for everything. In many Muslim societies, religion was a smoke screen for old-fashioned greed, tyranny, and hypocrisy, as well as numerous distortions of Muhammad's ideas for twisted political goals.

Among the worst examples of that last problem, obviously, is Al Qaeda, which has been a scourge in the United States, Afghanistan, Kenya, Yemen, and, more recently, Turkey and Saudi Arabia itself. Though Saudi Arabia, birthplace of the exiled Osama bin Laden, has been relatively safe from terror in the past, that changed after my pilgrimage, which took place in February 2003. On May 12, 2003, Al Qaeda truck bombers hit a housing complex in the Saudi capital, Riyadh, killing twenty-six Saudis and foreigners working in the country, eight Americans among them. On November 8, terrorists, probably linked to Al Qaeda, killed seventeen Arabs in a similar strike.

The hajj itself has never been the target of a terror strike, but according to published reports, in a raid carried out not long after the November bombings in Riyadh, the Saudis uncovered a plot by Islamic militants to booby-trap copies of the Koran, allegedly in order to maim and kill pilgrims during the hajj.

The Saudi government has to be worried about terror occurring under its watch, since its role as keeper of the holy places is a major pillar of its legitimacy. The closest thing to such an attack occurred back in November 1979, when a radical cleric named Juhayman ibn Muhammad and hundreds of followers barricaded themselves in the Grand Mosque for two weeks to protest what they saw as political and religious corruption in the House of Saud. Before it was over, dozens of soldiers and more than a hundred of ibn Muhammad's partisans had died in gunfights.

Even though the hajj was not in progress, attacking the Grand Mosque was an incredible blasphemy, and the punishment was swift. After their capture, ibn Muhammad and his band were executed in cities and towns throughout Saudi Arabia.

Throughout the international turmoil following 9/11, I remained a devout Muslim, and I found myself torn between my beliefs and my country. I've worried that President George W. Bush was too heavy-handed in his war against terror, both overseas and in the U.S. At the same time, I've felt oddly insulated from any anti-Muslim backlash. Too pedigreed to lose a job, too American-looking to be assaulted, I felt alienated from my fellow Muslims in Boston, some of whom were attacked on the street by angry locals. I was drifting, missing prayers. I worried that I was failing Islam. So, in late 2001, I started thinking about trying the hajj.

To prepare for my trip, I read narratives of pilgrimages to Mecca, beginning with the hajj chapters in *The Autobiography of Malcolm X*, the 1964 book about the political and spiritual quest of the famous black Muslim activist. In older books I found tales of desert caravans, raids by Bedouin clans, near starvation, and hard-won spiritual enlightenment. For 1,500 years the hajj has been the ultimate Muslim adventure. It remains a soul-rousing journey that, I decided, could snap me into shape.

The hajj itself predates the prophet Muhammad. According to Muslim belief, Abraham established it and built the sacred Kaaba—a fifty-foot-tall windowless sanctuary made of black granite—but over time the rites in Mecca degenerated. Pagan Meccans set up 360 idols outside the Kaaba, and Mecca became a center for worshipping cult, tribal, and polytheistic gods.

Muhammad, born in A.D. 570, received his call at age forty and risked his life to establish Islamic monotheism in Mecca. Persecuted and facing imminent assassination for teaching that there is no god but Allah, he fled with his followers to Medina in A.D. 622. Later, after several battles between Muslims and nonbelievers, the Meccans converted to Islam, and the prophet returned to rule. During his final hajj, Muhammad stressed the equality of man, respect for property, and the importance of prayer, fasting, and charity.

The pilgrimage itself is a twenty-five-mile trip, made by bus and on foot, that starts and ends in Mecca, with shifting dates determined from year to year by the Islamic lunar calendar. Pilgrims begin arriving two or three weeks ahead of time in Mecca, where they spend several days performing rituals and prayers inside the Grand Mosque. At this point, many hajjis take a multi-day side trip to Medina, the oasis city where Muhammad established his first community of followers.

In a transition that marks the official beginning of the hajj, all pilgrims start to converge on Mina, where they camp for the night. The next day they proceed five miles farther east to Arafat, to face the Mount of Mercy, a hill where they meditate on the day of judgment. The hajjis leave Arafat at sunset and walk three miles to the valley of Muzdalifa, to camp under the stars. There they pray and collect pebbles, which they'll take to Jamarat the next morning. At Jamarat, two miles northwest of Muzdalifa, hajjis throw stones at three fifty-eight-foot-tall granite pillars, symbolically warding off Satan. After completing this, pilgrims shave their heads or cut off a lock of hair, to mark the end of the hajj. Then they return to Mecca to complete their final rituals inside the Grand Mosque.

Initially, I'd wanted to do all this in the most rigorous way possible. My hope was to take a boat across the Red Sea from Cairo—where I was living for four months while researching my second novel—and then ride horseback from Jidda to Mecca, camping out in the vastness of the Arabian Peninsula.

But after checking in with the Saudi embassy in Washington, D.C., I discovered that the days of romantic pilgrimages were over. The hajj is too dangerous to allow everyone to chart his own course, and under Saudi law, to get a visa, every pilgrim who has the financial resources must make airline and hotel reservations. The embassy passed me on to the well-oiled D.C.-based hajj machine, Grand Travel, where I was informed that not only was a package tour required, but tours were segregated by nationality. I would be lumped in with ninety-eight other American Muslims.

Making one last stab, I asked the agent if he would book my flight and let me wing the rest. He laughed. "You want suffering, brother? You'll be suffering enough."

I set off for Saudi Arabia on January 28, 2003. Pilgrims prepare for the hajj by taking a ritual bath and putting on the symbolic robes of *ihram*, thereby entering a spiritual state in which differences of race, wealth, and nationality are erased. My robing took place in a hurry at the Cairo airport, where I followed a pimply-faced Egyptian skycap into a dimly lit industrial closet.

"Get naked," he said. For ten Egyptian pounds (two bucks), the young man expertly dressed me in two white sheets, one placed horizontally around my waist, the other over my left shoulder.

Afterward, I jumped on an EgyptAir flight to Jidda. From there I traveled by bus forty-six miles to the Al Shohada Hotel, in Mecca, where I met my tour group. Once in Mecca, hajjis immediately proceed to the Grand Mosque, a massive coliseum that contains the Kaaba, the cube-shaped granite shrine toward which Muslims all over the world direct their daily prayers. Pilgrims are required to circle the Kaaba seven times, counterclockwise, praying as they go. This ritual is called *tawaf*. At the end of the hajj, when they return to Mecca, they must complete the *tawaf* again.

Two nights after I completed my initial *tawaf*, inside the airy, luxurious lobby of the Al Shohada, I got a first look at the American hajjis as we assembled to meet our tour leaders. Studying them, I felt a painful rush of our collective inadequacy.

They were a collection of well-meaning people from all walks of life: taxi drivers, salesmen, mailmen, lawyers, doctors, and hotel workers. But they also seemed like a reflection of myself—slightly out of shape, self-conscious in pilgrim garb, clearly a little panicked.

We gathered in a hotel conference room, where Sheik Hussein Chowat, our spiritual adviser, paced before us, fielding questions. He's a squat, bearded, soft-spoken Arab in his forties who teaches Islam in northern Virginia. Here, it was his job to put the fear of Allah into us, stressing the need to do everything right. "You have to do the hajj carefully," he warned. "If you don't, Allah might not accept it."

Our group leader, Nabil Hamid, a grinning, Egypt-born chain-smoker from the Washington, D.C. area, also in his forties, sat by himself at a nearby table. He was the fixer, solver of the inevitable crises: lost hajjis, broken-down buses, sickness, emotional burnout. He fiddled with his prayer beads while Hussein responded to a question posed by a middle-aged woman, also from Washington, who had completed a hajj in 2002. (Like many pilgrims, this woman had returned to the hajj on behalf of another Muslim who couldn't make the journey.) She mentioned in passing that, at the end of her first hajj, she had not completed a final *tawaf* around the Kaaba.

"Sister," Hussein interrupted, "your hajj was invalid."

The woman was stunned. The sheik, with iron certainty, seemed to be telling her she had gone through great expense and weeks of pain for nothing. I wanted to find out the woman's name, but it wouldn't have done any good. I couldn't approach her or talk to her: personal contact between unrelated women and men is forbidden here.

Now, it's my third day. With a pair of new sandals, I wander down the rolling streets to enter the Grand Mosque and pray. After ten blocks of wading through crowds, I come to the mosque's towering granite minarets, entering alongside stone-faced Turks dressed in olive-green, African women in flowery headdresses, and a gaggle of tiny Indonesians dressed in white cloaks. The whispered prayer of millions sounds like rustling water along a riverbank. The Kaaba rises above the marble floor, and I move closer, meeting the stride of the floating multitudes and chanting along with them.

I exit onto Al Masjid Al Haram, Mecca's main street, which is thick with lame and disfigured beggars. Crying children from Africa kneel on the grimy road; when they don't cry loud enough, their mothers appear from street corners and beat them. One girl has wrapped a gauze bandage around her little brother's head and smudged it with lipstick to mimic a bloody wound.

Tired, and starved for a glimpse of the world beyond Mecca, I retire to a cafe in the back of my hotel to watch CNN, hoping to get the latest on the still-pending war between the U.S. and Iraq. Inside, I run into somebody from my tour group, Aaron Craig, a handsome African-American engineering student from San Diego. Aaron is a recent convert in his late twenties, and he's dressed like a Saudi in a full _jallabeyah_ — a flowing ankle-length gown worn by men. The robe isn't required for the hajj, but Aaron is signaling his burning desire to look 100 percent Muslim.

"You know," he tells me, sipping tea, "I've already seen lots of mistakes made by pilgrims. And the bumping and pushing and nationalism! And you wonder why we don't have Muslim unity."

This is Aaron's first visit to the Middle East. Like me when I converted, he seems convinced that pure application of Islam is the answer to everything.

"People are trying to change the religion, brother," he continues.

"What do you mean?"

"The sellout Muslims in America."

He's talking about moderates, people who live suburban lives, have non-Muslim friends, watch TV.

"Allah's religion is perfect. The sellouts want to say that jihad does not mean jihad. Meanwhile, Muslims are being attacked in Afghanistan, Chechnya, Palestine. You have to believe in it or you are a disbeliever."

This talk startles me. *Jihad* is a loaded word, referring to both armed resistance in defense of Islam and a private struggle to bolster one's faith. I wonder if he would think I'm a sellout. My jihad has always been intensely personal, concerning prayers, family, success, and finding the peace that lately has eluded me—peace that, so far, continues to elude me during this hajj.

In the evening, when the streets are empty, I call my wife, who's in the U.S., from a nearby cabin with pay phones. It's staffed by smart-alecky young Saudis dressed in Western t-shirts and blue jeans. They look like they'd rather be listening to Tupac or dancing in a club—anything but herding us pilgrims around.

"Why didn't you tell me the streets are filled with crooks?" I jokingly ask them in Arabic. "My sandals were stolen from the Grand Mosque."

"All Meccans are good, all Muslims are good," one replies robotically. He offers me a Marlboro, one of the few naughty pleasures tolerated in Mecca.

"No," the other declares. "Some Meccans are good. Some are bad."

It's three days later, February 3rd, and I'm standing in the hallway of the Dallah Hotel with Aaron. We have left Mecca, boarded a bus for Medina, and arrived at sundown, just in time to make the last prayers of the day. The ride here was soothing, with African pilgrims dressed in white walking the road beside us, chanting loudly, *"Labaik, Allah, labaik"* ("Here I am, Allah, here I am"). Medina is an oasis 210 miles north of Mecca. It's a smaller, more comfortable city, its streets cleaner and less congested.

The hotel is swarming with African-American converts and Kuwaitis. As we prepare to leave for the Prophet's Mosque, Aaron shares a big piece of news: His wife has been offered a position teaching English in Riyadh, and they're thinking of making the move.

"Murad," he says, "the Saudis—what are they like?"

There's a lot I could say about that. I spent a week in Saudi Arabia in 2002, and I was shocked by the restrictiveness of everyday life, where most pleasures, even innocent ones like G-rated movies, are banned. I've known too many American Muslims who studied in Saudi Arabia and found, alongside the unbearable dreariness, the same hypocrisies, vices, and bigotry that they thought they'd left behind.

In the end I say little to Aaron; I'm leery about interfering with his destiny. "The Saudis make loyal friends," I tell him. "But there is no social life here. I think you will miss the States."

Aaron sighs, then laughs. "I don't care," he says. "They've got Kentucky Fried Chicken and Burger King. That's all the culture I need. I just want to hear the call to prayer in the morning."

At twilight, Aaron and I wander down the windy street to the Prophet's Mosque. Set on flat land in the city center, its white granite walls are cast in beautiful greenish light. Six thirty-story minarets ascend from its corners, poking into the night sky. Inside, the shrine is huge, spanning 1.7 million square feet. At prayer time, each row of prostrate men extends nearly a mile.

Inspiring though it is, Medina does little to lift my sagging spirits during the six days we stay here. Aside from the physical discomfort—I'm suffering through my second case of flu, and my body aches from walking—something spiritual is missing. I cannot yet say that I'm feeling any different than before I arrived in Mecca, and I'm disappointed in the way the Saudis manage the whole thing, giving too little attention to safety and security. Not for the first time, I'm wondering if I'm crazy to be here.

After a week of Medina's prayer and quiet, our buses show up again on February 8th, a Saturday, to take us about 210 miles to Mina, where all 2 million hajjis are heading to enact one of mankind's grandest mass rituals, starting tomorrow. Bounded by mountains on two sides, Mina is home to a permanent tent city that sits between the plain of Arafat and Mecca's eastern boundary. It's a small metropolis of 44,000 identical fifteen-foot-high, aluminum-framed tents, placed on a square-mile quadrant. The Jamarat overpass—a huge two-level walkway that leads pilgrims to the three granite pillars representing Satan—sits roughly a mile to the northwest, in the direction of Mecca. A string of mosques borders the tent city in every direction.

We float into Mina, across the dirt roads between the tents, which are sectioned off by region and country. The bus stops before the entrance to what's called the Egyptian section. Nabil Hamid, our group leader, has placed us in an area called 42/2.

"Remember that number," he says sternly, pointing to a sign. "It's the only way to get back. If you are lost here, you are lost." We find our tent space, a 10,000-square-foot enclosure for fifty men.

After nightfall, Nabil leads us out to the site of Jamarat to show us the mile-long path from the tent and back. Just before we leave, Sheik Ahmed Shirbini, a forty-something Egyptian-born Muslim from Denver who's on his third hajj, issues a warning about the dangers awaiting us at the Jamarat walkway.

"If you lose your sandals, if you drop your money, your sunglasses, do not go back!" he says. "I was here four years ago, and I saw with my own eyes a man who'd dropped his wallet on the overpass trampled to death by the crowds."

Nabil carries a twelve-foot sign that reads USA. We wander across the dark dirt lanes, past patches of paved road where pilgrims sleep on the ground. We turn a corner, walking down a longer road, until we come to the infamous overpass, a mile-long, 300-foot-wide structure. You can get to the three granite pillars from this bridge or an underpass below it. The structure is built to hold 100,000 people, but three times that number will crowd it in the thick of Jamarat. This overload caused a collapse in 1998 that killed 118 pilgrims.

One of our group, a young doctor from Pennsylvania named Shakeel Shareef, points to the street under the bridge. "That's where all the people were killed," he says.

Hearing this, Aaron swallows and his voice goes big. "Allah is all-knowing and all-powerful," he says. "If we are supposed to die at Jamarat, it is part of his will. What better place to die?"

But I can see the fear on his face. It's oddly comforting to know that he's as scared as I am.

It's eight o'clock on the morning of February 11th, the day I'll perform the Stoning of the Devil ritual, and I'm lost. At the moment, I'm in Mina, walking on a street beneath the mountain valleys, surrounded by exultant pilgrims hustling toward Jamarat. On each side of me, the numberless tents sweep out beneath the mountains.

A lot has happened since this time yesterday. In the morning we left early as our bus raced toward the Mount of Mercy for the nighttime vigil. Hajjis in surgical masks streamed beside us in a fog of exhaust; young boys surfed the hoods of antiquated American school buses, their white robes flapping in the wind.

But this glorious motion didn't last long: We spent much of the day either stuck in traffic or walking around lost, and I got separated twice from my group. At sundown it looked like we might not make Muzdalifa by midnight. Sheik Hussein, our spiritual adviser, informed us that if we didn't get there by then, we would have to lay out cash for the sacrifice of a sheep in Mecca, to atone for this failure in the hajj.

When a pilgrim objected to this—shouldn't our group leader, Nabil, have to pay, since he is responsible for getting us around?—Sheik Hussein wagged his finger and said, "You do not understand worship! I don't care about the money! This is between you and Nabil! I am here to help you worship Allah!"

In the end we got there, but in these crowds, it's always easy to get lost again. Right now, pushing my way forward in the Mina morning, I have no idea where I am. I have a vague sense that my tent at the Egyptian camp is straight ahead, but Mina is so rambling, its hills so full of identical tents, that I can't be sure. I walk forward, pacing ahead of the crowds of half-sleeping pilgrims.

Two hours pass. When I finally get my bearings, around 10 A.M., I realize that I'm just one street removed from 42/2, but it's hard to get all the way there. Pushing through the crowds is like wading through waist-high water. I am caught on a street congested with pilgrims and tour buses, vans, and trucks on their way to Jamarat. Blocks away, pilgrims are flooding the street from both directions, coming back from Muzdalifa and racing toward Jamarat. Trapped in a hot, heaving crowd, I suffer the most terrifying claustrophobia of my life.

I force my way through the street until it is impossible to take a step forward. Suddenly there's an explosion of human pressure from all sides, and I find myself standing face to face with a small, neatly dressed Iranian hajj leader in wire-rim glasses. The Iranian's eyes go wide as pilgrims on each side of the road begin to rush toward us. Africans are shoving through. Saudi policemen stand on trucks and rooftops, doing nothing as they watch the street below them devolve into madness. Women shout "Stop!" in Farsi and wave their hands, but no one can stop the crowd from crushing in. I cannot move. I can only pray. The crowd erupts in frenzied screaming. A row of middle-aged Iranian women fall over like dominoes.

Nigerian pilgrims start pushing through violently. Feeble, veiled women shout the only Arabic words understood by every pilgrim: "*Haram! Haram!*" ("Shame on you!") Women and small old men are getting trampled in the mud. I find an opening through the maelstrom and hurry to a parked truck. I climb into the truck, my sandals left behind in the street mud, my bare feet burning on the truck bed's hot, rusty metal floor.

Nigerians crawl onto the truck from all sides. I can do little more than watch as screaming Iranian and Nigerian women are crushed on the street beneath us, a sea of white *burqas*, angled shoulders, crying, pleading faces, the flashing of out-stretched arms. I reach down and pull a young Nigerian woman into the truck. Like me, she is crying, her face racked with fear. An old Iranian woman in white clings to the Nigerian's waist as I pull her up, her body floating on a wave of white-cloaked women. In another language, she thanks me for saving her life.

And then, in what seems like just a moment, the street is somehow cleared behind us. Women lie moaning in the mud. The truck's engine chugs; it zips forward six or seven blocks down the now-empty street. I watch pilgrims in the distance climbing from the piled bodies to their feet on the muddy, empty road.

I jump off the truck and walk barefoot back to my camp through a cloud of diesel exhaust. The scene of the stampede is six blocks away, shockingly clear. When I return to it, the road has been swept of thirty or forty people who—I can only assume from what I saw—have been badly injured or killed. (I never find out, but the next day I read in the *Saudi Times* that fourteen people died a half-mile away in a different stampede at Jamarat.)

I am angry—angry at the Saudis for permitting such chaos. But beneath my anger, there is also exultation, something electric, happiness to have survived, the clarity that comes from facing death. Around noon, I finally reach 42/2, entering through an iron gate. Sheik Hussein is speaking with a veiled woman from the American group.

"I must talk to you," I tell him, sobbing.

He takes me by the wrist down a concrete path, and we stand in the shade of a fluttering tent. "I was almost killed, Sheik Hussein! There was a stampede in the street. I jumped into a truck. I pulled a woman up. I saved her life. I think people died there."

"It is O.K.," the sheik says. "It is O.K. if you touched the woman."

"No, no. I was not asking that. I wanted to tell you that I almost died today."

"Well, it is over now," he says, without emotion. Then he leaves me at the tent.

However deadly and frantic Jamarat is, it can't be worse than what I've just seen. Though I haven't slept in thirty-six hours, nothing matters now but completing this hajj. I step inside my tent and stare at my fellow pilgrims lying on a rug. Half of them have already gone to Jamarat and returned. They eat oranges or sleep blissfully on mats in the hot, cramped tent. The rest are waiting until evening, when Jamarat is safer.

I decide to go right now. I have lost all my fear. Along with Shakeel Shareef, the Pennsylvania doctor, and a few other pilgrims, I march to Jamarat in the midday heat, collecting pebbles along the way. The streets are congested, but we weave through the crowds. We watch a pilgrim coming back from Jamarat. He is bandaged and bleeding from the head, his *ihram* robes covered in blood.

We wander into a crowd of more than a million people. A couple hundred thousand pilgrims are striding on the overpass above. "Everyone is taking the overpass," says Shakeel, pointing. "The bottom level is safer."

We follow him, making our way through the rushing crowds to the smallest pillar to throw our seven stones, but we are too far away. Shakeel is not like so many other careless pilgrims. He will not throw at the first opportunity; he waits until he is certain he will not hit another person. I watch him, banged upon by rushing hajjis, measuring his throw, stopping, moving closer. I stand behind him, my hand on his shoulder, so that we stay together.

"We have to get closer," Shakeel shouts. "If we throw from here, we'll only be hitting pilgrims. Hurry."

We link arms and march into a wall of pilgrims. Hundreds of tiny pebbles pound against the sides of a granite pillar in little bursts of dust.

Right after Shakeel throws his last pebble, he is almost pushed down by a throng of Pakistanis. I grab him and pull him away from the scene. We run through the riotous crowd until we are outside again, safe, in the sun.

As we approach our camp, I turn and watch the arcing, sun-washed, overcrowded Jamarat overpass receding behind the tents. As I wander back, I realize I've made peace with the hajj, and with this rough, beautiful, holy place. Everything I have suffered seems almost necessary, because I am overcome with an unutterable serenity. How is it that, by some miracle, so many people can exist in the same small place at once?

We reach our camp, shave our heads, shower, change out of

our *ihram* robes into *jallabeyah* robes, roll out our mats, and sleep hard on the Mina dirt.

Murad Kalam is the author of the novel, Night Journey, *set in Phoenix, Arizona. He lives in Washington, D.C. and is working on a second novel set in Cairo.*

TIM MACKINTOSH-SMITH

⋆ ⋆ ⋆

Walking in Yemen's Terraced Mountains

A writer roams the storied hills of this other Arabia.

SOME WOMEN CALLED ME OVER FROM THE YARD OF THEIR house in the valley bottom. There were no men about and, although they were far from nubile, I sat at a demure distance on a wall. One of the women went inside the house while the other went on feeding a cow.

"Come on, my dear, eat," she said, coaxing a bundle of dry sorghum stalks wrapped in greenery into the cow's mouth.

"Can't she see it's a trick," I asked, "I mean wrapping all the sorghum like that?"

"Oh, she knows. But if you don't do it she'll eat nothing at all. It's a game." The woman held an unwrapped stalk out to the cow. It shook its head like a truculent child.

The other woman appeared with a tin bowl full of *qishr*, the discarded remains of coffee beans. All around, on large metal trays, coffee beans lay in the sun. I remembered *The Dispute between Coffee and Qat*, a literary contest composed in the middle of the nineteenth century in which each tree vies with the other in praising itself and belittling its opponent. The coffee tree says: "When my berries appear, their green is like ring stones of emerald or turquoise. Their color as they ripen is the yellow of golden amber necklaces. And when they are fully ripe they are as red as rare carnelian, or ruby or coral." The nearest jar of Nescafe was far away.

I said goodbye and set off on the track, which zigzagged up one of those stegosaurus backs like the one we had crossed in Surdud. I was still panting when I got to the yard-wide ridge. I hung my jacket on a prickly pear and sat down. Two men appeared from the direction of a solitary tower farther down the ridge. They were dressed in spotless white *zannahs*, lounge-suit jackets, and highly polished loafers. Not a bead of sweat showed on their faces. They greeted me without stopping, leaving behind them a strong scent of rosewater. The scent was still there when I looked up to the left ten minutes later. The men were far above, white flecks moving against the dark green of the mountain.

In an hour or so (a great deal of effort is compressed into those five monosyllables) I reached a village, unimaginative-ly—if appropriately—named al-Jabal, the Mountain. I propped myself up against a shop doorway and gulped down a can of ginger beer. Flavored with chemicals resulting from decades of research, packed in al-Hudaydah under franchise from a German firm in a can made from the product of a Latin American bauxite mine, furnished with a ring-pull which was the chance brainchild of a millionaire inventor, and brought here by truck, then donkey, for my delectation, it wasn't nearly as refreshing as the *qishr*. The ground was strewn with empty cans, each saying in Arabic and English "Keep your country tidy," and I wondered for a moment whether to put mine in my rucksack until I found a litter bin; but the nearest one was several days away, so I placed it at one end of the counter. The shopkeeper picked it up and threw it on the ground.

From al-Jabal to al-Hadiyah is downhill. At first the path was covered with rubbish, but soon there was just the odd sweet wrapper or juice carton as a reminder of the world of creation and corruption. The afternoon cloud rose, swirling past at speed, forced upwards by the cooling of Tihamah and channeled between the sides of the gorge. Everything but the rock wall either side of the path was cut off and I walked in silence. It was like swimming. Only once was the silence broken, by girls' voices singing a snatch of antiphony as they gathered fodder high above on the cliffs. The last note of each phrase was held, then let out with a strange downward *portamento*, like an expiring squeezebox.

About half an hour out of al-Jabal, a strange thing happened. For perhaps a minute the cloud parted, revealing two conical peaks directly in front and, below, a field of cropped turf, like a green on a golf course and perfectly circular. Then another column of cloud rose and shut out the vision. The precise geometry of the field's shape and its vivid color, and the way in which it had been revealed so unexpectedly and then veiled over, made it a mysterious sight. It had seemed to hover. It was the sort of place where you might bump into al-Khadir, the Green Man, a figure of lore variously considered saint, prophet, or angel, whose feet make green what they touch.

I half thought I had imagined the field and that the path would continue prosaically downwards, but I soon reached it. Once on it the perspective was different and its shape not apparent, a *trompe l'oeil* but seen too close to work. A few cattle lay round the margin of the field. They took no notice as I stood watching them and seemed anchored to the ground, oblivious of the intruder in their tiny, circular paradise.

After the field, the mist gradually disappeared and the other-worldliness was gone. Once more the path was beautifully maintained—it had to be, for it passed through an unbroken string of hamlets and carried a constant traffic of heavily laden donkeys. The boys who drove them had their *zannahs* hitched up and tucked behind their daggers. I stumbled down; so did the donkeys—but at twice the speed; the boys danced on stork-thin legs. Even the ones coming up danced.

I stopped to rest, and to look at the vista of receding mountain flanks sprinkled with little houses. Somewhere on this very path, Baurenfeind, the artist of the Niebuhr expedition, had stopped more than two centuries before to sketch the original drawings for the plate, "Prospect among the Coffee Mountains." It was the expedition's first experience of highland Yemen, and they were captivated by the scenery, the people, and the flora. The coffee trees, Niebuhr wrote, were in blossom and "exhaled an exquisitely agreeable perfume." It was a landscape in which, despite its natural ruggedness, the hand of Man could be seen everywhere.

Niebuhr's original *Beschreibung von Arabien* was at first ignored, but the French and then the English translations were hugely popular when they came out some years later. They had touched the spirit of the new age—the age of burgeoning Romanticism and the Picturesque. Up to then, the reading public had been given an Orient almost entirely of the imagination, colorful but savage. Now Europe began to look at the East through new eyes: Southey wrote of a garden "whose delightful air/Was mild and fragrant as the evening wind/Passing in summer o'er the coffee-groves/Of Yemen"; George Moore, in *Lalla Rookh*, of "the fresh nymphs bounding o'er Yemen's mounts." They had read their Niebuhr. Baurenfeind's plates, too, contributed to the new way in which people looked at mountains. Hitherto, mountains had been forbidding places, ignored or feared. Baurenfeind recorded a different image, of mountains dotted with folly-like dwellings, sculpted into terraces and covered with crops—in a word, humanized.

The light was beginning to go and the mountains were turning to amber, then carnelian. The humidity was increasing. The path leveled out and entered a *wadi*, snaking along the side of the valley through banana terraces which resembled a Rousseau jungle. I was half expecting to glimpse the shade of Baurenfeind sketching from a terrace wall, and when an old woman called out to me from above the path, I jumped. She laughed, and offered me some mouth-snuff. I was tempted but, not being used to it, didn't want to find myself retching for the sake of a quick nicotine fix.

After the airy peaks of Raymah, al-Hadiyah smelled fetid and unhealthy, although in Niebuhr's day it had been something of a hill-station for the European coffee merchants, a retreat from the even clammier heat of Bayt al-Faqih down on the plain. (The latter was sometimes rendered in English as "Beetle-fuckee"—probably a reflection of the merchants' feelings towards it rather than simple bad spelling.) I arrived in al-Hadiyah just after dark, knees jellified by the relentless descent from al-Jabal. I had arranged to stay in the English midwife's house; she had left the key with her neighbors as she was away—something of a relief, since it would save a lot of tongue-wagging.

The electricity went off early, interrupting me as I flicked through *Diarrhoea Dialogue*, the only reading material I could find in the house apart from *Where There Is No Doctor*—a book no hypochondriac should ever open, for it refuses to mince the strong meat of medical problems from leprosy to yaws. I made up a bed on the roof. A frog croaked softly from a pot of geraniums; elsewhere, geckoes clicked and the night was alive with other, unidentifiable, susurrations.

Not long after dawn the flies woke me. No trucks would leave for Bayt al-Faqih until later, so I walked to al-Hadiyah's main attraction, the waterfall. This plunges over a cliff in a single dizzy drop, then cascades in a series of deep pools. The path to it wriggled through rocky undergrowth and was home to dozens of glossy black millipedes; some were nearly a foot long and looked like pieces of self-propelled hosepipe.

When I reached the waterfall I found it empty. Little more than a dribble of moisture stained the rock. Only when it rained on the high places would the waterfall come to life, a roaring column of white against the dark cliff.

I sat there watching the dragonflies and thought of my absent hostess, delivering babies up in the mountains where the waterfall had its source. Horizontally she was no distance away; vertically, she was in a different world where climate, crops, dress, buildings, even speech, were different from those of al-Hadiyah. Any study, agricultural, ethnographic, or dialecto-logical, of Yemen's mountains would have to use a three-dimensional projection to map these variations. But in spite of the contrasts encountered over the vertical, the mountain people are bound together by a tenuous lifeline of water. Rain for the Arabs is *barakah*, a blessing; and it is particularly so for Yemen, where the great majority of cultivable land is rain-fed. In poetry, rain is a metaphor for human as well as divine generosity; historically, water is the reward of just government, and drought the punishment for profligacy. The beneficent rule of Imam al-Mutawakkil Isma'il in the mid-seventeenth century caused an increase in the water table, and even British policy in Hadramawt was said to have resulted in heavy rains there in 1937 (followed, it should be noted, by seven years of drought and famine); in contrast, Imam al-Mansur Ali made the wells run dry.

Barakah is for God to grant or withhold, but intercession can pay off. When there is no rain, the entire male population climbs to the high places and starts a litany—"Give us rain, O God. Have mercy on us, O God. Have mercy on the dumb beasts, thirsty for water, hungry for fodder." A sacrifice is made and left to the birds of the air. And if the rain comes, they do everything possible to hold it back. This is the function of the terraces which are so much a feature of the Yemeni landscape.

Yemen's terraces, its hanging gardens, contouring voluptuously round the flanks of mountains or perched, sometimes dinner-table sized, in what are often no more than vertical fissures, are not just a way of making a level surface. More important, they act like a cross between the pores of a giant sponge and the locks of a canal. The rain is trapped by them and contained in subdivisions separated by little bunds, before being released to the next level down in a slow and measured cascade. In slowing the downward flow of rainwater, too, terracing enables more of the *wadi* land to be cultivated. A torrential downpour, unchecked, runs away to waste and takes with it the *wadi*'s precious topsoil. The mountain men, as masters of the whole system, tend also to own the valleys and farm them out to sharecroppers. It is a system that calls for continual maintenance. The collapse of one terrace will affect the flow of water, and this in turn will lead to the destruction of terraces further down. Terraces must be kept planted so that the roots of plants consolidate the soil. The delicate balance can also be upset by the building of a surfaced road, which will speed up the flow of water and force streams into new channels.

People have to live at the top. If they didn't, the upper reaches of the wadis would also be uninhabitable, and cultivable land restricted to a few central plateaux, the hot and malarial coastal regions, and great inland wadis like Hadramawt and al-Jawf. The mountains would in time be stripped bare from top to bottom. Since the protective covering of forests was felled, the history of mountain Yemen has been that of a war waged against loss of land. The weather is, at the same time, the mountain farmer's reason for being and his antagonist.

And what an antagonist! Millions of tons of water, sizzled out of the Red Sea, fried off Tihamah, bounced up the wall of the escarpment and colliding with the cold highland air, pour down on Milhan, Hufash, Bura', Raymah, and the Two Wusabs. Evaporation and potential energy; blessing and destruction. This is why the Raymis live like eagles, why Yemen looks like nowhere else on earth.

Gazing up at the terraces hanging all around above me, this ultimate symbol of the Yemenis' co-existence with their land, I began to understand why al-Hamdani and the other geo-genealogists had turned mountains into ancestors. Lineage seems to have been relatively unimportant in pre-Islamic Yemen. It was the North Arabians, the rootless nomads, who developed the science of genealogy to give themselves a sense of continuity. At the same time, they looked down on settled farmers as peasants, with all the scorn that the word implies. As Islam spread over the Near East, the desert Arabs came across huge populations of settled serfs in Egypt and the Fertile Crescent working land which was not theirs.

Yemen was different. Here, the old civilizations had been based on agriculture. When these broke up, settlers moved further and further into the mountains, cutting down ancient forests and terracing the slopes. They were owner-occupiers, yeomen not serfs; and they still are—Yemen has remarkably few big landowners. Ali ibn Zayid, the Yemeni Hesiod, summed up their feelings: "The tribesman's glory is the soil of his home." Pride for the Yemenis is in land, not lineage.

To express these feelings and demonstrate the antiquity of the link between land and people—perhaps even to make a political point, that Yemen refused to be marginalized by a super-culture which idealized desert values—al-Hamdani and his school used the super-culture's own idiom: genealogy. By making place names the names of ancestors, they were literally planting the Qahtani family tree in the soil of Arabia Felix. It was an extraordinary landscape that they depicted, and—like the corner of it shown in Baurenfeind's plate—the most recognizable thing about it was the way in which it had been humanized.

And yet, for the West, the nineteenth century created a different image of Arabia. Explorers like Burton and Palgrave—and, more recently, the neo-Victorian Thesiger—portrayed a landscape of sterile sand where only individual qualities of honor and courage could ensure survival. Desert values were resurrected and romanticized, and they struck a chord with Europeans of a more puritan age. The chord still reverberates; received images have crowded out this other Arabia.

Tim Mackintosh-Smith is an Arabist, traveler, and writer. For the past twenty years his home has been the Yemeni capital San'a. His first book, Yemen: Travels in Dictionary Land, *won the 1998 Thomas Cook/Daily Telegraph Travel Book Award. His next, the best-selling* Travels with a Tangerine, *retraces the journeys of the fourteenth-century Moroccan traveler Ibn Battutah in the old Islamic world. His 2005 book* The Hall of a Thousand Columns *revisits the scenes of Ibn Battutah's Indian adventures. A sequel,* Worlds Beyond the Wind, *will trace the Moroccan's wanderings from the Maldives to China.*

SHANNON O'GRADY

Witnessing Ashura

An outsider experiences the passion
of a Shia holy ritual.

I CANNOT FORGET THE FIRST TIME THAT I MET ALAWI Al-Majeed, a well-known Shia Muslim religious scholar living in the old section of Manama, the capital city of Bahrain. Our first meeting took place along a road near the center of the souk, or marketplace, not far from the mosque where Alawi frequently lectured on Islam and politics. It had only been forty-eight hours since I had arrived on the small desert island when Sami, an old Bahraini friend, passed by my hotel and insisted that I accompany him to the souk, which was open late that evening. Sami needed to find a wedding gift for his cousin who had married one month earlier. I was still groggy from trying to overcome my jet lag, intense after the twenty-three-hour journey from the southwestern United States.

It was a warm night and I could hear the prayers from the mosque. My arrival coincided with the Islamic holy month of Muharram, when for ten days the Shia mourn the anniversary of the death of Imam Husayn, the Prophet Mohammad's grandson slain by his Sunni adversaries in A.D. 680, in what is known as the Battle of Karbala. The tomb of Husayn in the Iraqi city of Karbala remains a sacred shrine and a place of pilgrimage for followers of Shia Islam. The culmination of this holy time is the Ashura, the tenth and final day of the period, when Shia Muslims gather in the streets to publicly grieve the martyrdom of Husayn. The *souk* seemed particularly busy as people were coming and going from the central mosque. We found ourselves strolling in and out of the different shops. Sami was laughing as usual about something—he loved to tell jokes—but tonight I was too tired to catch them. The stores were about to close when Sami suggested that we pass by his friend Alawi's house, which was nearby.

We turned up the narrow road towards the rear of the souk where several of Bahrain's oldest houses stood side by side, composed of brick and mud—some with wooden lattice window frames and intricately carved wooden doors. Just a few yards in front of us was a tall, thin man with a black beard and dark eyes. He sat on the ground surrounded by young men who appeared to be listening attentively to his every word. Sami and I stood to the side, quietly waiting for Alawi to notice us.

Known for his poetry depicting the slaughter of Husayn, Alawi was barely forty years old, although the lines in his face made him appear much older. Sami had known Alawi since childhood and had told me stories about Alawi's life, mostly focusing on his dedication to helping the poor and those who had suffered. Alawi had gone to Iraq some years earlier to study Islamic texts in Najaf, another Shia holy city. While there he was arrested by Saddam's secret police for writing poetry that was deemed anti-government. Because someone in his family knew someone close to Saddam, he was released, but not without physical and emotional scars from the torture that he endured. Alawi was unable to use his right leg, but never spoke of his time in the Iraqi jail. Instead he chose to focus on what the Shia needed to do to improve their own lives. He was greatly admired for the manner in which he lectured about religion and politics, and for his passion for the Shia tradition of Azza, the public display of grieving that includes the ritual of self-flagellation and the chanting of poetry, songs, and Quranic verses to commemorate the death of Husayn. During Ashura, one could see the Azza ritual throughout the numerous Shia villages on the island, as scores of young and old men publicly shared their grief for their beloved Husayn. Alawi had written much of the Azza that was chanted by various groups from different mosques throughout Bahrain. Men of all generations from throughout the souk gathered to hear his impassioned recitations on the great Shia martyrs of Islam.

When Alawi finished speaking, he seemed surprised to discover Sami standing there. Instantly they were kissing each other on both cheeks. Alawi had a big smile and said many kind things, which I recognized as Islamic prayers that mostly the older people use when greeting one another. Although Alawi warmly acknowledged me, he did not look me in the eye. I knew that he was following the tradition of not making eye contact with a woman, as such behavior was considered disrespectful by more conservative Shia Muslims. When he spoke to me he stared at the ground, then looked to Sami, as though through Sami's eyes he was reaching mine. I was struck by Alawi's harsh face, with its sharp angular features, which made his extraordinarily kind eyes seem even more gentle.

Alawi glanced downward and asked Sami in Arabic, "Why don't you take Layla"—my Arabic name given to me by my Bahraini friends in the U.S.—"to see the Ashura processions tonight? It will be safe for her if she goes with your mother and sisters. She might really like seeing the Azza up close with your family."

I was taken aback. The last thing I expected from this traditional Shia sheikh was for him to invite me, an American woman who was not Muslim, to witness the Shia community's most passionate display of religious devotion. The Ashura observance involves processions of men, young and old, walking through the streets late into the night, mourning the death of Husayn by pounding their chests and chanting the Azza prayers and poems. In many cases, they practice self-flagellation to display their compassion and mourning for Husayn. Ashura also had the potential to turn into a demonstration, as some of the poetry recited also expresses political opinion that is not always favorable to the local government or the U.S.

In spite of my excitement to see the Azza, I had a moment of hesitation. I had seen the ritual once before from a distance and had wanted to be closer, but could not because security was too intense. Still, I remembered having been absolutely mesmerized by the level of devotion. Now, I imagined having the chance to witness it along with the women of Sami's family. But could it be dangerous for an American woman to be there given all of the political turmoil in the Middle East? That thought came and went as I comforted myself with the idea that I would be safe with Sami and his family.

On the eve of the tenth of Muharram, most of the women in Sami's family would be gathered at his grandmother's house, which was set far back inside the old narrow streets of Manama, directly along the path of the processions. It was the ideal location to view the processions, which would begin late and go all night into the early morning of the tenth, the anniversary of Husayn's death.

That afternoon when I returned to my air-conditioned hotel room, I pulled out my *abbaya* and *hijab*, one type of traditional Islamic dress for women, which I always took with me when traveling to the Middle East. I knew for this evening I would need to have my head covered with the *hijab,* a simple scarf, and wear the black *abbaya,* a long silk cover over my clothes. As I tried them on in front of the mirror, I laughed at myself. The scarf made me look funny, certainly not attractive, but I guess that was the point. I began to play with the scarf a bit and wrapped it more loosely around my hair, the way I had seen some of my more stylish students wear theirs. I put on my make-up, first using my black eye pencil to do my eyes the way Arab women do with the lower eyelid heavily lined. Then I put on some lipstick and stared into the mirror. At that moment I saw a Middle Eastern woman. I also had the thought that I looked more like I was going to a women's party with all the make-up on, rather than to mourn with the Shia during this sacred occasion.

Roadblocks were everywhere. The police had sectioned off the streets. After a lot of searching, I squeezed the old, enormous Mercedes Benz that Sami had lent me tightly into a parking spot not too far from the center of town. I shyly got out of my car, very self-conscious about arriving alone. It was unusual to see a woman dressed in Islamic clothing driving herself to watch the late night Ashura processions. The night was warm and it felt good to be walking. Although I had worn an *abbaya* and *hijab* before, I still wasn't quite sure how to carry myself in them, so I watched and imitated the women around me. I still felt rather clumsy.

Sami was supposed to meet me on one of the corners near the central mosque. Crowds were beginning to form. Groups of women walked together and chatted like schoolgirls. They were thrilled to be given a night out where they could legitimately stay up as late as they wanted, which most could rarely do. For the older women who viewed the crowds through their black veils, it was a time of mourning and great sadness. For the younger generations, it was also a time of mourning but additionally an opportunity to gaze at the young men who would soon be marching with great passion through the streets, slowly beating their chests while reciting the Azza incantations with profound emotion. Most of the men would wear black t-shirts, a few would be bare-chested, but all would be openly displaying their grief for the slaughter of their beloved Husayn. On this night, the Shia could cry out in protest against the injustices they had faced throughout history. Their words, as is also the case with many Arab traditions that predate the Islamic era, would pour forth as stories or poems, carefully woven into the cries of Azza. In these chants, poems, and prayers for the revered martyrs of Islam are cries for justice—justice for Imam Husayn who was killed 1,300 years ago, for the abuse of the Shia today, and for the end to the oppression in which so many of them live.

As I walked closer to the place where I was to meet Sami, the sounds of the drums, the chants, and the men beating their chests grew louder and louder. I felt excited and apprehensive as I walked through the crowd, bringing myself closer to the processions. Indian workers rode by on their bicycles, hoping to get a view of the event. There was a sense of danger in the air—danger of being caught in a public demonstration where emotions are extremely heightened. Public police forces were on alert. Out of fear for their own security, the government preferred to employ non-Bahrainis over the locals. Most of these guards were from other Arab countries and some were from Pakistan. All of these men had machine guns strapped to their shoulders.

I saw Sami's friend Mohammad standing on a street corner smoking a cigarette. I called out to him, and he looked towards me and stared blankly. I shouted again, and he suddenly recognized me, reacting with surprise.

"Layla?" said Mohammad, still a bit stunned. "What in the

world are you doing here? And look how beautiful you are wearing the *hijab*. You look like a Persian girl. Wow, you should wear this all the time!"

I felt slightly embarrassed by his comments. I had hoped he would be subtler, as I felt self-conscious enough in these clothes.

"Sami is around here somewhere," continued Mohammad. "I just saw him. Stay here and I'll go find him."

Finally having arrived, I suddenly had the feeling that I should leave. There was a palpable tension in the crowd. I saw older women crying while listening to the chanting and other groups of women talking softly as they looked for a place to sit along the road. I was alone, which felt peculiar given that no one was there alone that night, especially not women. Just as I started to walk away, I heard Sami laughing in the distance. Sami had a great sense of humor and loved to poke fun at others. He greeted me with a big smile. This time I was the object of his joking.

"Hey, *Hajia*, where are you going?" teased Sami. *Hajia* is a term used for women who have made the sacred Islamic pilgrimage to Mecca. "Layla," he continued, "you make a very good Shia. When my mother sees you, I know she will want you to marry me!" I resisted giving him a swift kick. He laughed at me again and said, "Come on, it's late. I've got to get you to my grandmother's house."

At last I was at ease in my new surroundings. I could relax and soak up the feeling of just being there. As we got closer to the center of town, the crowds grew larger. Soon we had to step over masses of people sitting on the roads and push ourselves through the mob in order to reach Sami's grandmother's house. It was an old house, built more than one hundred years ago, located on the corner of two of the busiest streets in the souk.

When we entered, the women rapidly approached me, told

me in Arabic how beautiful I looked in my Islamic dress, and asked if I was ready to be Shia yet. I smiled at them, feeling appreciative of their warm and welcoming manner. They joked a bit with Sami, then Rabab, Sami's sister, showed us to the second floor balcony that extended out the front of the house and overlooked the street. It was a small balcony, narrow, and very close to the neighboring one.

Rabab asked me in English if I would like something to eat or drink. I told her that I was fine and thanked her. She offered again, and I again replied that I was fine and thanked her. The third time she offered I accepted, knowing that it was customary to refuse a host or hostess until they have offered refreshments three times.

A few minutes later she brought tea. We sat quietly for a while until she asked me if this was the first time I had come to see Azza. I explained that I had tried in the past but could never get close enough, and that I didn't feel secure seeing it alone. She said I was right in that it could be dangerous if the crowds were out of control, especially if the police got involved for any reason. This house was a very good place for viewing, she said, because we were on the second floor.

In the distance I could hear the sounds of the Azza chants. Each time I heard the men in the procession hit their chests, a vibration resonated throughout my body. What I was feeling echoed a primitive part of my own being, awakened by this ritual from more than a thousand years ago. Old women peering out of the windows of dilapidated houses nearby looked sad, the tears on their faces a reflection of the deep faith they lived by. A traditional event such as this seemed a way to release their pain—pain for themselves, pain for their children, pain for the oppression of the Shia, and most of all, pain for the loss of the Imam Husayn.

The chanting grew louder and more fervent. I could now

see crowds of young men in black t-shirts pounding their chests as they led the procession into the square. Behind them, bare-chested men followed in an apparent state of hypnotic devotion. As the sounds of the Azza intensified, all the women in the house rushed out to the balcony with me. Sami's cousin, Zahra, who spoke English quite well, asked if I understood the chants. I said no, but they seemed very powerful. She told me they were cursing the Umayyads—the ruling Sunni family that held power from Damascus—for causing the death of Husayn. They were also praising Imam Ali, Husayn's father and the Prophet Mohammad's first cousin. Soon the beat of the drums took over and I could no longer hear what Zahra was saying. The men turned in circles, intensely beating their chests. I was mesmerized by the chants, the prayers, and the disturbing sound of flesh striking flesh.

The drumming was loud and sounded as if it was building to a crescendo when, suddenly, I began to smell the blood. I looked toward the square and saw droves of young men beating their bare backs with razor blades attached to the ends of chains. Zahra explained that their sorrow was for the loss of Imam Husayn and his followers' inability to protect him.

Now blood was everywhere. Some of the women began to feel sick. They could no longer watch this part of the ritual and went indoors. But I could not pull myself away. It was as though I was living a thousand years back in time. I started to feel full with grief. I wanted to cry. Suddenly I saw swords being drawn as some of the men began hitting the tops of their heads and chanting the name of Husayn's father Ali, who was also murdered by another opposing Islamic group, the Kharijites.

The crowd was wild, some men drumming, turning in circles, chanting, and beating their chests. Others were bleeding profusely from the lashes of the chains with razors. I could sense mounting tension in the crowd and began to feel afraid because I was so close. I watched, entranced, as the masses of men continued past, their tensions and passions reaching a fevered pitch.

My attention was drawn to a horse among the procession. It was painted green and had red-painted pigeons tied to a piece of black fabric draped over its side. The belief was that, because the ruling Umayyads had stolen Imam Husayn's clothes after murdering him, pigeons swarmed around and covered his bare body to protect him from the hot desert sun. I could hear the name of Zaynab, Imam Husayn's sister, being called out. It was Zaynab who made the trip from Karbala hundreds of miles back to Damascus on horseback, carrying only the head of her murdered brother. This horse was draped with black fabric to depict the sorrow felt by Zaynab, as well as the courage of her mournful and enduring journey. Again the name "Umayyad" was chanted and all the men got down on their knees and prayed. It was a very stirring moment. I felt myself melt into their sadness. Once this group passed, another came, and this time a softer chanting echoed through the night air. A group of old men passed by, very slowly beating their chests and reciting the most melodic of verses. It was almost as though they were singing, a moment that struck me as the softest of Azza that I had witnessed. It had a beautiful, soothing tone to it. Their voices drew me inward to a place of deep reflection. The power of their devotion and faith was overwhelming.

Umm Ali, Sami's mother, who had quietly been sitting next to me, picked up the bowl of fruit sitting on the table and offered it to me. We smiled to one another, then returned our attention to the men outside. Again I could hear the sound of flesh hitting flesh in the distance as each man forcefully brought down his right hand against his bare chest, producing a sound that echoed through the narrow streets of Manama. In unison, they continued passionately voicing the chants of Azza into the darkness of the warm night. I watched them, sharing their grief and feeling privileged to be a part of this great occasion.

This commemoration of the death of Husayn brings to life the rich history of Shia Islam. It unifies the Shia as a group in the same way the Islamic prayer unifies Muslims worldwide. There is a power to this practice that keeps Shia culture and traditions alive as it gets passed on to each new generation. Even after years of studying Islam, it wasn't until those moments of watching the Azza up close with the women of Sami's family that I felt I understood the true devotion of Shia Muslims.

Shannon O'Grady received her Ph.D. in International Education and Development from the University of Southern California. She taught at the University of Bahrain during the late 1980s and did fieldwork there a decade later, working to assist in developing HIV/AIDS education programs. She also contributed to the Middle East Human Rights Watch report submitted to the U.S. Congress and has worked as an editor of the International Encyclopedia of Women. *O'Grady lives in New Mexico where she teaches courses on Islamic Historyand Culture at the College of Santa Fe and has her own publishing company, Bookworks, Santa Fe. This piece was adapted from her upcoming book,* Petals of Jasmin—A Journey into the World of Shia Islam.

✦ ✦ ✦

In Jerusalem

*A pilgrim experiences the ancient
place for the first time.*

A DAY LATE, AND A SHEKEL SHORT. THAT'S HOW I FELT, AT FIRST:
overwhelmed by the ancient walled city. The historic air of
Jerusalem will never vanish, but how one longs for the days
before honking taxis, halogen lamps, and teenage soldiers with
automatic weapons slung over their backs.

People hurried by, racing the sunset, as my beer captured the
last rays of daylight. The western entrance to Old Jerusalem is
an extraordinary place; you can nod to black-cloaked Armenian
priests, watch Hasids trot by in their huge fur hats, smile at
dark-eyed girls hurrying home to help with the Sabbath meal,
salaam the elderly Palestinian with his checkered kaffiyeh and
worry beads. And all the while you're fending off shifty-eyed
touts, wolfish guides, taxi drivers, and other tomcats, all orbiting
past your small wooden seat, just down the cobblestones from
Jaffa Gate.

I left a few coins on the café table and wandered into the
labyrinth. The long flight of steps down King David and a
sharp left brought me into the Muslim Quarter. El-Wad was

crammed with a steady stream of Arabs, flowing toward the Dome of the Rock. Both sides of the path were lined with stalls, a frenetic Middle Eastern bazaar offering halvah and gummy bears, jeans and watches, perfumes, prayer beads, and PC peripherals. Ahead was Damascus Gate, where the coffee was cheap and strong.

Walled cities are worlds unto themselves; outsiders can take away only the barest notion of life within their borders. I walked miles and took as many pictures as I could, but never felt like more than a flat stone, skimming the surface of profound antiquity. It was like being handed a copy of *Anna Karenina* or *Catch-22* or the Bible, and asked to write a review based on one or two randomly chosen sentences.

Another hour of wandering brought me to the fringe of the Jewish Quarter, near the end of Western Wall Road. I hesitated. If I followed the path, it would take me to the Kotel, the foundation wall of the Second Temple, an immense synagogue built by King Herod and destroyed by the Romans in about A.D. 70. The Western Wall is the most sacred site in Judaism—but was I prepared? I had neglected to bring, on this first foray into the Old City, the satchel of prayers that I'd solicited from friends back home. Such missives, rolled up and tied with string, are pressed into cracks between the ancient stones of the Western Wall. Approaching the Wall without them felt awkward, like attending a housewarming without a bottle of wine.

Yet here I was. How could I resist?

I'd seen so many pictures of the Wailing Wall that I was surprised by how exposed, how stark it appears. My sense had been that the wall was in a grove, or on a platform, free-standing. But the single remaining section of the Great Temple is not an interior wall, but part of the building's foundation. It is enormous, and continues on well past the area where a sea of men in black skullcaps were bowing and muttering prayers with a rapid rhythm.

My single wish was to experience a moment in this holy place alone. But I was given no peace. From the moment I arrived, weary- and wild-eyed devotees competed for my attention. Some demanded I leaf through albums of their charitable deeds and make a generous contribution; others insisted that I receive a blessing from their reb and make a generous contribution. A dozen more, in fluent English full of zeal, tried to kit me out in *tefillen*: small prayer boxes that, tied to the head and arm with leather straps, affirm one's covenant with God.

The one place offering respite from these spiritual remoras was the Wall itself. I made straight for it and pressed my hands and head against the timeworn stone. The crevices were stuffed with bits of folded paper, all prayers, some many decades old. It took a few moments for me to find the wavelength, but after a few moments, the power of the site began emanating through the sandstone and into my skull. When I pulled back from the bricks, my face was streaked with tears.

No visitor to Jerusalem, Jewish or otherwise, should spend Shabbat, the Sabbath, alone. Seeking to avoid this fate, I strolled into the heart of the Jewish Quarter.

I found the flyer tacked outside the Jewish Student Information Center. A crude photocopy, it showed a scene from *Seinfeld*, with Cosmo Kramer leaning hilariously into the door of Jerry's apartment. "Drop in for a Shabbat meal," it said, and gave the number of Jeff Seidel, the social and spiritual ringmaster for visitors to Jerusalem.

Seidel's mission is to place every person who so desires with a local family for Shabbat dinner. I called his cell phone and was told to be at the drinking fountains near the Kotel at precisely 6:10 P.M.

"How will I find you?" I asked.

"Ask anybody," he replied.

Arriving at the Wall, I approached the first person I saw. "Do you know Jeff Seidel?"

"Of course. He was here a minute ago…. There he is!" Seidel is a short, bespectacled, action-packed figure. He was nearly hidden, surrounded by dozens of men and women. Most were in their teens and early twenties. I was told the drill: one stands directly in front of Seidel so he knows you are there. He appraises you for a moment, then assigns you to a family, apparently at random.

I assumed the position, waiting beside a young yeshiva student named Adam. After a few moments, Seidel pointed to us and fished a slip of paper out of a skullcap. He handed it to me, then leaned over with great curiosity. "So who did you get?" He read the tag. "Oh! The Helbfingers. They're very good. Very good. You're lucky!" Adam and I nodded gamely; he must say this to all the prospective diners.

Some of the families in Seidel's hat were a fair distance from the Old City, requiring a long taxi or bus ride. Ours—great luck!—was just around the corner, not two minutes' walk from the Wall. One of Seidel's colleagues escorted us, and we soon found ourselves rapping on the Helbfingers' broad wooden door.

It is impossible to overstate the rush of comfort and delight I experienced as Mrs. Helbfinger—a clear-eyed, kind-looking woman wearing a blue headscarf and modest white dress— invited us into her home. The large flat had been occupied since the Crusaders took Constantinople. It was 800 years old, with arched ceilings and simple white walls. The bookshelves were lined with religious volumes; Mr. Helbfinger, I learned, was a retired cantor from a Cleveland synagogue. The table was dressed with white linen and set for twelve. Besides our hosts, their son, Yaacov, and their daughter, Chaiyet, there would be eight guests as well.

"It's our pleasure to do this," said Mrs. Helbfinger, who made *aliyah*—the immigration, or "coming up" to Israel—in 2002. "Back in Cleveland, there were so few Jews passing through town that people would fight to host them on Friday evenings."

Dinner began with the candle-lighting prayers, but nothing resembling a formal service. The event was meant to welcome the Shabbat, the holy day of rest. For this, there was sweet red wine and dense, homemade challah. The other guests—all of them either friends of Yaacov's or local students of Judaism, steered to the Helbfingers by Seidel—knew the words and melodies by heart. Reb Helbfinger, a delightfully solicitous host with porcelain skin and a long gray beard, looked much older than his olive-complexioned wife. I was placed in the seat of honor, on his left. He frequently and eagerly leaned over to explain exactly what we were reading, and why.

Jewish prayers are unusual, he explained, in that they rarely actually ask for anything. They are not petitions to improve the circumstances of the devotee. The blessings over the wine and bread, for example, are simple statements of gratitude for the fruits of the vine and the earth. Even the somber and personal *yahrzeit*, recited when mourning a loved one, is a universal prayer for peace.

The meal was served. Our bread and wine, which begins every Sabbath dinner, were followed by olives and hummus, tabouli, gefilte fish with horseradish, chopped salad, falafel, pita bread, and many other small plates. I ate well, acknowledging that this easily prepared meal—a dozen courses of Middle Eastern *mezze*—was sensible, given the number of people the Helbfingers fed each Friday.

Imagine my astonishment when Chaiyet cleared off the table, changed our cutlery and brought out our actual dinner:

a fragrant roast chicken, steamed rice with Persian bean stew, roasted potatoes, green beans in curry, and the most delicious noodle kugel I've ever tasted. Then followed dessert: freshly baked banana bread and cardamom cookies.

No payment was expected for this feast. All the Helbfingers asked was that we share our impressions of Jerusalem. Our host began, speaking about the joys and foibles of life in the city. Helbfinger described how worried he was when, on renting this flat, he had learned it had once been a prayer room. "This meant, technically, that I would have to perform all sorts of elaborate rituals before making love here with my wife." Fortunately, various loopholes in conjugal law were discovered.

Adam, my companion at the Wall, was a sincere and open-hearted teenager, discovering his affinity for Judaism after a year in Israel. The other guests faded more or less into the background, but Reb Helbfinger was thrilled to learn that one of them—a painfully shy young man with handsome eyes, jet-black hair, and an unmistakably Semitic nose—was the great-great-great grandson of Reb Zushya from Anapoli, a beloved Hasidic rabbi of the late nineteenth century. Zushya gained great fame with a single anecdote. "I won't be worried," he once told his students, "if, when I die, God asks me, 'Why weren't you a Moses, or an Aaron, or a Joseph?' I will worry if He asks me, 'Why weren't you Zushya?'"

After half a dozen glasses of the nectar-like wine, my own tongue was loose. I told the story of my 1999 visit to Iran, and how gracious and generous the Persian Muslims had been. On one occasion, I recounted, I found myself held against my will in a Tehran diner, surrounded by fierce-looking locals. I was certain I was being taken hostage. True enough, I would not be permitted to leave—until my hosts treated me to an elaborate buffet.

As the most recently arrived guest, and as an American, I

was asked my views on many other subjects—including the Palestinian situation.

I found it difficult, in this Orthodox company, to express my empathy for the Palestinian cause. Still, I had to. Earlier in the day, walking through the Arab sections, I'd watched as elderly women selling fennel and sage from baskets were forced off the streets. I had seen Ariel Sharon's arrogant loft in the center of the Muslim district, the sharpshooters on the rooftops, the checkpoints, and the armored security cameras. It was difficult to view the workaday Arabs, most of them Israeli citizens, as anything but second-class citizens.

But the truth was that, after four days in Jerusalem, I found it impossible to fix blame anywhere. Every effect can be traced back to a cause, but every cause was in itself an effect. The cycle seemed endless, a cord running far back into the past and disappearing into the future.

The Helbfingers and their guests listened patiently. Everyone was amazed that I had spent part of the afternoon on the steps outside Damascus Gate, reading a newspaper among the pigeons and Palestinians. It was no mystery, I discovered, why so many Jews in Jerusalem do not fathom the Arab mentality. They have no Arab friends; they do not enter the Muslim areas, except to hurry through or do some quick shopping. An especially telling moment came when Yaacov, the Helbfingers' son, described in amazement how his Muslim classmates at Haifa University had refused all social invitations, clinging without compromise to their routine of daily prayers and forgoing the consumption of alcohol.

"Are they brainwashed," Yaacov asked, "or are they simply made differently?" It was an impossible question for me to address, of course—but it spoke volumes about the rift between these intertwined people and illustrated how difficult it will be, in the context of such bewilderment, to achieve peace in this part of the world.

There is a certain hubris to voicing almost any opinion in Jerusalem. At dinner's end, I begged my hosts' pardon for any presumption I may have betrayed. But the Helbfingers seemed grateful for my honesty and invited me to return whenever fate might allow. Our evening ended, I think, on a note of mutual respect.

It was now past nine, and the Old City was dark. I walked back the way we had come, returning to the now virtually empty Wall. A dozen men sat at the Temple's foundation, reciting blessings from large-type prayer books. This time, my cloth satchel of blessings was in my pocket, but inserting them into the Wall turned out to be more difficult than I had anticipated. Every single crack and cranny was crammed to capacity with prayers, scraps of every size and shape. It took me many minutes, and much studying of the Wall's crumbling architecture, to find resting places for my hopeful missives.

The final piece of paper in my cloth satchel was blank. It was meant for my own prayer, but I hadn't yet written one. Writing is forbidden on the Sabbath, and although I don't abide by this back home, it seemed best to be discreet while standing at Judaism's most sacred shrine. So I pressed the scrap of rice paper to my forehead, and conveyed my wish by direct transmission.

It seemed to take. I rolled the paper up tightly, found a narrow opening, and pressed my prayer so deeply into the wall that nothing short of an earthquake could dislodge it.

The traditional Jewish Sabbath begins with the blessings known as the kiddush. It ends with the lighting of a braided candle, in a ceremony called *havdalah*, the passage from the sacred back to the profane.

Twenty-four hours after my dinner with the Helbfingers, the three stars signaling the end of Sabbath appeared. I walked along the outer wall of the Old City and made my way to the Triangle, the tiny, lively district bounded by King George, Ben Yehuda, and Jafo streets. There, I found myself in the middle of a huge outdoor party, as if every Jewish teenager in the Holy Land had converged on this one spot. Hundreds of kids milled between the ice cream parlors, cafés, and falafel shops, while young Hasids whirled to the accompaniment of an electric piano. Everyone was talking to everybody else; nobody seemed left out. Kids with cell phones and hamburgers, girls in tight pants, boys with earrings and braids, and on every corner boys and girls with A-3s slung over their shoulders, smoking and laughing as if the deadly weapons were just part of a party costume. The military presence was welcome; just one week ago, right down the block, a bus had been struck by a suicide bomber.

The Jewish State is still, essentially, a state of mind, and the reverence of the Helbfingers' Sabbath night dinner found its perfect complement in these defiant, celebratory *havdalah*. There were no Arabs in evidence, as if this weekly ritual was a reassertion of the Jewish claim to Jerusalem—not just as a holy city, but as a place for cell phones and sundaes, glitter and raves. The scene seemed to embody the ironic, passive-aggressive motto on the country's tourist materials: "Israel: No One Belongs Here More Than You."

It had been a long time since I'd encountered anything so familiar, yet so strikingly alien.

Oakland, California-based Jeff Greenwald is the author of several books, including Scratching the Surface, Shopping for Buddhas, *and* The Size of the World. *He is also the director of Ethical Traveler, an international alliance uniting travelers to help protect human rights and the global environment (www.ethicaltraveler.com).*

WAYNE MILSTEAD

✦ ✦ ✦

Serendipity in Cyprus

A chance encounter yields delicious rewards.

SOMETIMES THE BEST LESSONS ARE UNPLANNED. SERENDIPITY is an intuitive teacher. It has a way of stepping in where course catalogs leave off, providing what you need to know when you need to know it. In our case, serendipity came in the form of George and Lara.

Sipping Cypriot brandy next to the fire at our hotel in Polis, Cyprus, on a brisk January evening, my traveling companion, Aaron, and I glimpsed two shivering figures emerging from the beach. As they stepped out of the darkness into the muted light of the bar, we could see it was a man and woman. The man ordered Commandaria, a popular sweet wine with a history spanning ten centuries. The woman ordered a warm drink of unknown origins. They spoke Greek, so I figured they were locals. They huddled near the fire to steal some warmth and immediately introduced themselves as George and Lara.

He was a handsome man with long salt-and-pepper hair pulled into a ponytail and a thick mustache of the same color. He had the sort of appearance that causes you to instinctively look for the guitar case and the rest of the band. The woman had a natural beauty and air of sophistication, like the women you see in films leaping white fences on thoroughbreds, doffing their equestrian helmet, and flashing a devilish smile.

To say the least, this was a marked difference from the two dour German couples in hiking boots and '70s-style mono-chromatic t-shirts who sat quietly in the bar each night and in the dining room each morning carefully avoiding eye contact or any other excuse to acknowledge our presence. It was off-season and the hotel didn't appear to have more than six guests the entire week we were there. This apparent desire for anonymity was considerably awkward with no crowd to blend into. While solitude on the hiking trails was a major incentive in planning our trip, it was nice to finally have someone to compare notes with.

George, who grew up near Polis, agreed it was a good time to visit. He and Lara were on vacation themselves. While it got chilly at night, during the day it was t-shirt weather. With few tourists, it was the perfect time of year to explore the natural beauty of this swath of southwestern Cyprus.

Dotted with citrus groves, overlooking turquoise seas, Polis is the least developed beach resort in the south of Cyprus. What is most striking is the variety of the landscape in such a small area. It ranges from rocky promontories to lush meadows and rugged forests to sleepy monasteries and quiet beaches.

The famous Akamas Peninsula is just down the road. Set aside as a preservation area, it is a wild finger of land jutting into the Mediterranean, with a network of nature trails and the Bath of Aphrodite, a waterfall and pool where legend says the goddess escaped to bathe when not entertaining lovers.

Lara asked what we had seen of the island.

We told her how we took advantage of several days of sun, during what is normally Cyprus' rainy season, by hiking through vineyards, orchards, and trails rife with wild herbs. The byproduct of the rain was a lush countryside. At the end of each hike we usually gorged on a meal of Cypriot specialties.

I'm a firm believer that you learn more about a place by eating its food and walking its streets than by staring in a thousand glass museum cases. It was the cuisine and the hiking that attracted us to Cyprus in the first place. So while we let our feet be the guide during the day, at night, our stomachs led the way.

The journey was tasty, but we wanted to learn more. Why was some *haloumi* cheese squeaky as the sole of your sneaker and others squishy like jelly? What's in season? Is *taramosalata* a native Cypriot dish? Why does it vary in color? How does Cypriot cooking differ from that in Greece and Turkey? We wanted to taste authentic dishes we had read about but not encountered in restaurants. The original pre-departure plan was to take a cooking class in Cyprus, but none were offered in January. As we soon learned, most Cypriots involved in the restaurant or tourist trade take the month off.

Enter serendipity.

"We own a restaurant in Yeroskipou near Paphos," George said. They only serve what he described as real Cypriot cuisine: uncultivated plants gathered from the verdant country-side and seasonal produce along with natural handmade cheeses, breads, and quality fish and meats. The types of dishes you would find in a Cypriot village home. "No chips or *taramosalata* at our taverna," George mused.

They were taking a break, staying in a villa at the hotel.

It was not long before George, sipping his Commandaria in the glow of the fire, began lecturing on "Cypriot Cooking 101." He explained the basics, the differences between styles of cooking, and how to find edible plants in the wild. He answered Aaron's *taramosalata* question. It originated in Thessalonica,

Greece but is common in Cyprus. George explained that the color varies from white to vast degrees of pink depending on the type of fish roe used and whether or not coloring is added. There was a time when *taramosalata* in the region was made from local roe. Now, with fishing stocks depleted, most roe is imported, meaning the type and quality varies widely.

Food in the south is eastern Mediterranean in spirit. Classics such as hummus, Greek-style salad called "village salad," eggplant salad, roasted meats, and fish (on the coast) abound. While feta is common, the ubiquitous local cheese is *haloumi*, usually served grilled or pan-fried. George said its texture varies based on the amount of sheep's versus cow's milk used. The traditional style of eating in Cyprus is called *meze*. It is best described as a revolving buffet, consisting of small portions of as many as twenty different cold and hot dishes served as they are prepared. Traditional Cypriot cuisine is quintessential village food. Simple, tasty recipes based on fresh seasonal produce and whatever meat is available.

When we finally said good night, George gave us a list of places to hike, including his favorite vineyard, along with the names and locations of open restaurants where we could sample the various dishes he had described.

We couldn't believe our luck. This was exactly the type of insider knowledge that brings a cuisine alive. We couldn't wait to head out into the countryside the next day equipped with a deeper understanding of Cypriot food, culture, and the natural environment. We had no idea that the fireside lecture included a practicum.

The next evening George was waiting for us in the parking lot when we returned from the hike in the mountainous Vouni Panayia Vineyards he had recommended.

"Did you get our note?" he asked.

"No," I said. "What was it about?"

"We want to cook for you," he said. He wanted to show us what he had told us the night before. No argument there. The best food talking and writing can't hold a candle to cooking and eating. We agreed without hesitation.

The scent of fresh herbs and garlic tickled our noses as we entered George and Lara's villa. Earlier, when he invited us to dinner, George mentioned they had gathered some "weeds" to eat. I thought he was joking. He wasn't. The kitchen resembled a greenhouse overflowing with a lush garden of fresh wild greens, herbs, vegetables, and fungi.

It was probably coals to Newcastle, but we presented our hosts with a couple bottles of wine we had bought at the vineyard.

"Thank you. I bought some, too. We have lots to drink," George said with a devilish grin, handing me the corkscrew.

Small dishes sprouted like mushrooms on the table: olives marinated in oil and coriander, fresh tomato and celery, and slices of bread topped with sesame seeds.

"These are called baby sparrows," George said, holding a dark green plant. "That's what the Greek means. In English you call it bladder campion. Sometimes customers get a frightened look on their face because of the name. They think they are eating baby birds." I understood the name when he stripped the leaves off. They resembled tiny feathers. He then fried them in a skillet with eggs, creating an omelet of sorts.

We helped chop, dice, and open wine, while asking questions, taking notes, and tasting the results.

"See these," Lara said, pointing to a clump of weeds in a colander. "These are wild mustard greens." She sautééed them in olive oil with fresh lemon juice. An exotic grassy aroma filled the room. *That's what fresh smells like*, I thought. I savored the refreshing chlorophyll flavor as I washed them down with Alina, the smooth waterlike white wine.

As we plowed through wild leeks sautééed with fresh thyme and olive oil, George filled our empty glasses with a rich, chocolatey limited-edition Cypriot red called Carmen. He bought most of the allotment for his restaurant. "It's not available anymore," George informed me. I was heartbroken. I drank slowly and surveyed the table.

There was *haloumi* made by hand in the village where George's mother lives. "It was still warm when it was delivered this morning," Lara said. There were also fresh *loukanica* sausages made by George's mother. We sampled a plate of fresh *anari* cheese. George served it deliciously plain, explaining that it is often eaten at breakfast with the locally made carob syrup, *teratsemelo*. With this new knowledge I tried this combination the next morning. It added a whole new dimension to the cheese.

Lara placed sliced avocado drizzled with olive oil, lemon, and herbs on the table. While an introduced species, avocado thrives in the region.

Next came a sautéé of fennel mushrooms with olive oil, fresh rosemary, and garlic. George explained that they got their name because they grow at the roots of wild fennel plants. I had seen hordes of fennel while hiking. George said the mushrooms only grow in certain areas and that you had to know what to look for. He picked these particular ones earlier that morning with his mother. "She has the eye," he said, referring to his mother's mushroom-hunting prowess. Lara agreed. "She just walks out and points and there they are," she said.

Lara followed the mushrooms with salmon broiled with lemon and fennel.

Our pace slowed. I glanced over at the counter with a strange mix of anticipation and dread. How could I eat another bite? How could I not?

Large mushrooms that grow at the roots of pine trees

roasted in the oven. They looked like golden upside down hats from a Dr. Seuss story. George served them drizzled with garlic, olive oil, and lemon juice. The infamous velvety textured Cypriot potatoes roasted with cumin and pepper followed.

George poured more wine and glowed with pride as we picked at the remaining morsels. He rubbed his back. It was sore from picking mushrooms.

As the conversation turned from food preparation to the relaxed banter of friendship, I couldn't help thinking about the power of food to unite. And to teach.

We didn't sign up for a class with George and Lara, our common love of food convened us. And the rest just happened.

Two days later George and Lara loaded their truck and headed back to Paphos. "Follow us out of town," George said. "I will show you where you should walk today."

We drove along the main road out of town, out past the beach and then turned onto the highway to Paphos. Our stomachs rolled as we barreled down the mountainous road trying to keep up with George. Finally we turned onto a gravel road and he slowed down. At the top of a hill, we pulled over and got out. We stood silent for a few minutes taking in the vista. A dam formed a small reservoir to our left and the road disappeared into the foothills to our right. An abandoned Turkish village crowned the hill before us. We turned around. The white stone ruins of a mill and medieval Skarfos Bridge contrasted against an organic green backdrop. George pointed out herbs and plants, many of which we had eaten that night in their villa. Rows of citrus and olive groves stretched along a small stream into the distance.

"Over there," George said pointing to a tree beyond Skarfos Bridge. "Before we married and had kids, we used to camp over there." His finger moved to the left. "Follow the stream along the road. Walk some, drive some. Whatever suits you. There's no traffic out here. Eventually you'll reach the edge of the forest where we picked the mushrooms."

We said our goodbyes and watched as George and Lara's truck disappeared over the hill.

We began walking. Past the oranges. Past the olives. Beyond the leeks and wild fennel. Finally, we turned back at the mushrooms.

Wayne Milstead writes from the colder climes of Europe, but thankfully it is only a few hours' flight to the eastern Mediterranean.

CHRISTOPHER K. BROWN

✦ ✦ ✦

Five-Star
Mussandam Bush

*An excursion organizer is determined to deliver
culinary perfection amidst an austere Oman setting.*

EVERY YEAR I REGRET ORCHESTRATING THE EVENT—AT
least until during and after the fact, whereupon delight muscles
in and overwrites the aggravation and logistical horror. But this
year I was particularly anxious as a crop of new friends had
been made, and they were expecting to be mightily impressed.
Once started, momentum sent the legend spinning wildly
toward ever-more-embellished heights. Old hands reveled
initiates with snippets: *Fabulous old dhow…bioluminescent algae…
vast pods of dolphins…campfire guitar strumming on a remote
beach…and the food! How does he do it?* For weeks we had been
discussing and delegating the details, and though the final list
of guests fluctuated wildly, as always, it leveled off at around a
dozen folk.

The contemporary UAE remains one of the most interesting
places I know of, full of an astounding range of people from
every possible background and station of life; my set in particular are fiercely united by a willingness to have a laugh and
pursue the unusual with gusto. Every time I get out of the

major cities, I remember again how compact the country is, and how much spectacular beauty resides so near at hand. Partly as a result of maniacal driving on monstrous motorways, just about any spot in the country is less than four hours away. Fancy the Indian Ocean and sea turtles? Go to the East Coast. Prefer mountains? The Hajar range rises up swiftly in the center of the country. Of course the red sands and impossibly large dunes of the Liwa Desert are to the south. But Mussandam, technically an isolated triangle of Oman, remains a special jewel in the crown of the region, a place of nearly mythical reverence among expats. The familiar, perhaps notorious, associations of the Strait of Hormuz, the unpredictable nature of border crossings in Arabia, and the prospect of a nearly uninhabited and fiercely rugged landscape all contribute to the appeal.

The invitation is always simple and enticing: *Mussandam IV, the legend continues. Meet at high noon at the Emirates Towers Hotel (Dubai) for three nights of dhow camping. Food and water provided, bring drinks and snacks.* While I delegate to others breakfasts and lunches, water and wood, my gift to guests is the best camping food they have ever had. It has become an art form over the years, my training beginning in high alpine environments where everything had to fit into a manageable rucksack. Being a food snob, even then gorp ("good old raisins and peanuts") and dried soups were not part of the equation. Over the years I have tested and perfected the art of feeding the troupe on delicious, even miraculous, vittles that tumbled out of a single—some have said magical—cool box. Mussandam is always my chance to play the epicurean conjurer and to revel in the fanfare.

The key is packing the cool box meticulously in reverse order of consumption and freezing as much as is possible in order that the box will stay cold for three days. Lovely fillets of beef, marinated for half a day and then frozen, reside at the bottom of the box for the last supper. Caviar and champagne rest on top for the first night, and between are all manner of delights in various states of semi-preparedness. Experience suggested to me that we would be able to find a fisherman somewhere along the way, with lovely fresh tuna and crabs to be bought; failing that, catching some pitiful tiddler or other was always possible. The cool box, sorted and groaning, always takes pride of place in the packing of the car.

Like all leisure activities for my set in the Gulf, luxurious temptations figure into every event. For those with money and time to spare—namely Western professionals—modest sums procure glories that would be unaffordable in cities like London or New York: spa treatments, attentive staff, frequent travel, and plenty of "boys' toys." While the drive from my villa in the capital, Abu Dhabi, to Dubai for the rendezvous point is at most two hours, in anticipation of somewhat less restful nights sleeping rough on a beach, we indulged, as usual. Why not drive in the night before, shack up at the Emirates Towers—our favorite hotel—and be fresh, ready, and caffeinated by noon for departure? Indeed, balancing camping with five-star luxury remains a great strategy, made all the easier by an endless array of "special deals" available to those of us who live here and know the right people.

In fact, that particular venue frequently serves us very well indeed and must be one of my favorite hotels in the world. Twin, diamond-topped towers rise proudly off the Sheikh Zayed Highway, a celebration of black marble, chrome, and glass. The rooms scream sophistication and business-traveler smugness with their low suede window seats, unbeatable views of the Cartesian chaos of Dubai, and wireless keyboards and high-tech gizmos. The tropical fruit bowl and orchids in the rooms concede a softer side of the decor. Of course the service is impeccable.

"Good evening Dr. Brown, we have not seen you in some time," gushes the reception clerk. "I see you will only be joining us for one night. That is a pity..."

Such obsequiousness, though flattering, punctuates nearly every interaction in this country. At times it can be grating, especially when hollow and unsupported with actually efficient service, but I know that at this hotel the service usually excels.

"Thank you, just a quick visit, we must be off again by noon tomorrow. But listen, I have a particular favor that you can help me with. You see, I have a large cool box," say I, gesturing to the smiling man with the baggage trolley, "that really does want to be kept cold. May we put the whole box in one of the kitchen's walk-in freezers for the night?"

His face falls momentarily; obviously this is a new request.

"Hmmm. Yes, well, um, let me call my supervisor."

An even more helpful manager bounds up, hears the story, and snaps his fingers: a claim tag is affixed and off goes the matériel for my culinary masterpiece into the bowels of the hotel.

Evenings in Dubai always pass swiftly and sweetly, so much so that one seems to blend into the next, a mighty collage of endless traffic, good food, sparkling new venues, multi-national people, and amusement of every sort. The whole place seems to change month by month, thus it is a markedly different Dubai every time I visit. Some call it fickle. I always sleep brilliantly in five-star hotels, and in spite of my best attempts I can never get my own bed to be quite as comfortable.

As requested, room service brings morning coffee and the papers on time, and the day begins slowly and softly. Anticipation thrills me, and wallowing in it puts me in the best of moods. Now the work is done and the fun can begin; nothing can possibly go wrong at this stage, gloat I to myself.

The bill paid, the valet seeking the truck, and another

fellow fetching the cool box, I begin to preview the drive in my mind. The lads insist upon loading the car, I suppose thereby increasing my sense of obligation to tip them. The first of my guests pulls up, swiftly followed by the rest. As if by magic, all are present and ready to go within five minutes of the allotted time. Mental note to self: *I like this punctual crew.*

The route northwards bounces between ever-less-impressive cities; as if receding into the bygone era, life gets simpler and more dated with every city. In many regards, such a journey is a whistle-stop tour of the seven Emirates by their eponymous cities: monolithic and glittering Dubai quickly gives way to tangled and under-developed Sharjah. Soon after, Ajman comes into view, its Etisalat telecom building identical to those in all the other cities, crested by a mammoth "golf ball." But the town is gone in a flash, almost before it is noticed. Umm Al Quwain teases a bit and takes some time to appear; it feels almost desolate and hugely remote from the globalized glitz of Dubai. The mountains arise in the east, and the country finally feels like the Arabia of yore: harsh but friendly, dusty but solid. By the time we race through Ras Al Khaimah, modernity seems a lifetime away as farm animals and shepherds vie with SUVs for space on the side streets. Even the waters of the Arabian Gulf to the west, visible intermittently throughout the journey, appear cleaner, clearer, and sparkling with potential.

Soon enough the border post looms; the usual nonsensical facade of high security and useless chits of paper aside, crossing is painless. Pulling away from the second checkpoint—we must stamp out of the UAE and then stamp in to Oman, each time laboriously copying the selfsame information that is on our passports and encoded on the magnetic strips—the world suddenly changes. Even the quality of the light feels different and the landscape possesses a tidiness and an untouched purity.

Whereas in the UAE there is always some structure, sign, non-indigenous flower, or "improvement" on nature, Oman seems to leave well enough alone. Though the tarmac is perfect and new, there really is little else by way of development: no pavements to nowhere, no poured concrete breakwaters, no sad tea houses, nothing but mountains, sea, sand, and whatever hearty foliage dares try to thrive. The highway is the only gesture towards progress, but, as if development were ambivalent, it lacks guardrails.

The ascent is swift as the unworn highway, nearly empty of cars, winds and cuts through the mountains, each curve revealing a new and more spectacular view of the sea. The afternoon sun casts deep shadows into the valleys, but at the higher points a golden warmth enlivens the matte-brown rocks. A fishing village appears below us, then disappears as the tortuous road meanders through the hills, only to reappear around us for a brief moment before returning to the sleepy contentedness with being unnoticed. Brightly painted boats are poised at the ready high on the pebbly beach; old, bearded men use both fingers and toes to complete repairs on impossibly green, nylon fishing nets. I feel decided serenity in this scenery; unlike the modern reality, this vision confirms the simplistic and Romantic expectations I once held for the region. I came to the Gulf mostly ignorant of Arabia, save for literary visions borrowed wholesale from Burton, Thesinger, and *1001 Arabian Nights*; for years I tried to reconcile what I saw in Abu Dhabi to what I imagined as the real Arabia. Over the years, the only places I have found vestigial traces of this fantasy world have been far away from the cities, joys discovered mostly by luck and patience. Doubtless, this is the reason I run the Mussandam trip annually.

The town of Kasab gives little warning of its approach; after one particularly sharp bend that loops absurdly out into the water, we arrive. The seaport also serves as the gate to the town, and we pass a motley collection of hulking teakwood dhows, souped-up speedboats—allegedly for the smuggling trade to Iran—and ubiquitous fishing boats. Clustered in a flat valley beneath impressively high mountains, houses and low buildings appear scattered by a whimsical child. The disused airport, a small strip, is the only logical use of space in town, its even geometry at odds with the rest of the town.

As the light is fading, it makes no sense to put out to sea tonight; the negotiations over a boat and the haggling over the price are much better done in the freshness of morning when time is not quite as precious. I lead our caravan through the village, back towards the mountains. Rather than being boxed in by a ridgeline, the valley curves sharply away from habitation and a gentle escarpment rises and tapers towards a large *wadi* (dry river-bed) that has breached the stone walls. A vast forest of acacia trees, squat and standoffish, spreads before us, naturally spaced in competition for scarce water as if planted meticulously by a diligent farmer. While Arab hospitality often remains true to its legendary graciousness, I seek a less visible place for our camp precisely to avoid curious and well-meaning visitors.

At the end of the forest, hard against the sharp sides of the ridge, I feel reasonably secure. The few hundred meters of elevation will help us to catch whatever small breeze there might be. We circle the wagons and dismount to set up camp. Silence braces us and reduces all voices to a strong whisper; the dry smell of dust and trees invites slow, deep breathing. Already the fun has begun. Amidst our laughter, curious—and pungent!—goats saunter near for a look. Our garishly colored tents—synthetic marvels in purple, orange, red, and blue—look strange and truly out of place in this setting. The cocktails have begun to flow just as the fleeting rays of day sweep over our camp.

Few smells are as evocative and reassuring as the burning of dry Arabian tinder. Though the evening is warm, and gas lanterns available, the ruddy light and crackling of the fire is essential. Some guests sprawl on the large Anatolian kilim that I have spread around the campsite, while others simply watch the sky as the first of a great parade of bright stars arrives. Amidst this contentedness easy smiles and intimacy bubble forth; the time is right to start the fun.

"Who fancies a bit of bubbly and some caviar blinis?" I ask smugly.

Answers are guttural and informal, more sounds than responses. With fanfare, I drag the heavy cool box near the fire and open the lid. As in a cartoon, my face falls absurdly, I close the lid, and then open it again. The box is filled entirely and solely with ice cubes. No one dares to laugh.

Six chattering conversations begin at once as I scan for other boxes that might really be mine; alas, there are none like it, blue and hulking. Apologetically, and angrily, I recount the story of checking the box into the hotel freezer, and only now do I notice that there is no baggage tag on this particular box.

I am torn between indignation—how could the hotel do this to me? Did they steal my goodies?!—and genuine concern: dinner is a serious matter, and dinner for three nights in the bush is essential. The prospect of living on bread and tinned beans proves unthinkable. Of course in the hills of Oman there is no mobile phone reception, so quick as a flash I am in the car driving for high ground. Atop the ridge I get a few bars of signal and ring the duty manager of the hotel.

Trying to keep my composure, I run through the story that obviously seems far-fetched to the Slavic night manager; she suggests calling the day manager to see if he knows anything. Ten agonizing and furious minutes drag past, enough to blast through two cigarettes in rapid succession, before she rings back.

"Hello, Dr. Brown, we have found your cool box. It must have been confused with one of the catering boxes in the freezer. We are very sorry for the mistake…"

Sorry indeed, but that does me no good whatsoever.

Firmly, I press the point: "Yes, well, I don't care how it happened. But what can we do to fix the situation? I am two hours away, in a different country, camping. What precisely do you expect me to do?"

"I am sorry, Doctor, is there no way you can come to the hotel to fetch the box tomorrow?"

"Impossible and unacceptable," though I am hard pressed to imagine what would be acceptable until a cheeky suggestion strikes me—"You really must have a driver bring the cool box to me in Mussandam."

This gives her pause, and I can nearly hear her debate the situation in her head. Perhaps she even checks my record on her screen to confirm the repeat status of my business.

"I am sorry, Doctor, our drivers cannot leave the UAE—"

Everything in the Middle East is a negotiated haggle, a give and take, life as carpet souk. My challenge is to know how hard to push: a delivery tonight, or first thing tomorrow morning? Knowing that the day manager must surely feel some cursory pangs of guilt, and recognizing that the night manager will be more likely to agree to a solution that will be passed on to her colleague, I strike.

"Let me be perfectly clear. I have a dozen people who are depending upon this box. I want your man at the UAE/Oman (Mussandam) border post at eight sharp tomorrow morning. I will hold you personally responsible if this does not occur. Tell me your name again…"

And so the deal is done and I can return to camp victorious, if tarnished.

To my delight, my guests have launched lustily into red

wine and one has begun noodling on the guitar. The French woman who has been charged with tomorrow's breakfast produces two fabulously rich quiches—God bless the French at times like these. I relate to the troupe our general success, and the evening proceeds unblemished and merrily.

Just after seven A.M., with dew on the tents and goats devouring anything left out unsecured—edible or not—my wife and I leave our groggy guests and depart for the border post, forty-five minutes down the lovely road. I am anxious and nervous: very little in Arabia happens how and when it is supposed to, and a significant delay will cause considerable disruption.

When we near the border, my wife, always the practical and logical one, notes to me an issue I had not imagined heretofore.

"So we have to stamp out of Oman and then drive through the neutral zone to the UAE side. Does that mean we have to buy a new visa?" Christ, she is right; it will take at least half an hour and a new fee to secure visas again, all for the sake of traversing the 500-yard neutral zone. My blood pressure has just rocketed off the charts. I briefly debate talking sense and logic—in pidgin Arabic—to the Omani border guards and realize the impossible folly of this option. Before I can formulate a viable plan, we are at the border post.

My attempts to explain the situation fully come to naught, and increasingly frustrated, I proceed with an inspired notion. I cannot say why we all seem to revert to broken, even accented English, when speaking with a non-English-speaker, as if talking as they do will be the key to comprehension, but I confess that I do it as well.

"Five minutes. I go. Come back. Keep my wife here. No stamp, five minutes, I come back."

Although I have no reason to suspect that they understand,

I proceed as if they must. Priceless is the look on my wife's face as I leave her as security deposit at the Omani border post. Often swift, bold action is enough to avert opposition in this part of the world. At every level, decisions are made not based on the spirit of some clearly articulated rule or procedure, but according to the likelihood of repercussions or reprimand. Implying that you have some vague authority to do something usually works, especially if accompanied by a dropped name or a multiply-stamped paper. As soon as logic or guilt are brought into the equation, the battle is lost; I usually rely on bluster and a nonchalant projection of entitlement and suggestions of very high authority.

Just down the road, I can see the UAE post; parked at the post is a gleaming white Mercedes emblazoned with the Emirates Palace logo. A bored chap in hotel livery is staring at his shoes. I park just before the exit gate, arousing the guards from their slumber.

"Hallo, I believe you have a cool box for me," I hail to the clerk.

"You are Dr. Brown? Yes sir, I have your box. My manager is very sorry for the inconvenience..."

The disheveled fellows in the guard house have now come out to try to ascertain the situation; obviously they can make no sense of this and resort to gawking silently as the bellman and I slide our heavy boxes under the gate. Why they do not assume it is their duty to examine the contents is still a mystery to me. We all smile and thank each other.

My wife has made herself comfortable in a chair outside the Omani guard house, and I fetch her on the way in. She winds down the window and smiles coquettishly to her newfound friends, "*Shukran*, boys!"

By ten o'clock all is right in the world and we have assembled an embarrassing amount of gear on the quay. I am in friendly negotiation with a diminutive captain of a boat, and we both know that we are going to do a deal, but it is about graciously compromising towards a price. At last we settle on one—about the cost of two nights in the Emirates Towers— for the entire boat on a three-day voyage, petrol included. Before long his first mate, a snot-nosed and weedy boy, has humped our gear into the hold of the dhow, and the lubbing diesel has been cranked up. The boat is sturdy and will happily limp around the fjords of Mussandam.

The weekend passes at an odd pace, at times the hours race, at times the minutes expand pleasantly to the cadence of the waves and the engine. As expected, the snorkeling is grand around Telegraph Island, the dolphins frolicsome, and the sunsets divine. But as always the most memorable events are the journey itself, the miscommunications, the instantaneous decisions that make all the difference, and the graceful ease with which friendships develop away from the noise of normalcy. All told, three days feel akin to weeks, and new acquaintances have become fast friends. The beauty of our scenery will be most stunning only through the lens of nostalgia and the sharing of photos after the fact; during the trip, how-ever, the scenery is simply a gorgeous backdrop to fantasies of old Arabian traders and meandering conversations that occur in spurts over days. And, of course, who will deny that the best restaurant in the region—though very difficult to book a table—must be that small nameless beach in a cove.

Dr. Christopher K. Brown is Associate Professor of Literature and Assistant Dean of the College of Arts and Sciences at Zayed University. He has worked and lived in the UAE since 2000. His scholarly work includes authorship of The Encyclopedia of Travel *and three volumes about the UAE.*

CHRIS KIPINIAK

* * *

Magic Carpet Ride

*The rug you can afford but the hospitality
might set you back.*

"This," said my guide, "is a rug school." The van had
pulled into a parking lot and stopped in front of a stucco cube
with dusty banners on either side of the front door, sloppily
painted with the same outlines of Horus and Isis and the
Pyramids that decorated all the other businesses I'd seen
around Cairo.

"Rug school?" I asked, stepping out onto the gravel. "Not a
rug shop?"

He shrugged, "A school. This is where they teach to weave
rugs. We're very proud of our rugs."

He must have detected my wariness.

"It's not just a rug school," he said and pointed, "but the best
rug school in all Egypt."

I looked to where he was pointing and, sure enough, there
was a billboard at the far end of the lot with a faded sphinx and
the legend, "Best Rug School in All Egypt!"

I didn't want a rug. Of course, I didn't want a guide either.
Yet somehow, the day before, not five minutes off the plane in

Cairo, I had been booked with one. Egyptians in the tourist trade have a way of politely forcing you to do things. Hire a guide, for instance. Or visit a rug school. And so on. The glass doors opened and a tall Egyptian man, flanked by twin attendees, minced out into the lot. He wore linen trousers whose cuffs spilled over new loafers and a crisp, white, short-sleeved shirt with thick primary-colored stripes. His hands were held up as if to display the splendor of all the world behind him.

"*Aaaaaaaaaaaaah*," he said, drawing out the sound. You could hear the echo of a voice that had once been deep and sonorous but had started to scratch a little with age.

"Welcome," he continued, "to our," and then leaning forward at the waist, "rug," separated for emphasis, "school."

"Thank you. I hear it's one of the best in Egypt."

"Ah," he flapped back and forth at the waist with false modesty, like a bird on a leash. "Well, we do not like to brag but it is, in fact, *the* Best Rug School in All Egypt," and he gestured toward the sign.

"Please," he said, bowing slightly and throwing his hand toward the door, as if to summon a lush red carpet that would snap to and eagerly roll itself out over the tiny stones and broken glass. None did. We stood there in the lazy heat looking at the door and the air-conditioned shade beyond it. His arm wobbled a little and he struggled to keep his smile intact.

"Please," he said again, and bowed a little lower.

What?

Then I realized—they were waiting for me. I was supposed to go first. I apologized and hurried toward the door. As I reached for the handle, the man sprang to life, dove forward, thrusting his arm over my shoulder, and elbowed me out of the way before politely opening the door.

"Please," he said. In I went.

We went into a large open room with three pairs of "students" working on rugs. The man stopped me with a hand on my shoulder.

"Now, first: What is your name?"

I told him.

"Good. My name is Michael. Where are you from?"

I told him.

"Good. You know, I have many friends from there."

Of course.

"Well, here we are. Welcome to our rug," again, for emphasis, "school. You have heard, of course, of our famous Egyptian rugs? Well, this is where they come from. From this and many other schools in Egypt that are like this, but not this, because this—" Michael lifted his hands. "This is The Best Rug School in All Egypt."

He dragged me to the right where two little girls knelt in front of a half-finished rug.

"These girls come from homes nearby and come to study and work here." He leaned close to my ear as if to take me into his confidence. "We pay them a little something. They bring it home to help their families. Most of their families are all very poor. Very poor."

The girls worked nimbly, only slowing to show the simplicity of the knot they used as Michael explained the process to me. The girls turned and smiled up at me during the explanation; it was obviously a show, a pantomime that they had to go through often. It was likely that neither of them understood the words being said, but they recognized the cues in Michael's pitch—cues to look up, to smile, to display the pre-cut thread, and finally, to let me have a try.

"Would you like to try?" Michael asked me.

"No, thank you."

A little girl with a lazy eye pinched two of the vertical

threads between her fingers, holding a half-tied knot. She looked at me eagerly, waiting for me to move.

"Are you sure? You can. It's very easy."

I shook my head. "Thank you though."

I turned my head and looked around the wide room. There was a lot of space. Like Egypt itself, everyone was in one section of the room, and more than 85 percent of it was empty. Like the desert. Along the next wall two boys worked on a larger rug and in the middle of the room was a large wooden contraption being operated by two men. I turned back to Michael and the girl, who were looking at each other. She still pinched the loose loop.

"Are you sure you would not like to try? It's really very simple."

"Quite sure." I was going to stand my ground.

Michael seemed unable to go on. He took a breath in the pause, "You're sure?"

I looked from Michael's scared smile to the girl's lazy eye to her delicate fingers bowing the guide threads. I wouldn't even be tying it, really. I mean she had already. All she had to do was pull. I wouldn't even be making the actual knot!

The girl was cute, though. She had eyes like polished onyx. She was not going to tie the knot. I had to do it. *Come on, dude*, I read in her smile, *my arm's getting tired and I gotta finish this stupid rug by Friday. I know you don't want to and Michael's kind of a dick, but don't make this your Alamo. I don't want to go down fighting your damn fight. Now quit being such a hard-on and tie the damn knot.*

I pushed my bag onto one shoulder, cradled my guidebook, and, with one hand, was somehow able to take both of the ends of the thread and pull. There. There is my knot.

"Aaaah, very good," he said, having finally gotten his cue. "If you stay, we'll have you making rugs very soon, hmm? You have a talent, you know that?"

"Yes, thank you."

"Would you like to try again? Maybe I take a picture? You have a camera?"

"No thank you."

Michael shrugged and turned toward the boys. As we moved away from the poor girls, Michael reminded me again how poor the poor girls were. He made a special point of it— how poor they were. We arrived at where the boys worked and watched as they mechanically looped the cuts of string into knots. Their faces were blank. They appeared to neither enjoy nor dislike their task. They looked like they had hypnotized themselves with their own actions. In contrast, the rug that was growing on the wall before them was lively and intricate. They didn't react to my standing there or to Michael's patting of their shoulders or to my questions or to the way Michael stuck his finger into the rug as they worked.

We walked from there to the center of the room where the two men sat. Their faces were like those of the boys, only with sagging cheeks and puffiness around the eyes. A cigarette dangled from one man's lips. With his feet he clumsily pressed the pedals while his rough fingers ran the thick fraying camel hair between the threads suspended in the frame.

The smoker jerked his head quickly, whipping the ash from the tip of his cigarette. It flew to the side, over the loom, past his partner, and into a developing pile of ash.

Michael led me up the stairs at the far end of the room to the second floor. While the room below was bare except for the three pairs of "students" practicing their skills, this room was bursting with colorful carpets. They hung on the walls, on pillars, many lay on the floor, and hundreds sat in piles, flopping over each other like the layers of the pyramids, showing off their fringe, their edges, the craftsmanship and the designs, each of which was repeated over and over, in different materials and in every size. Michael maneuvered me over to a bench against the wall.

"Now you will get a chance to look at some of the many rugs that we have produced here at our rug...school."

"You're going to try to sell me a rug, right?"

He shrugged his shoulders and made a face, "I would just like to show you some of the rugs that we have made. If you find one that you like, then perhaps…. But, now," he went on before I had a chance to refuse, "what would you like to drink?"

"Nothing, thanks."

"It's hot out. You're not thirsty?"

"Well—"

"Then what would you like?"

I tried to stand up, "Look, I'm really not interested."

But I couldn't. He was standing just close enough, and leaned forward just far enough, to keep me seated.

"I don't want a rug," I said with certainty.

"Of course not but I am offering you something to drink," and then, as if anticipating my next question, "It does not cost anything. This is Egyptian hospitality."

I turned my head and looked across the length of the room, through the windows, and saw the intensity of the light and heat outside. Dust hung permanently in the air until a car sped by setting the whole cloud whirling in place like dirty pinwheels. It made the drink sound very inviting.

Michael sent someone somewhere to get me something. While we waited he stood over me, looking at me and rubbing his hands together, not saying a word. His smile was friendly and frantic, like a child standing at the school room door waiting for the clock to make the final tick to recess; he wanted to say something but couldn't. Not yet. He waited, one row of teeth set firmly atop the other, silently. And, in the same way that the schoolboy will go tearing out into the playground as soon as he hears that bell—*BOOM*—so Michael waits until his minion places the bottle on the bench beside me and—*BOOM*—he's off.

"Now," he starts, his voice lowered, belying the speed with which he speaks, "I have shown you the process by which we hand make all of the many, many rugs you see here in this room, all handmade by the students, like the ones that you have seen downstairs working on the beautiful, handmade rugs. Do you remember the rugs? Of course. And we have many like them here, of many sizes with many different colors and designs and now, if you like, you can buy one. What sort of rug would you like?"

No words were coming out of his mouth but that's not to say he'd stopped. His engines were still running. In his eyes you could see that, whatever was going on outside, he was still going at the same frantic pace inside. His forehead started to glisten as he waited for me to respond, to say something, to give him his cue, to unleash him.

I took a sip of my soda.

Silence.

"They're very nice." *BOOM*!

"They are all made from the finest materials and, as you can see, the students are all very good workers. Many of them come from far away to study here. They are from very poor families. If we sell many rugs, I can sometimes give them money to take home. It helps them and their families. They are all very poor but do very good work. Which one do you like? The silk is very beautiful, isn't it?"

"Yes."

His hand shot back and grabbed a large silk rug. He whipped it in front of me. It was a picture, ornamented around the sides with symbols and hieroglyphics.

"This is the 'Day of Judgment,'" he said.

I said nothing.

Michael threw the rug behind him and grabbed another.

"Ah," he said, lifting another which pictured…"King Tut. My uncle." He cocked his eyebrow and smiled at his own joke. I smiled politely.

And then another. "This is the 'Tree of Life.' These birds represent the stages that we all go through in life…"

"Michael?"

He stopped, holding the rug in front of him like a matador's cape. The old pro had the scent: A sale! A sale!

"Can I have another 7-Up?"

I thought this would have thrown him. But no. After only the slightest pause he nodded to the young boy who had brought me my first drink and continued bringing forward new rugs.

"Now. Is this the size rug you wanted?"

"I'm really not interested…"

"We have larger. How do you like our country?"

"Fine—"

"We have many different styles and sizes," he continued, "Perhaps one like this? Or this one? Very nice, yes?" he kept whipping out rugs from nowhere and laying them on the pile which he'd then shuffle like a deck of cards before displaying one that I hadn't seen.

"Yes, very nice," I said, or "They're beautiful but—"

But "but" would signal him, and he'd go for another rug. I was trapped. Somewhere in there I got my soda. It was a little warm.

"I really can't afford silk—"

"AH!" he exclaimed and, in a feat of Herculean strength, he grabbed a whole stack of rugs from behind him and plopped it in front of me. Before I could protest, he turned and grabbed another. I was walled in behind three staggered stacks of Egyptian rugs.

"Perhaps then the camel hair. We have many kinds of designs." He held one up. "King Tut. My Uncle." He cocked his eyebrow and smiled at his own joke. I smiled blankly again.

Across the room sat a round woman wearing bright white with a pixie-style haircut. She sat holding a cup of tea and munching on a wafer, watching her salesman work himself into a sweat, whipping carpets back and forth at an alarming speed, desperate to catch her fancy. I could tell that it would take a while. She was very American in the way she sat. Her tooth-white tennis shorts, the new canvas sneakers—items insultingly out of place—and the casual ease with which she sat in them, all conveyed a feeling of tacit ownership. I will never know how she looked in the U.S., among so many rich and richly-fed people, secure in the knowledge that everything was O.K. and that tomorrow would be, too; there she might not seem so regal or sit so still. It might have been her who sat on the floor faking a smile and displaying her worn and fraying wares to an even richer, even more blasé customer. But here, in this country, with her plump ass, her prosperity, and her American dollars, she was Queen. One of us must have caught the other's eye because we started talking over the heads of our salesmen and their kaleidoscopic displays.

"Hi! Where you from?" she asked.

I told her.

"That's great. I'm from California—just outside L. A.," and then looking down, "No, thank you. I don't like it."

"Are you enjoying your trip?" I asked, trying to peek around the carpet Michael was pushing into my face.

"Oh yes. We went through Europe, my husband and I," she paused to shake her head at the salesman, "and afterwards we thought we'd try something a little different," and then, without the least attempt to lower her voice, "it's just hard to find any restaurants, you know, that you can really trust."

"Of course. Has everything been O.K. so far?"

"I said NO!" and then to me, "I'm sorry, yes, everyone's been very nice. They're a bit dirty, but—" and I loved this, "it's just a different culture," and she stroked a few crumbs from her lip, rubbing them from her fingertips to the floor. "You can't judge them by the same standards." She smiled. I did, too. She then punctuated the conversation by telling the salesman that there was no way she would pay more than thirty dollars.

"Well, have a nice trip," she said and decisively got up and plowed over her salesman. The poor guy never stood a chance. It was like watching someone get hit by a tidal wave. She left, which left me alone with Michael, who at that second was saying, "…my uncle."

"I'm sorry, who?"

"What?"

"Who? I was asking who is your uncle?"

"King Tut," Michael said, smiling slowly at his own joke. I smiled smugly.

"We have this rug with his picture on it."

"No, thank you. Look, I'm really not—I—"

"O.K." He was ready to start over; seriously, now—no more fooling around.

"How much are you willing to pay?" he asked, this newly serious Michael.

"I'm traveling—I don't have much cash," I pleaded.

"We take traveler's checks."

"I don't have much of that, either."

"We take credit card."

I was running out of excuses and, apparently, not wanting a rug was not a good enough reason not to buy one. I frantically tried to construct some other explanation, but he must have caught me thinking and was ready to head me off at the pass.

"How much will you pay?"

"I told you already—"

He waved his hand quickly in front of his face, as if I were making an offensive joke.

"Just tell me, how much?"

"I'm not—"

"How much?"

And then, out of my mouth, without thought, understanding, or strategy, "Thirty dollars."

Of course, now I couldn't back down. I had given a price and, according to my guide book, I was bound to stick to it. If he offered to sell me something for thirty dollars then I was duty bound to buy it. It could have been a used handkerchief with his initials, and I'd have to buy it.

"Thirty dollars," I said again.

"But you have seen the work…the children."

"I'm sorry," I said, "but that's it. I will be on the road for quite some time and can only afford to spend thirty dollars."

He looked around at the scattered rugs and grabbed a red rectangular one. It lay on his arm with the easy flow of silk. The fringe fell seductively toward the floor. The design was an ornate abstraction, unfolding into smooth loops and voluptuous curves. His smile was sly.

"It is very beautiful, yes?" he asked.

I was mesmerized. The rug's bottom bobbed back and forth as it lay prone on Michael's forearm. *Take me*, the rug seemed to say. *Make me a symbol of your conquest of the exotic East.* The rug somehow purred at me and seemed to writhe.

"You like?" he asked.

"Yes," I croaked.

"Have you ever seen a rug so smooth, so beautiful as this?"

"No," my voice was less than a whisper.

"It can be yours."

"Oh…"

"Fifteen hundred Egyptian Pounds," he whispered, "Three hundred dollars American."

My reverie was over.

"Three hundred!?!" I stammered, "I just said I couldn't pay more than thirty!"

"What? You are American. You have money."

"That's not the issue, I—"

"All right." He threw up his hands. Michael's about to make a deal. "Two hundred seventy-five."

"Thirty."

"Two hundred fifty."

"Thirty."

"Two hundred sixty."

"Thirty!"

"I cannot for thirty. The material, the time…the children."

I think he saw that the rugs-for-humanity tactic was not working with me.

"The material itself costs more than thirty dollars."

"Then show me something in another material."

"How about," he started, "something," searching through the other pile of camel-hair carpets, "like," and he pulled out a long carpet with an intricate scene from Pharaonic lore, "this?"

"How much?" I asked. Wordlessly he went back to the pile.

"I don't understand," he said, "why you will not buy?"

"Jeez," I was feeling sorry for the guy, "what about one of the smaller ones?"

We looked through the pile together.

"Perhaps this. It is King Tut," Michael looked at the rug. It was ugly. The king's face was set against an off off-white background that made it look unfinished. In the smaller size much of the detail was lost and what remained was distorted. He looked like a boxer with a round shapeless face and a nose, pounded into a dense pulp, stuck onto the middle of his puss.

"My uncle," we said in unison, and both found ourselves unable to smile.

"The picture rugs," I told him, "don't translate well into the smaller sizes."

He looked at me blankly. In one hand was a little version of the "Tree of Life," which looked like a dead branch, and in the other a miniature of Cleopatra, which looked far more like King Tut than the rug he had just shown me.

"Don't you think? I mean, you can't get the detail—it's not…it's too…"

He was still silent and I started to feel bad, which made me forget my point, which I still contend was probably perfectly legitimate.

"How about," I began, "you show me a rug with a more…abstract design? Just…no pictures…just designs…and small...and no silk… "

"How about something like this?" and Michael, from some secret pile kept in a nook somewhere between time and space, pulled out a small, camel-hair rug, with a red diamond-based design that bloomed from the center and spilled out over a blue-green pool, toward a thin golden border.

It was love…in a medieval, arranged, political, marriage-of-economic-necessity sort of way. The rug was everything I wanted; it was red, I got it in Egypt, it wasn't ugly…it had, after another ten minutes of argument, a thirty dollar price tag…Most importantly, though, it was my ticket out of there.

Yes, I bought a rug. But I don't think of it as a defeat. Or, that I was pressured into it. I mean—yes, I was pressured. But it's like traveling. I came away with something I didn't expect. Or realize I wanted. Until it happened.

And I like it. It's on my wall right now.

Of course, that wasn't how I felt as I stepped back into the parking lot and saw my guide bullshitting with the driver. He could see the tube sticking out of my backpack.

"I bought a rug," I told him.

He just nodded and flicked the butt of his cigarette out the window.

"It's nice," I told him. And myself, I guess.

He smiled and nodded.

"What's next?" I asked.

"Well, I thought we'd go by a famous Egyptian Perfume Museum," he said as he settled back into his seat, "but I think you've already had enough for today."

Chris Kipiniak is an actor and writer, but does not want to make a big deal out of having performed on Broadway ("Metamorphoes"), off-Broadway ("Kit Marlowe"), at the Soho Theatre in London and the Edinburgh Fringe Festival ("How to Act Around Cops"), or at myriad other theaters around the U.S. He has written several plays including Stalled, *which was performed at the Kraine Theatre in New York, as well as at the Hangar in Ithaca. He's currently writing* Marvel Adventures: Spider-Man, *and has already written the comics* Amazing Fantasy *and* Nightcrawler.

* * *

Shlonak?

What you don't know can entertain others.

I LIVE IN KUWAIT AND I STUDY ARABIC. I DON'T TAKE FORMAL language lessons in a classroom. I take informal lessons at the barber shop.

Hair salons in Kuwait are called hair saloons. I don't know where the extra "o" came from. Maybe it's because they're the Arab equivalent of the corner bar. They're more than just barber shops; they're little social clubs. Everybody sips tea and talks while they wait for a haircut, and they hang out for a long time after they're done. Some of the customers don't even get a haircut; they just stop in for a chat.

None of the barbers at my saloon speak English. The older guy—I guess he's the owner—speaks Arabic. I'm not sure where he's from, but he looks like he's been there since the day he was born. As soon as you walk in the place, it's obvious that this is *his* saloon. The other barber is a heavy-set Turk who speaks Arabic and Turkish. They used to have an Egyptian who spoke a little English, but he went home last year. So I always practice my Arabic when I'm in the saloon. The barbers and their customers are really nice people, and they all want to teach me the language. I forget most of it, but I always walk out with at least a few new words.

I went in for a cut last week. The old owner was the only guy in the shop. He was finishing up a plate of *shwarma* and watching TV. I said, "*Salaam Alakam*," and shook his hand. He smiled and said, "*Wa Alakam Salaam. Shlonak?*" He gestured toward the chair. I thought, *shlonak?* What does *shlonak* mean? I had heard it before, but I couldn't remember where.

He didn't have any tea, so he went next door and bought me a Pepsi. "*Shlonak?*" he asked again. I just smiled and thanked him for the drink. *Shlonak, shlonak*, what the hell is *shlonak?* Then I remembered where I'd heard it—it was here, in the saloon, about a month ago. The Turkish guy had started to cut my hair and said, "*Shlonak?* Same-same?" And I had said yes, and he had given me my usual cut. That's what *shlonak* must mean: same.

I ran my hand through my hair and said, "*Na'am, shlonak.*" The barber looked a little confused, but he didn't reply. He finished his lunch and stood up and asked again, "*Shlonak?*" I said again, "*Na'am, tamaam. Shlonak, menfadlak.*" He got a pair of scissors and a comb. He laughed to himself and said, "*Shlonak.*" I switched to English, repeating my request: "Yes, please. *Shlonak.* Same-same."

Halfway through the cut an English-speaking Kuwaiti came in. We all said hello, and the barber said something in Arabic. He laughed at me and said, "*Shlonak.*" The Kuwaiti laughed as well and asked me, "Do you know *shlonak?*"

I said, "Yeah, it means 'same-same,' right?"

He got a kick out of that. He translated for the barber, and the barber laughed so hard he had to stop cutting. The Kuwaiti said, "No, *shlonak* means 'How are you'."

I said, "I thought 'How are you' is '*Keef halak*.'"

He replied, "Yes, yes. *Keef halak, shlonak*, same-same."

"Now you're really confusing me."

"*Keef halak* is Arabic for 'how are you,' but in the Gulf we say '*shlonak*.' It's a Gulf dialect, like when people in Texas say 'howdy.'"

We all cracked up. I replayed the (translated) conversation in my head.

"Hello, sir."

"Hi, how are you?"

"Hello."

"How are you?"

"Yes, yes."

"You want a Pepsi?"

"Yes. Thank you. Pepsi good."

"How are you?"

"Yes, yes, O.K."

"Ready for a haircut?"

"Yeah, O.K."

"How are you?"

"Yeah, yeah, O.K. How are you, please."

Another customer walked in. Before anybody could say anything, I jumped out of the barber's seat and yelled, "*Shlonak!*" The customer said in English, "Um...fine. How are you?" The Kuwaiti laughed. The barber patted me on the back. This is how I learn Arabic at the saloon.

Michael Cornn is an American writer from the Midwest. In 2004, he traveled to Kuwait to experience a year in the Persian Gulf. While there, he learned a bit of Arabic, picked up a little culture, and made a lot of new friends. He currently lives in Honduras and plans to return to the Middle East.

WALEED AL-SHAMMA'

✳ ✳ ✳

A Damascus Cab Ride

*An expat's encounter with a taxi driver transports
him to the wonderment of childhood.*

MY FIRST VISIT TO DAMASCUS WAS NEARLY TWENTY YEARS
ago. Satellite dishes were illegal and the cell phone era wouldn't
descend upon Syria until the turn of the century. In the eyes
of a newly minted nine-year-old who had scarcely left his
home state of Michigan, traveling to Syria may as well have
been an interstellar voyage to the planet Raldoor 7. But
instead of apprehension and fear I was filled with wonder and
amazement. Everything was different. The people made funny
sounds with their voices. My dad would make these sounds
on the phone a few times a year; often I thought he was just
clearing his throat.

"*Salam aley-kum.*" "May peace be upon you." This was how
people greeted one another. Strangers in the street! And they
would say it again when they took their leave. I was hooked.
God help you if you ran into someone you knew on the way
to an appointment:

"*Ahlan! Keefuk? Schlounuk? Keef sahtuk? Shoe sarmak? Shoe
akhbarak? Ensha'allah bikhair?*" (Hello. How are you? How is

your health? What is new with you? God willing, everything is going well?) All of this might be replaced in the States by, " 'sup?"

My dad spoke with the cabbie all the way from the airport to my grandparents' house in Shora. An outside observer might have thought they were old friends the way the driver asked about us, my dad's family, and the way my dad told him about the last twenty-plus years of his life since he'd left Syria. The half-hour cab ride passed swiftly, even for this impatient youth. I was hanging on every word as though I actually understood what they were saying. I may not have understood the content of their conversation, but I did understand that this exchange of warmth and sincerity among strangers was unlike anything I had ever known.

The next stranger we met was a shopkeeper next door to my grandparents' home. Our cab driver was unable to break the Syrian 500-pound notes my dad had gotten at the airport foreign exchange, so we went into the nearest store to get change. After a warm welcome and another oddly long exchange of pleasantries, my father asked the man behind the counter for change.

"Can you break a 500?"

"How much is your cab fare?" the *Sahib Al-Halout* (the shopkeeper) asked.

"Twenty pounds."

"Welcome home to you and your family," the man aggressively shoved 20 pounds into my dad's hand as he vehemently refused to accept any money from him.

"*Ahlan wasahlan, ahlan wasahlan, ahlan wasahlan…*" "Welcome, welcome, welcome…" the man kept repeating.

"What just happened?" I asked my dad as we ascended the seemingly endless flights of stairs to my grandparents' home. He tried to explain the customs and traditions of the old country to me, and I listened earnestly, as my little legs tired further with each step.

My age, like the population of Damascus, had tripled by the time I returned. This time I was staying for months, perhaps years, rather than weeks, and living rather than visiting. Many things had changed. Every rooftop had at least a half dozen satellite dishes and, much like the rest of the world, it seemed *everyone* had a cell phone.

I had been in Jordan for the past two months studying Arabic at the University of Jordan in Amman. I was about to continue the elusive pursuit of mastering the Arabic language, or at least attempting to graduate from the stage of neophyte, at Damascus University. In Jordan I'd had no problems with my ATM card, but two weeks into my stay in Syria I had yet to find a bank that would accept it. I was down to my last 200 Syrian pounds (about $5 U.S. at the time) when I was told about BEMO, the Saudi-Franco bank that was on the same world network as my ATM MasterCard. So I hopped in the nearest cab and in my broken Arabic told the driver which bank I was looking for. Thankfully he knew where it was, because I didn't.

"*Yeslam idayk,*" I said to the driver as he drove off after dropping me in front of the bank. This basically means "God bless your hands" and is typically said in place of "thank you" to cab drivers, or to anyone handing you something. Arriving safely at one's destination after a cab ride may indeed seem like a blessing until you get used to the traffic in Damascus.

Anyway, I went to the bank with about 200 Syrian pounds before giving 50 to the cabbie. I waited patiently, as one must learn to do in Syria, as the bank teller converted thousands of dollars into millions of Syrian pounds and vice versa for the stream of businessmen flowing in and out of the bank. Upon my arrival in Syria I thought everyone was slow, except when driving. I began to realize, however, that this perceived slug-gishness was more the product of my American impatience than some ineptness on their part.

A favorite word among Syrians seems to be "*bookra*," which technically means "tomorrow," but in practical usage means, "at some point in the future." The first time I came to realize the true meaning of *bookra* was during a search for German muesli I had bought at a market near my apartment. I had purchased and consumed both bags that had been on their shelf, so I asked when they would be getting more.

"*Bookra,*" they told me, so I checked back the next day, but no muesli. Again I asked and again I was assured, "*bookra.*" After the fourth such encounter I asked a Syrian friend to explain this to me. He told me they didn't know when it would be in and that I'd do well to check every couple of weeks.

Things generally don't happen quickly or on time here because people don't concern themselves with time. I have found that Syrians are generally happier and more relaxed as a result. I still get frustrated sometimes that the post office is closed by 1 P.M., but I have come to appreciate the fact that most of my "immediate needs" are little more than wants that can wait a day or three.

By the time I reached the front of the line I realized I had forgotten something. Maybe I wouldn't need it? I wanted to believe that…

"Passport, please."

"Umm, yeah…how late are you open?"

Ugh, back into a taxi for a minimum of a half hour round trip to get my passport. Oh well, at least I can practice more Arabic with an unsuspecting cab driver.

"*Salam aley-kum.*" I said in obligatory fashion when I got in the front seat, as is customary for men, and closed the door of the already moving cab.

"*Wa aley-kum salam, wa rahmatallah, wa barakatu*" (And the blessings and the mercy of God). Where to?"

"Rawda, near Rawda mosque, please."

"Where from?" Abu Maher asked in English on par with my Arabic. "Abu" is a title given to men with at least one male child meaning "father of…" It is a handle of respect, though it is used very casually. He introduced himself to me as Mohammad, but I immediately switched to Abu Maher when I learned his eldest son's name was Maher.

My answer to the ubiquitous "where from" question has become second nature. "I am from the States, but my origin is Syrian." This was one of the few responses I could give in Arabic at a normal conversational speed without errors. We proceeded to talk about families, his and mine, work, as a cab driver or a restaurant manager, language difficulties, of which there were plenty, life, in Syria and in the States, and everything else we could come up with. At least in so far as our limited time together, and indeed linguistic abilities, allowed.

When we got to my place I went to pay him and he said, "Go ahead and get your passport, I'll wait." By that time I'd been thinking I might hang out for a while, maybe go back to the bank the next day, but this was better. I would hurry and get this tedious task out of the way and stop living this impecunious lifestyle.

I got back in the car with my passport and we resumed our conversation. Were it not for the distinctive yellow and the "taxi" sign on top, I might have thought I was getting back into an old friend's car. By the time we got back to the bank I almost didn't want to get out. Maybe we could go to a café and *ishrub argilas* ("drink" water pipe) and *la'ab toulay* (play backgammon), as was a favorite pastime of men in Syria. I couldn't help but think about that cab ride from the airport with my family nearly twenty years earlier. Had I taken my father's place riding shotgun and talking with the cabbie about my life and his, my family and his?

I offered Abu Maher my last 150 Syrian pounds, easily triple the fare, but he refused payment entirely. Upon my insistence this man, who works far harder than I do for considerably less money, refused again by simply saying, "*Ahlan wasahlan, ahlan wasahlan, ahlan wasahlan…*"

Waleed Al-Shamma' was born in northern Michigan to a Syrian-born father and an American-born mother. As a Syrian- Turkish-Hungarian- Scotch-Irish- German- Welsh- English- French-American with a Muslim, Christian, Jewish, agnostic, atheist background it is little wonder that Wally, as he was known growing up in rural America, developed an interest in differences and, indeed, similarities among diverse cultures and peoples. He is currently winding through life's journey in an attempt to combine his passions of traveling, writing, and food.

UMUR ÇELIKYAY

* * *

An Afternoon
in Kavaklıdere

One can be spontaneous in Turkey's second city.

IF YOU WERE FRENCH, YOU WOULD REFER TO ME AS AN
Ankariote, a dweller of Ankara. Yet, every time I hear this, I
secretly smile because I think it sounds like *Ankara Riot*. Take
my word for it, Ankara is *not* a riot. Instead, it is the calm and
solemn home of government officials, retired teachers, journalists, trade chamber representatives, young professionals, and
university students. So, the second irony is this: I am in fact
Turkish, but I was born not here, but in another corner of the
Middle East. My father was a diplomat with the Turkish
Foreign Affairs, which is why I spent the first two decades of
my life in Belgium, Saudi Arabia, and the United States.
Eventually, I realized that I was getting a bit too old for being
dragged all around the world, and that I needed to settle, to
throw my anchor down. I just happened to be in Ankara when
I made this decision, which must be why I made it my home,
almost by default.

Today, the sun is pale and it's rather cold, but I don't really
mind. I am in my favorite destination, pacing up and down the

Tunalı Hilmi Avenue in the neighborhood called Kavaklıdere. Frankly, I know very well that this is no Jewel of the Orient and that most people would probably perceive it as just a shopping district. I imagine that tourists would prefer visiting the Ulus/Citadel area, where they can get their dose of "genuine" Turkish delights: souvenir shops, a bazaar worthy of the name, authentic Turkish cuisine, the Museum of Anatolian Civilizations, and so on. Not me. I want to be right here, even though I have no particular reason for it. In fact, I identify with this locality more than I identify with any place in the world— and did I even mention that this is the third time I have come here today?

I stop briefly to provide directions to a foreign couple looking for a place where they can exchange currency. Somehow, people in need of directions always manage to find me, each and every time. I take pride in this because I know precisely how many meters they have to go, where they need to turn, what they should look for.

I resume my walk on the lively Tunalı, which was named after some forgotten Young Turk who had spent a considerable part of his life in Europe—a bit like yours truly. People are everywhere window shopping, enjoying themselves, walking around, meeting friends, and sitting in cafés. I pass countless phone shops, bars, pool halls, restaurants, hairdressers, cafés, kebab houses, expensive clothing stores, patisseries, pharmacies, banks, and fast food joints. Unfortunately, it is true that the place could use a few more bookshops.

I see the blind pencil seller standing in his customary spot, right in front of the bank. As I reach Kuğulupark—literally "Swan Park," a little cliché of a park, complete with a pond, swans and ducks, rides for children, and the whole shebang— I do an about face and head right back into the direction I came from. Clearly, I have not had enough yet. I turn into the next street, Bestekâr, an exclusive bar zone, and a scaled-down clone of Tunalı. On the sidewalk between the Guangzhou Chinese restaurant and the orthodontist, I spot a few of my students hanging around with beer bottles in their hands. They seem pleasantly surprised to see me.

"*Hocam*! What brings you out here?" *Hocam* (pronounced *ho-jahm*) is the proper, formal manner of addressing an instructor or a teacher. At least it used to be. In the past decade or so, the expression has become vernacularized, and it can now be used as a safe way to address any person, regardless of status, gender, or age—there goes the only proper title that I have ever held!

I laugh. "I don't live in the classroom you know. So? Isn't it a bit cold to be doing the Riviera?" Cold and a wee bit too early for my taste, even on a weekend. They all look puzzled. One politely asks, "Excuse me, *Hocam*?"

"I mean, you're drinking in the street, treating it like a waterfront."

"Yeah, we're just hanging out in the minibar. Want a beer?"

"No, thanks. I haven't had my coffee yet. Well, great talking to you. Just make sure that you make it to class on Monday morning."

I would not be caught dead drinking on the street, a principle I must have picked up in the United States. But I cannot really blame them; doing the Minibar has got to be cheaper than partying in one of those upscale places. When I was younger we did not have to drink on the street. We could just go to the infamous Sleaze Palace, only a hundred meters down. But that was way before the gentrification of the area, when it could tolerate disgusting, unsophisticated rock bars.

I remind myself, perhaps for the hundredth time, that Kavaklıdere translates as "Poplar Brook," which could have been the name of a chic suburban development in northern

Virginia or Maryland. There must have been a tiny brook here, ages ago. I read in some ancient novel that there were once cottages and vineyards here. And I clearly remember the huge wine factory that was located where the imposing Sheraton Ankara currently stands. Idiotically, I close my eyes in a vain attempt to visualize the ghosts of the past. I should stop before I run into a tree.

And then the inevitable happens: I run into a couple of friends, Ergun and his wife Aylin, and we get a table in one of the innumerable cafés. I am glad for this opportunity; I hardly get to see them since they have moved to Batıkent, to the "West Town," the hideous new highrises in the suburbs, where rent is supposedly cheaper. They have two kids now, and they bought the mandatory family sedan. I think they are still paying for it. Personally, I fail to understand why anyone would want to drive in this city, but that is easy for me to say since I live only five minutes from here.

For some reason, the menus are all in English. We order Mexican Chicken Wrappers, and before we get the chance to exchange a single meaningful sentence, some guy I barely know sits down, uninvited, and hijacks our conversation. "I have been busy designing a sculpture for the Municipality of Paris, and…"

Miraculously, he leaves only ten minutes later.

"So, who is the *gereksiz eleman*?" asks Ergun.

"Sorry about that," I reply. "The *gereksiz eleman,* the persona non-grata is just some…. Oh, forget it." I almost said *some pathological liar.*

A bit later, I get to ask them the question that I have been contemplating all day: "So guys, why do we hang out in this neighborhood? What is it that we like about it?" Ergun replies, "Actually, I should be asking you that…after all you're the one who is the *muhtar* around here."

The *muhtar* is traditionally the elder of a Turkish village, elected to act as leader. Ergun is using it in the figurative sense, implying that I know everyone in the neighborhood. And I suppose, after so many years as a visible regular on these streets, he has a point.

In the meantime, we are all staring at what the waiter has just brought. For some strange reason, the food has been served in small baskets rather than plates. Aylin looks disappointed with hers. "What's this? This is just a standard Turkish *tavuk dürüm*." What did she expect? *Tavuk dürüm* is chicken wrapped in thin dough, no matter what language you say it in. Before taking her first bite, she adds, "I like this neighborhood, it is not like Istanbul. It is modest. And honest. Not pretentious."

"Yeah, Ankara's just one big café," I say. But, as ever, I dutifully avoid committing the cardinal sin of comparing Ankara to Istanbul. But if you must know…Istanbul has a glorious history as an imperial and cultural capital. It features endless attractions for tourists: a beautiful Bosphorus, splendid palaces, mosques, and bazaars. But it is, after all, a large, chaotic metropolis, and life is frantic there. What's more, you could end up spending hours getting from one place to the next. On the other hand, Ankara is a compact, modern city that allows you to be spontaneous. You can leave your house at nine in the evening and catch a movie just fifteen minutes later. You can walk to your workplace. After work, you can meet all your friends in a single location. And nobody will steal your taxicab. If Istanbul is a jungle, then Ankara is a carefully manicured private garden.

Time to pay the bill. Not pretentious? Not cheap either. "Maybe we should have gone to the minibar instead," I say. It is their turn to be puzzled, so I try to explain.

"Ergun," says Aylin, "we better head on home, it's getting dark. We have to pick up the kids." She turns to me, "We would drive you, but we didn't bring the car. You know it's impossible to park around here."

"Don't worry. I can walk. And who says I'm going home yet?" They leave in a rush.

But I'm actually tired after having spent the better part of a day out here. There are plenty of distractions, and if I'm not careful, at any moment someone might still lure me into one of the bars. I have to make sure that *I* make it to class Monday. Five minutes or not, I need to flag a taxi…but first, I stop by a kiosk and say "*İyi akşamlar*," and ask for a pack of Marlboro Lights. The guy smiles and returns my greeting, "Good evening." It is a tolerant and knowing smile, as if I have just committed some horrible faux pas. "*Hocam*," he says, "your Turkish is wonderful. How long have you lived here?"

Oh my God! I might not be the *muhtar* after all; I'm more like the village idiot. I end up walking on Tunalı for fifteen entire minutes before I can find a free taxicab.

Umur Çelikyay was born in 1967 in Jordan and has lived in Belgium, Saudi Arabia, and the United States. He has published a volume of poetry (in English), but his two novels (in Turkish) remain unpublished. He is currently publishing a fanzine and working on a "photobiography." He has also done considerable work as a freelance technical translator. Though he describes himself as "a trilingual/multicontinental citizen of the world," he considers Ankara his hometown.

JOEL CARILLET

✦ ✦ ✦

Half Truths and Olive Trees

Yes, even here, the beauty of humanity can be salvaged.

HAVING WORKED FOR SEVERAL MONTHS IN JERUSALEM AND the Palestinian Territories, I could confirm much of what I saw on the news. I had heard Palestinians express support for violence toward Jews, and I had witnessed the shattered remains of a storefront after a suicide bombing. I had ducked behind walls as Israeli soldiers shot at stone-throwing children, and I had looked on as angry soldiers—someone had thrown a rock at their jeep—shot holes in the water tanks of innocent Palestinians. In so many ways—a thousand more than I can recount here— the "Holy Land" was a difficult and ugly place to live.

Yet I loved the place and its people passionately, because more lay behind the scenes than what was covered in the news. In the midst of the brokenness was hope. It emerged daily in laughter and hospitality. I witnessed it in the parents who, knowing that the only Jews their children had ever seen were holding guns, told them stories of other Jews with whom they had been friends in better times. "Do not hate," the parents would say. "The world is more than what you can see now." And I witnessed it as well in middle-aged Israeli women who traveled daily to stand at military checkpoints notorious for abusing Palestinians. They stood watch like observant mothers, reminding the soldiers that in protecting Israel there was no need to humiliate or abuse their Palestinian neighbors.

Part of what I loved, then, was how this complicated sliver of land along the Mediterranean illustrated what every traveler already knows: the view from up close is never the same as the view from a distance. A television or newspaper, seen or read 6,000 miles from the place it is attempting to describe, is limited in what it can do. It is incapable of leading us to *know* a place, especially in the ancient Hebrew sense of the word. The Hebrew implies an intimacy with the subject that is known, or, as I once heard a professor describe it: *knowledge is connected to responsibility is connected to caring.* Knowing, then, is not the collecting of facts and figures and opinions; it is to care.

One of the underreported tragedies of the conflict in Israel and Palestine is the demolition of more than 14,000 Palestinian homes by Israeli authorities since 1967. Of the various kinds of demolitions, the most controversial are those carried out when a Palestinian has built without a proper permit. These are known as "administrative demolitions." A visitor walking the streets of East Jerusalem will undoubtedly pass Palestinians who are selling souvenirs, slicing *shwarma*, and shouting out prices at vegetable stands. But the visitor will also pass countless people who are wondering, *Will my house be demolished this year?*

The people who first brought this aspect of the conflict to my attention were not Palestinians but Israelis. Angered by the institutionalized racism they believed pervaded their government's interaction with Palestinians, they had made it their business to speak out against it. Rabbi Arik Ascherman, executive director of Rabbis for Human Rights, complained that "the Israeli government is one of the few governments in the world that uses the destruction of homes as a political policy tool.... I, as a rabbi, feel that to destroy homes in this way is to trample on the Torah and on everything we hold dear in the Jewish tradition."

Perhaps the most vocal critic was Professor Jeff Halper, co-founder of the Israeli Committee Against House Demolitions (ICAHD). "The bulldozer," he writes, "certainly deserves to take its rightful place alongside the tank as a symbol of Israel's relationship with the Palestinians. The two deserve to be on the national flag. The tank as symbol of an Israel 'fighting for existence,' and for its prowess on the battle-field. And the bulldozer for the dark underside of Israel's struggle for existence, its ongoing struggle to displace the Palestinians from the country."

Here is the situation: In order to build a home in Jerusalem (or in those parts of the West Bank administered by Israel), a landowner is required to obtain a building permit from the proper government office. For Palestinians this process is not only expensive—in the West Bank an applications runs about $5,000, and in Jerusalem it can be considerably more—it is also exacerbating. Even if they meticulously navigate their way through the entire process, in the end their application is likely to be rejected. Then, having been denied access to a legal permit, they are left with three options: give up and move to a country where they will be allowed to build, move into a Palestinian administered portion of the West Bank but risk losing their right to enter Jerusalem again, or stay where they are but build illegally.

And this is why Israelis like Rabbi Ascherman and Professor Halper are angry. Today, most Jewish neighborhoods in the Jerusalem area are preplanned by the Municipality or private developers and then housing is sold. Hence, because they do not face the same bureaucratic challenges a Palestinian does, it is easier for a Jewish resident to procure legal housing. Human rights groups argue that the system is designed to facilitate the movement of Jews into Jerusalem while hampering the ability of Palestinians to stay.

Early one August morning a taxi dropped me off at a construction site in the West Bank village of Anata, a Palestinian community just outside the Jerusalem city limits. The day was already a fast evolving into a scorcher, and I found forty-seven-year-old Salim Shawamreh, a Palestinian, sitting in the shade of an olive tree. With him were one of his seven children and two Jewish friends, including Jeff. We were the first of some two dozen people who would gather at the construction site today. While we waited for the others, Salim told me his story.

Born in Jerusalem's Old City in 1956, Salim married in 1981 and moved with his new wife to Saudi Arabia. There he worked as a construction manager to save money so he could eventually build a home in Jerusalem. But upon returning to Jerusalem, the cost and challenges of obtaining a building permit—even for a native Jerusalemite—led him to purchase land just outside the city. Over the next three years he twice applied for a building permit—an expenditure of $10,000—but both times he was rejected. Like thousands of other Palestinian families who were not granted permission to build on their land, Salim eventually began construction anyway since he had a family to raise. That was in 1994. The following year Israel's Civil Authority ordered the home demolished, and the order was carried out in 1998.

Jeff continued Salim's story. When the soldiers came to destroy the house, they dragged Salim out and beat him. Salim's wife, fearing for her family's safety, locked the door behind the soldiers, who then hurled tear gas through the windows to remove her and the children. With the house now vacated, a bulldozer moved in to tear it down. Jeff threw himself in front of the bulldozer, but he too was dragged away and beaten. "If the authorities sent a bulldozer to destroy a Jewish house," Jeff explained, "there would be a revolution—this is absolutely unthinkable."

In the non-violent tradition of Gandhi and Martin Luther King, Salim, with the assistance of ICAHD, committed to rebuilding his home as an act of resistance. Predictably, the house was demolished three more times in the five years that followed. This, of course, is why Jews, Palestinians, and others were descending on Anata today. We had come to rebuild.

But this occasion was unique because Salim had decided to lease the land to ICAHD and, instead of a home, build the Beit Arabiya Peace Center. Dedicated to the memory of two women who had been killed during home demolitions earlier in the year—Rachel Corrie, an American trampled by a bulldozer, and Nuha Sweidan, a pregnant Palestinian killed when a wall fell on her—people from all walks of life had come to take part in its construction. One couple came from Santa Fe, New Mexico. "My husband and I are retired from the CIA," the woman said, "and when we heard about this project, we knew we wanted to be here." Another volunteer was a Muslim, a twenty-six-year-old Briton of Pakistani descent who had taken two weeks off work in London. Several other foreigners would be here later in the week, and all of us shared the conviction that travel, at its best, is not a self-indulgent foray into foreign lands; it is to help our global neighbors in the modest ways we can.

Elizabeth was the youngest member of the group. An eighteen-year-old Palestinian with flowing dark hair and braces, she had met Jeff the day a bulldozer came to demolish her neighbor's home in Beit Hanina, a Palestinian district of Jerusalem. "My family is originally from Ikrit, a Christian village near the Lebanese border," she said. "Do you know the story?"

I had read about this village before; it was one of more than 400 Palestinian communities that Israel leveled in the years following its independence in 1948. While the destruction of Ikrit occurred years before Elizabeth was born, it was part of her story, and this contributed to the beauty of what was happening now in Anata. As we worked, she conversed about the history of the region and its political dynamics with a maturity beyond her years.

The sun climbed higher and I joined two young Israeli men in moving garbage and heavy stones—mostly rubble from the last demolition—away from the building site. One of the men, twenty-four-year-old Michael, had recently finished four years of active military duty. We talked about his years as an Israeli officer in Lebanon and the West Bank. We also talked about my impressions as an outsider who had friends on both sides of the political divide. When I mentioned that for three months I had lived in a village adjacent to the West Bank town of Jenin, he told me his unit had fought in Jenin and that some of his men were killed there. "I wasn't actually in Jenin," Michael said as he held open a bag so I could toss in some faded plastic Coke bottles. "A few days before the invasion we were in Nablus, and I was hit in the head by a rock. I was in the hospital while my men went to Jenin." He paused a moment and then said, "But maybe being hit by that rock was one of the best things to happen to me in the West Bank. I should have been with my men, but Jenin would have been a moral nightmare."

Michael was referring to the 2002 Israeli invasion of Jenin that left at least fifty-two Palestinians dead and many more injured.

As we heaved the last few stones downhill and wiped the sweat from our eyes, bad news came. In the last hour, Palestinian suicide bombers had struck two locations, one outside a Jewish settlement in the West Bank, the other within Israel itself. This vicious storm of violence had taken its latest turn, slamming against another set of lives and taking them away.

Not only were lives lost, but tomorrow's news headline had been made. Media consumers around the world would read their papers and watch CNN, and many would shake their heads at the hatred here. But this is precisely why the evening news is sometimes a culprit in conflict: it trawls the world for tragedy and then beams this half-story into our living rooms, leaving the other half abandoned among the olive trees. But when we are robbed of hearing good news—no matter how small that news may seem—our imagination withers, and we become too content to view the world from a distance. With sickly imaginations we fortify our walls, even though there are gaps where people are already coming together—and where we could too, if we wanted.

The hour's bombings did not interrupt our work. As Michael handed some tools up to a Palestinian laboring on the roof, the Palestinian serenaded Michael with a Hebrew song he had learned in an Israeli jail. Another Israeli, who like Michael had also recently completed his army service, shared a bottle of water with a thirsty Palestinian who was shoveling gravel. And at midday, when a group of Canadian Christians arrived for a short visit and sang "Amazing Grace," all of us—Jew, Muslim, and Christian—stopped our work and listened.

At 2:30 P.M. we set our work aside and, under a canopy held up by pieces of the demolished home, dug into lunch: chicken schnitzel, hot dogs, and veggie burgers. Our appetites were ravenous.

After eating, I lay down to rest by an olive tree, where rugs had been spread across a shaded portion of ground. With my head propped up, I watched several Palestinian boys sitting with Michael, playing. After a while one of the boys, Salim's son, pointed to the yarmulke worn by Michael, an observant Jew. Michael removed it from his head and gave it to the boy, who promptly put it atop his own head. Here was a Palestinian boy—a boy whose home had been destroyed four times by a Jewish government, whose father had been beaten by Jewish soldiers—wearing atop his head the religious head covering of a Jew. And here also was a Jewish man—a man whose friends were killed in combat with Palestinians, who had served as an officer and would still be called up for reserve duty once a year—sitting with his head uncovered before God because he was sharing his yarmulke with an inquisitive Palestinian child.

The Israelis and Palestinians meeting today did not have to travel far to reach Anata, but the words of Maya Angelou were as true for them as they were for the rest of us: "Perhaps travel cannot prevent bigotry, but by demonstrating that all peoples cry, laugh, eat, worry and die, it can introduce the idea that if we try and understand each other, we may even become friends."

Relaxed by hard work and good food, and with the heat reaching its afternoon peak, I grew sleepy. As I drifted from wakefulness, happy for the beautiful coat of dust and dirt that covered me, I dreamed I was in a land full of good news, where enemies ate veggie burgers and played together. Some would call this a hippie's vision, a fantastic dream that doesn't mesh with reality. But as for me, I only wished that the *New York Times*, the *Jerusalem Post* or anyone else with an audience—had been here in Anata, even if only to write one line: *If you want to behold an incredible gathering of individuals, the West Bank may be just the place to be.*

Joel Carillet has taught at a college in Ukraine, worked on the staff of a study abroad program in Egypt, and has done human rights work in the West Bank. In December 2004, he completed a fourteen-month overland backpacking journey from Beijing to Istanbul, which he recounts in a recently completed manuscript tentatively entitled "Sixty-One Weeks: A Journey across Asia." His work has appeared in several publications, including Touchstone *magazine,* The Kansas City Star, *and* The Christian Science Monitor, *and he regularly posts written and photographic travel essays at http://jcarillet.gather.com. His story "Clutching My Soul in Paradise" was included in Travelers' Tales* The Best Travel Writing 2006.

* * *

Clothes, Camaraderie, and Qat

When the doors close behind them,
Yemeni women live it up!

FOREIGN MEN CALL THEM "WHISPERING SHADOWS." ARAB MEN call them "BMOs," or "black moving objects"—Yemeni women, swathed head to toe in black.

As I walk through the winding, cobblestoned labyrinth of the centuries-old city of Sana'a, the lavish gypsum friezes decorating the old stone houses remind me of a gingerbread fantasyland. Yemeni women swish past in flowing black gowns, scarves, gloves, and face veils, some covering their eyes. Men wear the ubiquitous *jambia*, or dagger, whose varying styles denote regions and still-strong tribal loyalties.

Located on the Arabian Peninsula's southwest tip, Yemen is a land of mountainous stone villages, virgin coast lines, and an ancient history reflected in cleverly designed architecture. Its economy, once based on frankincense and myrrh, sprang from its place on the Old World's incense route.

Today, with 60 million guns—three for every Yemeni man, woman, and child—and a penchant for the occasional kid-napped tourist, Yemen feels like some kind of Wild, Wild East.

In recent years, Yemen has been routinely labeled as "the ancestral homeland of Osama bin Laden." Not surprisingly, most Yemenis prefer their magical homeland to be known for its historical names such as "Arabia Felix," or as the land of the Queen of Sheba, a figure so legendary that she makes appearances in both the Bible and the Koran.

Hotels, restaurants, and stores pay homage to Sheba or to Arwa, the country's famous eleventh-century Islamic queen.

Yet, perplexingly, Yemen's contemporary Shebas and Arwas remain segregated from male society.

Wedding celebrations are segregated by the sexes. In one of the world's poorest countries, female illiteracy runs near 70 percent; women in the work force are minimal. Even the bridal shops are operated by men, and Yemeni women must try on white bridal gowns over their black robes.

An urban myth in Yemen, my friends tell me, holds that only a dozen Yemeni women go outside without wearing a veil covering their hair.

A dozen, in a country of 20 million people.

Jamila Al-Rajaa is one of that famous dozen. She is a striking, dark-skinned, strong-willed, and intelligent woman, a former Yemeni diplomat-turned-development worker committed to rescuing child laborers.

When Jamila asks me to join her at a women's afternoon *qat* party, I jump at the opportunity to see a world men aren't allowed to experience.

I take a taxi from Old Sana'a to her home in Hadda City, a suburb that some now call "the Beverly Hills of Sana'a." Once graced with terraced walnut and almond orchards, peach and apricot trees, it now is being redeveloped with modern mansions that lack the charm of the city's old stone houses. Many are being built for Yemenis who are returning from abroad with ample cash to re-establish themselves in their homeland.

My reed-thin taxi driver wears a *futa,* the Yemeni man's traditional skirt. His *jambia* is tucked into a leather belt around his waist; a threadbare blue sport coat tops off his outfit. He is busy digging into a plastic bag for branches of *qat*, plucking off the little leaves and stuffing them into his mouth, enlarging the golf-ball-sized bulge already tucked into his cheek. Then he tosses the stripped branch out of the taxi's open driver's window.

He offers me a branch. "Do you want some *qat*?"

"No, thank you."

"You have to try it," he insists.

"I will, later," I assure him.

The driver has quite a cheekful of *qat* firmly in place before we travel very far. Despite repeated cell phone calls to Jamila for directions to her home off of Zero Street, he can't seem to absorb the information—most likely due, I surmise, to the *qat's* half-narcotic, half-sedative effect. Finally, Jamila tells him to stay where he is, and she will pick me up.

Safely in her hands, Jamila tells me about a meeting of the Women's National Committee. It will be a good place, she explains, to learn what Yemeni women are up to these days.

Though of Yemen's upper class, these women are not the hyperelite in a jet-setting Paris Hilton kind of way. Many of them have pushed through boundaries in this conservative society to become educated, others have returned from studies abroad. And they are remarkable in that they use the opportunities afforded through their class and education to work in the trenches in fields of human rights, journalism, development, and even politics to improve the lives of Yemeni women less fortunate than themselves.

As we leave Jamila's house, she tosses a red-and-black scarf around her neck. "This is my chastity belt," she says, smiling and gripping the ends of the scarf. "In case of an emergency, it will keep me chaste."

I assume the "emergency" would be some conservative Muslim man giving her a hard time on the street for not covering her head.

The meeting turns out to be a women's party at the home of Rashida Al-Hamadani, president of the Women's National Committee. Black-veiled women enter the house and remove their robes. Underneath, they are dressed to the Yemeni nines, in full-length gowns of vibrant, multicolored, and sequined silks, satins, and chiffons.

At this and other parties, it's all about the clothes, the camaraderie—and the *qat*.

Some women wear updated versions of traditional Yemeni dresses. But one woman's dress could have come straight out of America's Old West, with its laced-up bodice, ruffles and bows, and white petticoat peeking from the hitched-up hem. Another woman wears a forest-green taffeta dress with small red bows that reveals a fire engine red crinoline petticoat around her shins, all capped by a crownlike green-and-gold brocade headdress that is more reminiscent of a medieval European court than of the gauzy dresses and veils in an old Arabian harem.

As the guests arrive, they greet each other affectionately, hugging and kissing each other on the cheek. Then they stroll into the home's *diwan*, a carpeted rectangular room bordered by floor cushions. The smoke and scent of *bakhur*, or incense, hang thickly in the air.

A dark-skinned singer wears a dress that is traditional to Yemen's southern port city of Aden, a translucent pink sheath with a pink shift underneath; her outfit is complemented by a gold belt, a dowry gift at marriage. A woman wearing white pants, a colored sweater, and a headscarf, smiles and reveals a gold-capped tooth. She begins to dance, hiking up her pants and shaking her hips, as the other women laugh.

Jamila explains that at these women's parties one woman acts as a clown to make the other guests relax, laugh, and dance.

The women sip sweetened tea made with evaporated milk and talk a bit of politics. Many comment on the recent news that Jamila's sister, Sumaya Al-Raja, has decided to run for Yemen's presidency, a first in this male-dominated nation's history.

"We have to support her," says Huria Mashour, the editor-in-chief of a monthly Yemeni newspaper. "She has broken the taboo. Not just for women, but for men who are afraid to do that."

Soon, more of the women move to the middle of the floor and begin to snap their fingers and dance. One of them gyrates in an Egyptian-style belly dance as another woman wraps a scarf around her hips, to emphasize her movements. Others, watching, hold their right hands over their lips and ululate, a piercing wail that Arab women often let loose during celebrations.

Amal Basha sits cross-legged on a cushion against a wall, leaning on one knee to smoke a water pipe. A passionate human-rights activist, she says the separation of the sexes is the biggest problem that Yemeni women face today. She blames it all on the conservative Islamist view of women.

"Here, they relax and let go," Amal says, pointing to the women who are dancing in the center of the room. "Here, they show their beauty, their femininity. Here, they laugh and dance, and they can smoke and chew *qat* and tell bad jokes."

I tag along with Jamila and Amal as they head out to another, smaller women's *qat* chew. Walking into the next house, I ask them about the urban myth of the twelve Yemeni women who are not veiled.

"No, there are more now—twenty-six," says Amal.

She and Jamila fall into a debate over whether the country's six female television broadcasters are veiled. They decide that all six routinely wear a headscarf, or *hijab,* and finally settle on twenty as the correct number who are unveiled.

The new party we head to is similar to the many gatherings taking place around the country.

In early afternoons, all around Yemen, men and women gather in their homes, mostly in segregated groups. They often retire to the top floor of their stone houses, in a room known as the *mafraj,* or "room with a view."

Guests enter through the ground floor, passing under a stone archway that in an earlier time would have sheltered the household's animals. Old grinding stones sit in a courtyard grain-storage area. A spiraling stone staircase leads up the floors to the *mafraj.*

Inside the room, windows on all sides offer guests one of the finest views of the city, its skyline perforated by minarets and the towers of old stone palaces. Small stained-glass windows decorate the room's walls nearer the ceiling. As night slowly falls outside, the old city of Sana'a shimmers with colored lights.

Guests sit on cushions and are served water, Pepsi, or Fanta soda. They dig into plastic bags for the ubiquitous *qat* branches holding the leaves that virtually everyone in Yemen chews and stuffs into their cheeks, to enjoy the narcotic yet stimulant effect.

This party is not only smaller but more informal; the ten or so women in attendance gather together every night except Fridays, alternating among each other's homes.

Nagat Yousef Qussami is a former United Nations worker and mother of two daughters who have grown into successful professional women. She takes me under her wing, picking leaves for me to chew and dropping the stripped branch onto the carpeted floor.

"Eat the soft leaves and the little red ones, they will soothe you," she instructs. She says the *qat's* buzz is similar to drinking several cups of coffee, except that "the coffee goes quickly, and you have to drink one more cup."

"I do all my housework at night," she says.

Another woman leans over, conspiratorially, and adds with a broad smile: "It's great for sex."

A native of Aden, Nagat is proud of her daughters, one a dentist in Cairo and the other the owner of an investment company in Dubai. "I didn't let them marry until they had their master's degrees," she says proudly.

She explains that I must first chew the leaves, then store them in my cheek. I try the leaves, but the taste is lip-puckering bitter. She pulls a small purple-and-gold beaded coin purse from a pocket and picks out a nut, a cardamom seed, and colored sugar-coated fennel seeds. "You put these in your mouth to take away the bitter taste."

Arabic music plays in the background, and conversation swirls around us.

"In old times, women in Sana'a used to wear dresses that showed their cleavage, but it was forbidden to show their legs and ankles," says Najwa, a slim yet serious young woman.

Jamila shares her water pipe with me. The grape-flavored tobacco flows through the tube, a relief from the bitter taste of the *qat*. Another, larger water pipe, called a *madah*, is brought into the room. It stands three feet high and its leather smoking tube, covered with furry red and black wool, stretches some six feet, snaking across the room. The tobacco is plain; Jamila warns me to be careful when inhaling, because it takes so much air to bring the smoke to my lips and could choke me.

Sumaya Al Raja, Yemen's first female presidential candidate, arrives to join the party. Women greet her with *"Ya, Raisa!"*— "Oh, President!"

Sumaya, a brown-eyed woman who carries herself with the grace and style of a middle-aged French actress, smiles widely. The talk in the room quickly turns to her newly announced candidacy and to other women who have achieved positions of power in the modern world, such as Benazir Bhuto and Indira Gandhi.

Her candidacy is possible in this strict Muslim country "because of the history of the queens, the women working in the fields," Sumaya says.

She calls her and Jamila's father a visionary because he obtained permission from the country's ruling imam, or religious leader, to allow his daughters to go unveiled. "We were the first women to go out without a veil. Our father believed in the *hadith*"—a collection of sayings attributed to the Prophet Muhammed—"that says you should teach your children to swim, shoot a bow and arrow, and ride horses." Sumaya learned to swim and to ride horses.

"We missed out on a lot of prominent marriages," she says. "The men would come to ask for our hand, and our father would tell them that in Islam the girl had to agree to the marriage. The men would be so scared they would run away." She laughs heartily at the memories.

Sumaya tells me she has a lot of hope for Yemen, despite its place near the bottom of the world's economic rankings. But Yemeni women must be taken seriously first, she says.

"We are loved, we are protected. Now we need to participate.… It is time to go back to our matriarchal traditions."

Some of these traditions I experience myself, as Nagat takes the comb out of my hair that she had worked in earlier. The women in the room pass over a square incense holder with a long, upward-curving handle. Nagat pulls up my hair and puts the incense underneath the blonde strands, letting the smoke drift into them. Then she sprinkles me with perfume as the women around us recite Yemeni poetry. Yemenis love poetry and use it often, including on wedding invitations.

"Many Yemeni women may be illiterate, but they know more oral history and poetry than more modern women," Sumaya explains.

The women at this second party chew *qat*, their cheeks beginning to bulge, and smoke water pipes while touching on a variety of topics. Despite Yemenis' widely-held belief that America will attack their country one day, these women welcome me into their homes with the warm customary Arabian hospitality.

"You have more freedom when you are just with women," explains Najla Foud Attif, a Yemeni actress. "You feel freer to talk." Her brown eyes sparkle as she describes her role in an award-winning film, *A Brand New Day in Old Sana'a.*

Acting in a Yemeni film, in a country without theaters or cinemas, was a dream-come-true for the diminutive beauty with thick black hair and a dazzling smile. Her film role required her to go without the traditional robes and veils. "It is good to see different faces of Yemeni women. It makes us more human," she says.

Toward evening's end, the conversation turns to men. The women all agree that Yemeni mountain men are best, because they are comfortable with themselves and enjoy strong women.

The next day's gathering is held in honor of female human-rights activists from several Arab countries. The women dress in new gowns; Maemona Taha, a woman from Aden who plays the oud, a Middle Eastern-style lute, sings and strums Arabic music as the party begins.

One striking woman with long black hair, wearing a black velvet dress with spaghetti straps, demonstrates the Sudanese Pigeon Dance for everyone. She stands with her back arched backward, face in the air, arms back, and chest out. The African music starts and she shakes her hips, raising one cupped hand up to the side of her face.

"Very sexy!" the enthralled guests shout.

But that will be another Yemeni night. To end my first Yemeni girls-night-out, Jamila hands me a glass of warm milk to help settle my stomach after all the *qat* chewing. Her strapping son, Muhammed, takes me back to the magical old city and my charming hotel, the Arabia Felix. On the way to my room, Ibrahim, one of the workers at the old stone palace-turned-hotel, smiles and asks if I tried *qat*.

"Yes, I was at a women's *qat* party."

"You won't be able to sleep tonight," he says with a smile.

I climb the large, uneven steps of the spiral staircase to my cozy fourth-floor room. Snuggling under fuzzy blankets, and in spite of Ibrahim's prediction, I fall asleep with a smile on my face—and the scent of perfume in my hair.

Betsy Hiel has been the Middle East correspondent at The Pittsburgh Tribune-Review *since 2000. She is the co-author of* The Islamic Revival Since 1988: A Critical Survey and Bibliography. *She studied Arabic at the American University in Cairo and at Hebrew University in Jerusalem. She obtained a master's degree in Arab Studies at Georgetown University, and a bachelor's degree in Middle Eastern Studies from the University of Minnesota. She is proficient in written and spoken Arabic.*

KATHERINE BELLIEL

* * *

Instant Mother,
Just Add Tea

Hospitality unchecked makes for a rough ride to Istanbul.

THE PAIN WAS AGONY, AND I COULDN'T HIDE IT ANY LONGER. I imploringly looked at the woman sitting next to me, willing her to speak English so that she could help deliver me from this dilemma. I had been living in Istanbul, Turkey, for just a few months and still had only a basic, hodge-podge grasp of the language. How could I desperately convey in my non-native tongue, "I will wet my pants if we don't find a toilet soon"?

I was aboard a bus from Bursa to Istanbul, a normal journey of three to four hours. Returning from a visit to my Turkish "family" who resided in Bursa, also a welcome mountain retreat from the hustle-bustle of Istanbul, I silently cursed my Turkish "mother," Sevil-teyze, for treating me like royalty and preparing a massive, three-hour-long leisurely breakfast with a bottomless teapot. I cursed the luxurious bus that was clean, replete with a waiter serving tea and cakes, yet lacked a toilet. Even the horrible Greyhound buses found in the U.S. were endowed with a commode, however dubious. But most of all I cursed myself for drinking so much tea, for getting onto the bus without first using the bathroom, and for not knowing enough of the language to get myself out of this ridiculous quandary.

I braced my arm against the seat in front of me as another spasm ripped across my bladder that threatened to spill its contents at any moment. *God, Allah, whoever is there, please help me!* I turned again to the woman next to me and asked, "*Tuvalet nerede?*" Where is the toilet? She looked sympathetically at me and replied, "*feribotta.*" On the ferry.

We still had another twenty minutes before the bus would reach the ferry station, where it would board a transport to take us across a narrow slip of the Marmara Sea before continuing on the road to Istanbul. *You can wait twenty minutes,* I told myself encouragingly. I looked out the window and tried to focus on passing scenery. The mountains had given way to gently rolling hills, some brutally cut open by marble mines, exposing red flesh beneath. "*Su ister misiniz?*" Would you like some water? asked the waiter, standing in the aisle with a rickety cart atop which coffee, tea, soda, and water accoutrements jostled with each other as we bumped down the road. *You have GOT to be kidding me!* I thought, as I refused his offer. *How did Turks do it,* I asked myself in wonder, as I looked around at everyone happily sipping tea, with no idea of the agony I was in. *Did they all have bladders made of steel?*

To receive a mother's touch I frequently visited Bursa, located in "Anatolia" (literally translating to mean "land full of mothers") to visit my best friend, Sechil (pronounced "Say-cheel"), and her mother, Sevil-teyze. I had met them when I traveled to Turkey as a tourist, and it was their friendship that helped me decide to move here. Sevil-teyze treated me like an adopted daughter and through her touch, ministrations, and love I realized I missed something that had never before existed for me. From giving lessons in the art of preparing delicate cups of bitter Turkish coffee to the timely task of making *mantı* (small meat-stuffed pasta), she not only has educated me in the culinary aspect of her culture but also demonstrated the love and dedication inherent in the preparation of Turkish food. A woman who suffered an early loss of a husband and young child, she knows the importance of expressing affection, such as offering random kisses on the cheek, pats on the knee, and gentle caresses. Under her tutelage and in only a short time I learned more about the values of life than I had at my blood mother's knee. My current bladder predicament was due to an expression of her love and acceptance, and my thirsty consumption of the love that her endless cups of tea and carefully prepared breakfast represented.

We finally reached the ferry station and, to my horror, our bus parked at the end of a line of cars, trucks, and buses all waiting to board the ferries, which bobbed in the rough waves. Our driver turned off the engine and vendors selling *simit* (hard, sesame-covered rings), *pismaniye* (a sweet similar in texture to cotton candy), and tissues boarded our bus and gave us the bad news as they sold their wares. I looked at the woman next to me questioningly.

"*Feribot chalishmiyor.*" The ferry is not working, she said. My face burned and my stomach dropped at the news. "*Bekliyoruz.*" We are waiting, she said and shrugged her shoulders.

I could no longer sit and was forced to stand in order to relieve any extra pressure on my poor bladder. Everyone stared at me as I made uncontrolled facial expressions. As I broke into a sweat, I knew I had reached the limit of my resolve and needed to take desperate action. In Istanbul I had learned from a friend that a good way to ask a taxi driver to slow down was to tell him you were pregnant, and that was one of the first phrases I learned to say in Turkish. I hoped it would help here as well.

With a deep breath I nudged the woman next to me, put

my hand on my stomach, and whispered, "*Hamileyim,*" I'm pregnant. Her eyes widened in shock and sudden understanding as she stood up. She did not call the steward and discreetly explain my situation, nor did she keep my "secret" quiet. To my horror she announced to all forty-six passengers that the foreign woman next to her was expecting and needed to use the toilet immediately. This was an emergency that suddenly everyone knew how to handle. The driver hurried down the aisle and made reassuring motions towards the ferryboat. The men jumped from their seats and left the bus, while the women squeezed down the narrow alley to crowd around me. I was shocked as hands reached under my shirt and squeezed my stomach, although with how swollen my bladder currently was it no doubt gave my story credibility.

"You speak English?" a young girl sitting a few rows behind me queried.

"Yes," I replied, my voice winding around the bulk of humanity surrounding me.

"Men went to other buses, toilet looking. I speak little English, I'm sorry," she apologized.

I nodded in embarrassment as other sympathetic mothers attempted to comfort me by patting my back and stomach. This affinity for physical contact and touch—widespread in Turkish culture—never ceased to amaze me. These women saw nothing wrong or strange with putting their hands on my bare stomach, squeezing my cheeks, or patting and holding my hands despite the fact that I knew none of their names, nor they mine. I had been drawn into the circle of motherhood through a selfish lie I had told for instant relief from a problem caused by a fellow caring mother.

Within minutes the driver returned to the bus, a triumphant expression on his face. He announced something to the passengers in rapid Turkish as he started the engine, and everyone settled into their seats. I looked out the window and saw that the queue of cars and trucks on our left side was being directed away from our bus, clearing a path that led directly to the ferry. We slowly drove onto the boat, the only vehicle allowed to board since it was still being repaired. As the last wheel precariously eased onto the ferry, the bus driver stopped and the steward rushed to my side to assist me off the bus. He gingerly guided me by the elbow as I made my way down the three steps. He then escorted me to the most horrific toilet I had ever seen and stood guard outside the door as I prepared to release my burdened bladder. There was no time to roll up my pant legs, nor for much of a concentrated effort in how to navigate the hit-or-miss rusty hole in the floor that offered heavenly relief. As I squatted shamelessly and without grace, the faithful steward patiently waited outside the rickety door until the process was complete.

Everyone applauded as I re-entered the bus, not only cheering because I was out of agony but also happy that my predicament had landed us at the front of the line, sparing a delay of one to two hours. After a short wait the ferry was fixed and started to move. We continued our journey to Istanbul, although I was not delivered from my plight despite my recently empty bladder. I was now subjected to a deluge of questions, all asked in basic Turkish that I could easily understand and respond to. Do you live in Turkey? Is your husband Turkish? Where do you live? What is his job? An engineer! *Mashallah!* Which company?

I continued the snowball effect from the first lie and created a fantasy husband who was a computer engineer for Microsoft whose office was in Nishantashı, a chic Istanbul neighborhood. I thought I might as well make it worthwhile.

We arrived in Istanbul and as I disembarked from the bus I

realized a fatal error in my plans. In order to furbish my new house in the Tarabya district of Istanbul, my trip had also included a major shopping spree to purchase sheets, towels, bedding, and other home textiles that Bursa is famed for. Due to the sheer amount of packages I knew I would be bearing, I had asked my friend Utku and his wife if they could pick me up from the station and drop me off at my home. As I got off the bus I saw Utku's face attempt to hide expressions of shock as passengers surrounded him, congratulating him on his beautiful foreign wife and the baby we were supposedly expecting. They also questioned him as to his Microsoft contacts and other matters relating to the fantastic tale I had spun on the journey—all while his real wife was waiting in the car. Women and men scolded my poor friend for allowing his "wife" to travel unaccompanied in her delicate "condition." Utku murmured to me out of the corner of his mouth, "What the hell is going on?" He gracefully made our excuses and rushed my packages and me to his waiting car where I related my story amidst much laughter.

As soon as I arrived home my telephone rang, and I heard Sevil-teyze's voice on the other end of the line. After I assured her of my safe return I related my story to her and Sechil. Dutifully, Sevil-teyze taught me on my next visit to Bursa how to put the teaspoon across the top of the tulip-shaped tea glasses to signal that I wanted no more refills, thereby avoiding another unwelcome bathroom predicament.

Despite the humor of my situation that day, I was shocked by the generous response of everyone around me. I had never been "mothered" to this extent until arriving in Turkey, and I was overwhelmed. Despite living alone in a foreign land with basic understanding of the language and customs, I had been nurtured as though one of their own. In this nowhere I felt what it was like to live somewhere, and I never wanted to leave.

In Turkey, as the name Anatolia suggests, you will never have too many mothers.

Grand Rapids, Michigan native Katherine Belliel continues to drink tea and visit her Turkish "mother" in Turkey. She lives in the Tarabya district of Istanbul, where she researches and writes about the Middle East. She is a regular contributor to the English language daily Today's Zaman, *and is also featured in the expat anthology* Tales from the Expat Harem. *She hopes to complete her Master's degree soon and master the Turkish language shortly thereafter.*

LAURENCE MITCHELL

✳ ✳ ✳

From the Oasis
to the City

Cairo races on, but Egypt's deserts
and shores rush for no one.

THE EARLY MORNING BUS TO MARSA MATRUH LEAVES ON time but we have a puncture just ten kilometers out of the oasis town of Siwa in western Egypt. All of the men get off to smoke cigarettes as the driver and conductor efficiently exchange one balding tire for another. It is still quite cold after a cloudless desert night. I am wearing a jacket and pullover but the cold-blooded Siwans are dressed for the Arctic, with woollen scarves wrapped around their faces and collars turned up to the chill. As we gather round the crew in the universal habit that compels all males to watch other men at work, the low morning sun creates strange Giacometti shadows of our forms in the sand: big-footed phantoms that stretch westward like strings of glue.

After a couple of hours motoring through unremitting, dreary desert, the bus stops at the same half-way restaurant we called at on the way out, although "restaurant" is perhaps too grand a title for a filthy, jerry-built pit stop. I risk a cup of tea, and then even regret that when I investigate the toilet block: a temple to excrement, the floor decorated with the sorry cairns of errant customers.

The place is teeming with soldiers who have just ended their tour of duty in Siwa. For the majority of the recruits, farmers' sons from the Nile Delta, the Siwa posting must have felt like an awful long way from home. Egypt has one of the world's largest standing armies, with an annual budget twice that received by the nation's schools but, despite military conscription, concessions are made for special cases. The prescribed term of national service is reduced for high school graduates, and even more for university alumni, while only-begotten sons do not have to serve at all. The consequence of this is an army composed mostly of poorly educated *felaheen*: the sons of large traditionalist families from the farming villages of Upper Egypt and the Delta. Joyful to be returning to their families after their enforced desert sojourn, it is no wonder that these young conscripts are in such high spirits.

At Marsa Matruh I am in luck—there is a direct bus to Cairo at midday. I have an hour to kill, so I go for a walk along the seafront. As in Alexandria, the buildings that line the corniche are uninviting concrete blocks that have been expunged of any color by an unyielding sun; the sea itself is a perfect shade of ultramarine.

Instantly, I am the focus of attention for a bunch of young students who see few foreign visitors this far off the usual tourist circuit. There is little to draw travellers here, although I am aware that, for many Egyptians, the words *Marsa Matruh* conjure up notions of an elegant resort that holds the same romance as Cannes or Capri. I parry the usual line of questioning. What is my name…my line of work? Do I like Egypt? I tell them that I am on my way to Cairo but this does not prompt a favorable response from these provincials.

"Cairo, bad place. *Fuggin'* bullshit Cairo," one of them says with a sneer.

On the bus to Cairo I meet Omar, a doctor from Marsa, who is going to the capital to catch a plane to Britain the next day. I make the usual joke about Omar Sharif, the Egyptian everyone knows, but my short list of other famous Egyptians falls flat when I realize that he has not heard of the former UN leader, Boutros Boutros-Ghali. Boutros Boutros- (so good they named him twice) Ghali is a Copt, and not especially popular with many Muslim Egyptians, so Omar may just be in denial. Instead, he asks if I know of Doctor Magdi Yacoub, the world famous London-based surgeon. I say that, yes, I have heard of him, but I think what Omar really means is: do I know him personally?

Omar is going to Newcastle-upon-Tyne for a month, to attend a medical convention. I tell him that he will like Newcastle; that it is a friendly, down-to-earth sort of place, even if the wind does trip off the North Sea a little too freely at times. Somehow, I cannot see Omar walking around Newcastle in short sleeves in February, as any self-respecting Geordie might. But Newcastle holds no romance for him. He is far more interested in London and I am bombarded with questions about what he should see and about the cost of living, which I think he has quite worryingly underestimated.

"What should I see in London as tourist? What number one?"

I am at a loss for words, never really having been a tourist in my own capital.

"Big Ben," I reply. "You know; the big clock that you hear on the BBC?"

"O.K. Big Ben, number one. Number two?"

I deliberate, "Umm…the Houses of Parliament—where the government is, next to Big Ben."

"OK. Number three?"

"What about Buckingham Palace?"

"*Bucking Beless*?" Omar looks confused.

"Yes, Buckingham Palace—where the Queen lives."

"*Aiwa. Bucking Beless*. Queen's Kingdom. O.K. Number one: Big Ben. Number two: House *Barliment*. Number three: *Bucking Beless*. Number four?"

"I think three is enough. *Talata kifaaya, mush kida*?"

I realize that his English is not as good as I had first thought, so I try to intersperse a little pidgin Arabic into our conversation as he continues to grill me about prices in England. He seems genuinely taken aback by my attempt to estimate the current cost of a rail ticket from London to Newcastle. Recovering from the shock, he asks:

"I will need to buy camera to make pictures of my visit. How much will it cost: two pounds, three pounds?"

I do not have the heart to disabuse him any further: "Maybe a little more."

Before the conversation dries up, and we both return to staring at the desert speeding by outside, Omar extends to me the usual vague but well-meant invitation:

"If you come to Marsa Matruh again you can ask for me. They all know me here; I am famous in this town. Ask for Doctor Omar. I can ask for you in London, yes? I can ask for Laurence? O.K.?"

"O.K., Doctor Omar."

We bypass the lackluster sprawl of Alexandria and take the desert road to Cairo—a dual carriageway with advertising billboards running alongside, which act like a sort of mercantile sand barrier. Sporadic building development shadows the highway, with numerous untidy, half-finished projects dotting the roadside. Angular heaps of cinder blocks pile up drifts of sand behind them. The steel worms of concrete support posts protrude from recently cemented roofs, an indication that another story may be added at a later date if funds permit. By any stretch of the imagination, it is not a pretty sight. I am starting to come to the realization that much of Egypt is comprised of scattered pockets of beauty connected by long corridors of unabashed hideousness.

Traffic police appear intermittently along the length of the road, standing around in groups, seriously underemployed— bored but not really wanting any more action either. We pass a group of them gathered together for a communal meal. The food is spread out on a large tin tray that has been placed on the trunk of a car, and they disdainfully ignore the constant stream of speeding traffic as they concentrate on their shared lunch of bread, *fuul* beans, and sliced tomatoes. Lunchtime must be a good time to commit a traffic offense around here.

Sooner than anticipated, and with little warning of its approach, we arrive in Giza at Cairo's outskirts. Here, I get my first view of the Pyramids. (I did not catch sight of them at all during my first brief visit to the capital.) The tombs disappear from view as we veer east towards the metropolis; then, five minutes later, they offer another teasing glimpse, this time towering hazily above Giza's commercial streets like the improbable mountains of a child's painting.

I get off the bus at Midan Tahrir (Tahrir Square) near the Egyptian Museum, where I am immediately misdirected by a succession of guides who would prefer to take me to a hotel of their own choosing rather than the one that I have selected. I shake them off easily enough but soon become lost among streets that should not even exist according to my tourist map. It probably serves me right for bucking tradition. Eventually, I am rescued by another solicitor who is good enough to take me where I want to go.

It is a good choice: the hotel is central, clean, and cheap, and for next to nothing I am given a large double room with polished wooden floorboards and a giant, rock-hard bed. The only problem is that every time I leave the antique lift on the fifth floor I become disoriented by the hotel's warren-like corridors, and it takes me a full five minutes to find my room. This would not be so bad if I were to do this unobserved, but every time I wander off in the wrong direction I am spotted by the night porter, who gently leads me to my room as if I were a country bumpkin unused to buildings higher than one story. Cairo has that effect on me—I really do feel like a provincial here.

I have just one night in Cairo before heading out to the desert once more, so I go upmarket and treat myself to dinner in a smart downtown restaurant that resembles a pasha's palace. The restaurant's ambience is nothing less than that of a lavishly-decorated Turkish harem: the lighting is refreshingly discrete for neon-crazed Cairo; there are low tables covered with enormous copper trays, and the room is divided by delicate *mashrabiyya* screens of intricately carved mahogany. The faux-oriental décor reminds me how Egyptians constantly seem to be reinventing themselves through romantically-skewed memories of their past. On the bus today, one of the videos played for our entertainment was a Hollywood version of the *Arabian Nights*, with Christopher Lee and Milo O'Shea decked up as sultans. I try to imagine the opposite scenario: native Egyptians playing English aristocrats (although perhaps Omar Sharif could pull it off).

The table across from me hosts a group of ten Japanese girls, coyly perched on low benches facing each other under the watchful eye of a bored-looking Egyptian minder. They have ordered the set meal, which is probably just as well given the difficulties of communication between them and their Egyptian chaperone. The Japanese girls giggle with embarrassment, while their host waves his hands around a lot and gestures in a protective, avuncular manner.

"What you like to eat, ladies?"

"Oh! Don't mind; something typical, but no more falafel."

The minder smiles understandingly, fully aware that the Japanese palate differs greatly from the simple bread and mashed bean tastes of his own country. Nevertheless, he feels obliged to defend his national cuisine:

"What? You don't like falafel? It is delicious."

The spokesperson for the Japanese, not wishing to offend, coos gently: "Yes, delicious, but already had for lunch...and breakfast…and yesterday, falafel, too. Too much falafel!"

I savor the serenity of the restaurant's slightly bogus oriental atmosphere and enjoy a slow, well-cooked meal of grilled pigeon and *baba ghanoush*. The bill is four times what I would normally pay, which seems reasonable enough.

Back at the hotel, exhausted, I fall asleep almost immediately on the huge, hard bed. Already, I am missing the quiet of the desert, but this is just a brief interlude and, it has to be said, I am quite enjoying Cairo's metropolitan clamor. I enjoy contrasts like this. I must be a man of extremes.

*Laurence Mitchell is a British travel writer and photographer with a preference for destinations that are firmly off the beaten track. He is the author of two guidebooks to Serbia (*Serbia: the Bradt Travel Guide *and* Belgrade: the Bradt City Guide*) and his story "The Road to Urfa" was included in* Travelers' Tales Turkey.

JASON WARD

✳ ✳ ✳

The Neon Night of the Emirates

A British expat in Dubai takes a nocturnal dip into a simmering fondue of exoticism, exploitation, and the Eagles.

FROM BENEATH THE IMPASSIVE GLARE OF FIVE-STAR HOTELS and shopping malls, we clambered onto the bare wooden deck of a dilapidated taxi-boat crowded with exhausted migrant laborers. As the small ferry chugged across the black steaming creek, the workers stared impassively and the hyper-real skyline of Bur Dubai opened up behind us; post-modern windowed obelisks and illuminated mosques shimmered through a putrid cloud of diesel. On the other side of the creek was the old Spice Souk, a typical Middle Eastern street market bathed in neon and towel-dried in saffron. We dodged past endless stores and street traders hawking powders, perfumes, trinkets, fabrics, carpets, and toy camels that sing the call to prayer with red flashing eyes aglow. Then we reached another futuristic hotel, just like the ones we'd left behind on the other side of the river.

In the hotel was a Mexican restaurant that cooked up half-decent enchiladas served by Indians, with musical accompaniment provided by a nasal English DJ who appeared to have escaped from a Yorkshire mining town in the 1980s—and hadn't bought any new music since. A couple of margaritas later, I wandered over to the bathroom and was shocked to find myself greeted and ushered into the men's room by a four-foot-high, overfriendly Indian man in a tight white suit. He gleefully guided me towards the urinal but I quickly darted into a cubical and bolted the door. When finished, I looked under the door to confirm my anxious suspicion. Undeterred, he lurked on the other side of the cubical door patiently awaiting my return. I opened the door quickly and gave him my sternest eyebrow, but he continued to beam broadly and was now gesturing grandly towards the sink where I was heading. He lunged forward to turn on the taps and, as I washed my hands, activated the soap dispenser on my behalf, passed me a paper towel when I'd begun to rinse off, and swiftly whisked its soggy remnants from my hands as I turned my head to look for the trash. When he shuffled backwards and started bowing, I made a sharp exit.

As I wandered back to my table, I pondered why anyone would actually like to have a strange, servile man following them around in a toilet. As a post-colonial Brit, I'm like many others from predominantly self-service cultures who are discomforted by having people running around doing mundane stuff for them. However, this is quite the norm in the Emirates, so I'm making a concerted effort to adjust. To this end, since I moved here from Turkey four years ago, I have never even filled my own car with petrol. As soon as I pull into a gas station, an attendant takes care of everything while simultaneously swabbing all of the windows. Washing the whole car is an even more slothful experience. I sit in an air-conditioned room reading glossy magazines about Dubai's latest record-breaking skyscraper, shopping mall, ski slope, or man-made island while dozens of workers from the subcontinent swarm all over the car in a frenzy of foam, polish, vacuum hose, and matching jumpsuits. During a busy spell at the gas station, I once made the fatal faux pas of trying to pump my own gas. Unfortunately, by the time I had managed to locate where to put the petrol in my car, I was almost wrestled to the ground by a smiling, nodding pump attendant. I have faced similar challenges trying to pack groceries in supermarkets, push buttons in elevators, or pour water in restaurants. My idleness is now so chronic that I'm starting to appreciate the necessity of a little guy in a white suit to attend to one's toileting.

The UAE is a place where every extravagant whim is catered for. Despite summer temperatures reaching 122 degrees Fahrenheit and chronic water shortages, everywhere fecund flower beds and lavish lawns are attached to elaborate sprinkler systems tended by armies of shamefully poorly paid immigrant laborers toiling around the clock. According to the U.S. State Department, 93 percent of the country's total workforce is foreign and only 15 to 20 percent of the population is actually from the Emirates. This is probably why, in most of the major cities, the global language of English is more commonly used than Arabic.

Tourism cashes in on Dubai's global culture in numerous ways, most notably during Dubai's month-long shopping festival, which features the gigantic "Global Village" on the outskirts of the city. This oversized county fair boasts a giant fun festival set amidst dozens of stands and sideshows elaborately constructed to represent the UAE's most prominent populations and their most notable landmarks. Several new mega-malls in Dubai have also been developed along similar themes. However, one of the best ways to truly appreciate the post-modern global mishmash of life in the Emirates and its frequent contradictions is to head beyond the malls and out into the night.

Anticipating roads that haven't been completed yet, we four-wheeled across the desert between traffic-clogged mega-highways and construction sites to make our own shortcut to the first call of the evening: an Irish pub. Due to the alcohol licensing laws in most Emirates, booze is only served at hotels or private clubs. Our selected watering hole consisted of old-world-style Irish storefronts stuck to the side of a huge tennis arena. Surprisingly, this Emerald Isle theme park is one of the more authentic and comely drinking holes in Dubai. It has a huge and popular beer garden and serves up a pint of draft Guinness comparable to any in colder climes. The resident guitar strummer, who seemed to have been plucked fresh from the streets of Dublin, played note-perfect acoustic renditions of Coldplay and Radiohead as we indulged in fish and chips served up by an Australian waiter and washed down with hand-pulled pints of the finest British ale.

Next we headed to a hotel bar with cheaper beer where a Filipino band fronted by a cannonball-breasted Russian woman modestly dressed in a bikini top and spray-on skirt took to the stage. Eyebrows were raised further when we noticed that every woman in the place seemed to share a similar wardrobe, but had a mobile phone instead of a microphone and the roving eyes and over-familiar questioning smile of a professional. Those interested in Dubai's less exclusive nightlife will soon notice that despite the country's conservative moral agenda and strict censorship laws, prostitution is huge here. Some of the more notorious bars are so packed with sex workers that it is impossible for men not accompanied by women to grab a quick beer without getting propositioned!

Our next stop turned out to be one such place. This club in an infamous hotel had a loud Filipino band, but no one appeared to be paying much attention. Many clubs in the Emirates have Filipino bands and although many of the bands deserve much better, some are destined to provide little more than background muzak for brothels. Although many of the

Filipino bands I've seen in Dubai know how to put on a storming show, most play the same clichéd repertoire of classic rock covers. An expat American friend, a veteran of Dubai's seedy nightlife, sagely revealed that a good way to keep a pub-crawl mobile is to stay in a bar until the band plays "Hotel California" and then to repeat the routine in a different bar with a different Filipino band.

In this particular hotel club, the clientele were checking out all the time. Most notably lobster-faced, beer-bellied expats on package holidays and shaved-headed GIs on shore leave were coming and going with young ladies decked like rock stars' girlfriends—often without even stopping to buy a drink. In a bizarre reversal of pub life from my own culture, seductively dressed groups of single women were leering at every passing male. It was like a teenage boy's dream come true; a veritable chocolate box of exotically beautiful ladies from all over the world seeking sex *sans* commitment.

As soon as we walked in the door a group of about five heavily made-up and tattooed Chinese girls tottered over to our quartet and started to shout questions above the din: "Where you from?" "What your name?" "What he name?" We attempted to deflect questions and made polite conversation while ordering drinks from a weary-looking Indian waitress who drifted in and out of the huddles of girls that filled the club. Our drinks arrived and as we made to move around the room, the girls became more insistent and the conversion shifted abruptly from inanity to intimacy. "You not like me?" "I give good sex." "You like my friend?" "You wan two for one?" "You like sucky suck?" As we moved around the room, we heard much of the same banter from other non-native speakers hailing from Thailand, Tanzania, and Russia. As a language teacher, it reminded me of the importance of using stimulating content to quickly acquire a foreign language.

Those in the club who had not yet mastered the basics of *English for Sexual Commerce 101* were employing body language to dramatic effect. The room was an almost comical eye-averting chatter of smouldering stares, seductive pouts, over-familiar winks, and wet red pearly smiles. The joke soon wore thin. As we moved through the crowd, we were stroked, patted, tugged, tapped, and squeezed. Rapidly, what had started out as a deludingly flattering ego-massage began to feel like the slow-motion, claustrophobic panic of a zombie film. Everything was wrong. Why were we here? The band seemed to get much louder and shriller. As we recognized the liberating notes of "Hotel California" through the distortion, we were already halfway out of the door.

In need of a change of tune, we decided to check out what my expat veteran friend described as a "sporadic dancing bar." These Indian clubs are famed for their bizarre stage show of intermittent Indian dancers draped in Hawaiian-style wreaths (leis). We found a club in the neighboring Emirate of Ajman that confirmed he was true to his word. Inside a garishly decorated hall blasting out distorted Bollywood tunes, dark-skinned bachelors, most with well-oiled hair and bushy moustaches, stared intently at the stage and nursed expensive drinks. On stage, a row of ten shockingly pretty, dangerously young Indian girls in beautiful saris faced the audience. They all had chairs from which one or two would occasionally arise at random intervals to dance half-heartedly, swinging arms back and forth as they looked at the far wall in abject boredom. The other young ladies sat staring into space, and a couple were reading what appeared to be schoolbooks. As the girls danced, a painfully smiling older lady meandered around the tables with a stack of Hawaiian leis. Occasionally she would be flagged by a patron who would hand over a wad of notes and point to the sporadic dancer that he wanted to receive the lavish paper neck adornment. He would be repaid by the occasional cheeky smile or meaningful stare from his chosen beflowered beauty, as she swayed distractedly or glanced up from her algebra into the smoky darkness fingering the paper petals on her bosom.

Our ears were ringing and we soon discovered that there would be no reprieve from the Eagles here, so we paid a small fortune for our Sprites and left. Next, we wandered into a dingy bar connected to what appeared to be a long-gone beach club and discovered it contained several groups of local middle-aged Arabs adorned in national dress (the white *dishdasha* robe and *gutra* headdress). Many were red-eyed from cigar smoke and whiskey. This was doubly surprising because not only do locals not usually mix with foreigners, but they are not often seen drinking in public given that the consumption of alcohol is generally considered a sin. In fact it is illegal for a foreigner to buy alcohol for an Arab and clubs in Dubai enforce a strict no *dishdasha* policy, which is a shame. The white robes look spectacular under UV light.

Parallel to our table, a group of heavily-bearded older gentlemen in *dishdashas* reclined on split and peeling leather sofas in an expensive smelling fug of blue smoke—accompanied by what appeared to be half a dozen blonde prostitutes. On a low stage, a tired-looking Filipino band was working through a dirge of standard lounge tunes. After a turgid rendition of a Dusty Springfield classic, the mini-skirted singer was pulled aside by one of the bearded Arab gents for a shady-looking *tête-à-tête*.

The next song was "My Way" and the same old local was now up on the stage, lazily prowling the footlights in a luminous *dishdasha* with a glass of Jack Daniels in one hand and the microphone in the other. He cruised up and down the front row milking the anticipatory applause and closed in on our table of conspicuously white faces and nervous laughter. Then, with a heavy stare and heavier accent, he slurred the opening words: "And-a nowa de end is neeeear…" It really felt like it was, so we applauded with great gusto until he turned away. Then I attempted to get the waiter to bring the check with equal enthusiasm. At the end of the song, instead of the check, unordered glasses of whiskey appeared at our table, and we scanned the bar to find our scary hairy crooner and his party saluting us with cheeky toothless grins and glasses raised aloft a sea of *gutras* and bleached frizz.

Originally from the grim north of England, Jason Ward has lived and worked in universities in the sunny Middle East for the past eight years. His hobbies include travel, music, film, and literature. He is happily married and one day hopes to gain a Ph.D. in Film and Literature and to pump his own gas.

A M A N D A   C O F F I N

✦ ✦ ✦

Repatriation and Regret

*A hotel manager leaves the land of opportunity
and laments the permanence of his choice.*

IF YOU CHECK INTO A CERTAIN SMALL HOTEL IN DOWNTOWN
Amman, Jordan, between 5 A.M. and 5 P.M., on any day of the
week, you will meet Nabil, the general manager. The day I
arrived, he strode out from behind the reception desk, looking
crisp in shirt and tie, well-pressed trousers, and black Oxfords.
I asked if he might have a single room available. "For how
many nights?" he asked.

"A month," I replied.

"Please," he said. "I invite you to sit and drink some tea with
mint." He brought me the tea and promptly disappeared. I
wandered around the lobby, responding as requested to the
signs in both English and Arabic, "Please Smile!" Does he have
an available room, I wondered, or not? He hadn't said. And
where is he? Many minutes later, Nabil hustled back into the
lobby and handed me the key to Room 601. I believe he had
been upstairs cleaning it.

He looked twice at my address and passport information
in the registration ledger. "You live in Turkey, but you are

American?" I was sorry indeed about the latter, especially in light of the recent Iraq fiasco. I rather wished for a passport from Liechtenstein, or any other neutral and unpronounceable country. Nabil was quick to assert that Americans were most welcome.

"What brings you here?" he asked me.

"Turkish Airlines frequent flyer miles," I replied. I didn't see any point in dissembling. It was use them or lose them, and there were only enough of them to take me from Istanbul to Amman. I was unequipped to profess a long-held fascination with Jordan, a country about which I knew embarrassingly little. It's wedged between Israel to the west, Syria to the north, Iraq to the east, and Saudi Arabia to the south. I'd assumed that Jordan, like its Arab neighbors, has petroleum resources. It hasn't: potash and phosphates are the big things. (Ever heard of a potash magnate, or a phosphate sheik? Right.) Jordan is poor, and it is small. The total population is about 6 million; 70 percent are Palestinian. This area's tumultuous history could easily justify hatefulness toward Westerners, but as in Turkey, I couldn't walk down a Jordanian street without being peppered with smiles and greetings. "Hello! Welcome! Where are you from? How are you? Ah, I have relatives in America..." My real connection to Jordan, however, was to come through my conversations with Nabil.

Nabil and Mahmoud, a young Egyptian, do whatever needs to be done in the hotel during the daytime hours. Hanni is the night manager; he and Ashraf cover the evening shifts. These four men are the entire staff of this twenty-four-room hotel, working twelve-hour days, seven days a week. Nabil goes home every night to his rented apartment; he cooks dinner, watches some television, sleeps, and repeats it all the next day.

He lived in the United States for seventeen years. His American ex-wife and teenaged son still live there. He managed a 7-Eleven in Chicago for some time, then opened his own shop. One day he and I sat in the lobby with a Jordanian couple who also spoke English. Nabil recalled the ethnic slurs he'd run across while living in America. "They call us camel jockeys over there," he said. "They call Mexicans wetbacks. They call black people niggers. They have names for everybody."

The woman was shocked. "Is this true?" she asked me. I admitted that some people do use these terms and asked if it wasn't the same in Jordan. For example, do Jordanians have derisive names for the Palestinian and Iraqi refugees who have flooded the country? The woman and her husband shook their heads resolutely.

"Our culture forbids this," said Nabil. "If you see an ugly person in the street, you cannot even comment upon his ugliness. It is a sin."

Nabil was born in Nablus, in Palestine. He wanted to return to his family's home in the West Bank when his mother was dying last year, but the Israelis wouldn't permit it. He also wants to return to the U.S. to visit his son, but the Americans won't permit that. I asked him why he'd left the U.S. five years ago. "Because I was stupid," he said. "I missed the culture here." The cost of applying for a U.S. visa is $100, a considerable sum in Jordan. The consulate pockets the money whether it grants the visa or not, and the officials aren't obliged to explain why they reject an application. Nabil has applied and been rejected three times now.

"I have thought about trying to go to Mexico and then sneaking across the border," he told me, "but if they catch me they will say I am Osama bin Laden's cousin and throw me into the prison at Guantanamo Bay. They won't say I'm a hotel manager trying to see his son." I went to the web site of the U.S. consulate in Amman. It was an educational but very discouraging venture. I knew that immigration was a pipe dream, but Nabil wanted only a tourist visa. The Department of State, however, views all foreigners traveling to the U.S. as potential immigrants; it's easier to keep them out than to track them down should they overstay their visas. To obtain even a tourist visa, Nabil must present some undefined but compelling documentation to convince the consular officials that he'll return to Jordan. Examples are lucrative employment, extended family, or an owned home or business. Nabil has none of these. He would be hard-pressed to convince anyone that he has reason to come back, having gotten to America again. Having a family member in America is no advantage, either. In that case, the consulate asks, how often has the family member come home to Jordan to visit, "as is normal?" Nabil's son has never been to Jordan, and his mother is afraid to send him. I didn't even bother to visit the consulate's immigration section. I see Nabil as an industrious, entrepreneurial, well-spoken gentleman who thrived in America once, and who could do the same again. I, however, don't work for the State Department.

"We cannot get ahead here," Nabil says. "There is no hope." The economic conditions in Jordan allow the average citizen to survive, but not to save, or prosper. The CIA World Fact Book reports that the average per capita income is $4,500 per year. Unemployment is at 30 percent, but Nabil believes that figure to be low. Less than 3 percent of Jordan's land is arable. America is an arena for innovation, hard work, and creativity. Nabil knows from his own experience that he can work very hard there, scrimp on his expenses, and put away enough money to grow his business. In Jordan, he can merely keep his head above water. "The Land of Opportunity" is a jaded phrase for most Americans, but not so for him.

I mentioned to Nabil one day that I was going to walk a half hour to a café in the more modern part of Amman, where I'd read that women can smoke a *nargileh*, or Turkish water pipe, in peace. The cafés in the old city are definitely the province of men. "What? You want to smoke a *nargileh*?" he asked me. "We have one right here in the hotel. Mahmoud!" In a few minutes, Mahmoud set the *nargileh* behind the reception desk, its coals glowing. The three of us pulled chairs around it and enjoyed a leisurely smoke, the gentle bubbling sound lulling us. Arabic music videos played on a TV in the lobby's corner. "You see what they do?" Nabil asked, pointing to a siren in a slinky red gown on the screen. "They just want us to think about sex—not about politics, not about economics, not about war or peace, only about sex."

Nabil is not a prude, nor is he a misogynist. "The woman is the boss here," he says. "She runs the family, but she does not humiliate her husband in front of the children." Some Jordanian women cover their heads in public; others don't. I joined them in covering my arms and legs; loose cotton clothing is excellent protection from the sun. Women in Jordan vote, drive, and enjoy a 90 percent literacy rate. "In America, women want to be just like men," laments Nabil. "They work on construction sites, they drive trucks. They are not like women anymore." This doesn't strike me as a plea to keep women in the kitchen where they belong, but rather an Arab version of *vive la différence*.

A young woman came into the hotel one afternoon, veiled in black and accompanied by a rotund young man. I watched as they sat in the lobby, a coffee table between their seats and the chair Nabil occupied. I wrongly assumed they were his acquaintances because the woman, during their twenty-minute stay, chain-smoked five of Nabil's cigarettes, and at one point pulled up her sleeves to reveal scars, possibly burn scars, on her elbows. Nabil later told me what had transpired between them. The woman was looking for a job in the hotel; the man was her cousin. "I am not a nice guy, I told her!" Nabil said later. "I tell her, you work in this hotel, there's no foolishness. No visitors here! One visitor comes to see you at my hotel, and you are out the door. If you work here, you show up at 8:00. Don't bother coming at 8:05. And all that black veil and so on, that comes off. You want to put it back on when you go home, fine. But you don't wear that foolishness in the hotel." Nabil must have seen my eyebrows heading for the stratosphere, because he put his hand on my arm and said, "If that woman was religious, fine, she can wear whatever, but she is not religious. It's bullshit with her. I don't want her in my hotel like that. It makes people uncomfortable."

"So will she be working here?" I asked.

"We'll see if she shows up at 8:00 tomorrow morning," he shrugged. "Her cousin will explain the situation to her father. If her father allows her to come, then maybe…her father does not treat her well," Nabil added, pointing to his own elbows. Suddenly I saw the situation very differently. A devout Muslim woman would have neither smoked Nabil's cigarettes nor showed him her bare arms. Nabil no doubt worried that this girl would get out from under her heavy-handed father's control and start to sow her wild oats, thus his warnings about receiving visitors while she's working. He's a perceptive man. Nabil manages this budget hotel as if he were running the Hilton. (Either the woman changed her mind, or her father nixed the idea; she never returned.)

I told Nabil about an inadvertent detour I took one Sunday morning in Amman. I'd been walking to a café-bookstore when I stopped to ask for directions. Downtown Amman, the old city, is in a rift valley, surrounded by hills which are prone to dropping off into sheer cliffs. Consequently, only crows can travel as the crow flies; the rest of us must navigate serpentine streets and hunt for unmarked staircases. A middle-aged man at an intersection pointed the way, and I walked on. A few minutes later, the same man pulled alongside me in a large BMW. He told me he was going toward the café and gestured to me to get into the car. I would never have done so in America or Europe, but in Turkey or Jordan, it's a different story. I got into the sedan and we sped off. The driver introduced himself as Jamil; he pointed at the café as we zoomed by it. But, but...I looked questioningly at this balding, grey-haired, well-dressed man with a scar extending from the corner of his mouth to his right ear. He merely smiled and asked me why I was going to the café. "For coffee," I told him. He swerved sharply to the opposite side of the street and slammed on the brakes. An old man had a booth there with a samovar on a bench in front. Jamil returned to the car with a plastic cup of sweet, dark, cardamom-flavored coffee, and off we went again. Terrific, I thought, it could be that a Jordanian gangster has abducted me, but damn! This is good coffee.

Jamil spoke very little English, and I little Arabic, so it was a quiet drive. We roared around Amman for an hour in his shiny silver car. This is the hospital, this is Abdoun, (a district where the few rich Ammanis are building their ostentatious homes and drinking coffee at Starbucks), this is the courthouse, and here is a nice park.... I enjoyed this impromptu tour, but I was never without a twinge of fear. If this was, in fact, simply a random act of kindness, I'd feel guilty for having been suspicious. On the other hand, if I came to harm, how stupid I'd feel for having been so trusting! It's the traveler's constant balancing act. As we neared the café again, Jamil pulled up to a shop. He returned in a few seconds with his friend, Adnan, who spoke English. "Jamil just wanted to show you the city," Adnan told me. "He hopes you weren't worried. He's a good guy. He will give you his number, and he wants you to call him at any time—night or day—if you need anything. If you need a ride to the airport, to Petra, any help at all." I took Jamil's card, thanked both men, and walked to the café. The next day, I shared this story with Nabil, who nodded, nonplussed. "It is like this here," he said. "In Chicago I had to carry a gun to protect myself. You have to be so careful in America. Really, I feel so sorry for Americans sometimes."

I had just finished breakfast one day when Nabil, who had been watching TV news, went on a pro-Saddam tear. "He was good to his own people!" he bellowed. "Everything was free: hospitals, university, electricity—even telephones were free!" (I guess the Kurds and Shiites Saddam murdered didn't count as "his own people.") Nabil's voice is hoarse from his three-pack-a-day smoking habit and tirades like this one.

I strenuously opposed the invasion of Iraq, but I don't think Saddam was on the short-list for canonization, either.

"I would support Hitler if he took such good care of his own people!" he railed.

This was a monologue, with no room for reply (assuming I had one), so I just walked back upstairs when Nabil answered the phone. Does he really mean what he says? Partly, I suppose. The cost of living is prohibitive in Jordan—any government that provides free services to its people gets a lot of leeway. And like so many of us, Nabil feels raw and helpless watching the daily Iraqi fatality reports and news of the civil mayhem that's tearing the country apart; the images are inescapable in Jordan. I'd be astonished if anyone living here didn't occasionally say, "And this is supposed to be an improvement?"

As my time in Jordan grew shorter, so did Nabil's temper, and he often took it out on poor Mahmoud. "They don't *think*, the Egyptians! I must always tell him what to do, or he does nothing. An Egyptian has enough money in his pocket to buy a glass of tea, and he's happy with that. They're not like us Palestinians. We're always thinking of how it could be better." I wasn't sure it was such a gift, this propensity to "think," especially for this Palestinian whose options appeared very limited.

"I'll die here in this hotel," he groused. "Dig a grave for me out in the garden, because I'm going to die here." He laughed as he said this, but it was a bitter laugh—I almost looked around to see if Mahmoud might be trudging out with a shovel.

Nabil's desire to return to the United States seemed to grow more frantic as he beheld an American citizen just as determined to avoid it. In a wistful moment, he told me his daydream of retiring to a small farm in the southeastern States, complete with an orchard and a few cows. In a heartbeat, he turned and snapped, "Why don't you go back there? You're being an idiot!" I reminded him of the reasons he'd returned to Jordan—because he missed the culture. Had he forgotten that? I didn't want to end my time in Amman wrangling over the pros and cons of living in America or in Jordan. At the heart of it, I finally realized, was the ineluctable fact that one of us has choices, and the other hasn't. Nabil eventually tumbled down to the same bottom line, and we spent a couple of days with more coffee, less controversy.

We parted ways in the garden. "It's not a bad place to be buried," I said, and we laughed. But I was wrong. In the garden, Nabil would spend eternity just as he spends every day right now: watching hotel guests coming and going, heedlessly presenting their passports, taking for granted their luxurious freedom of movement.

Amanda Coffin is a writer, reader, Braille transcriber, and whatnot. She has reduced her life to what is highly portable and lives a completely nomadic existence, moving along when visas expire or restlessness sets in. At the moment, she is quite fond of Kuala Lumpur.

PAT WALKER

✦ ✦ ✦

Oh, Little Town of Bethlehem

*A biblical site's mystique dissipates in
the haze of war and commerce.*

*Oh little town of Bethlehem,
How still we see thee lie!
Above thy deep and dreamless sleep
the silent stars go by.*

UGLY CHUNKS OF CONCRETE AND DUST-COVERED ARMY TRUCKS
block the road into Bethlehem. At the main checkpoint, two
young soldiers wearing silver sunglasses and machine guns pore
over passports and papers. Snapping in the October breeze is a
blue and white Israeli flag. Off to the left I see a new Israeli settlement—a treeless jumble of block-like apartments and condos.

This is Bethlehem?

The Bethlehem of my youth, the little town I sang about at
Christmastime, was a place of safety and promise: a child set
lovingly in a manger, a mysterious star, wise men with exotic
gifts. This Bethlehem is a war zone.

I am here on impulse. After wrapping up a business trip in
Jordan I decided, against the advice of my Jordanian hosts, to

cross the formidable and unwelcoming border into Israel. Bethlehem is only an hour and a half by car from Amman, and sweet childhood memories of religious lore tempted me to make the trip.

In Jerusalem I had hired a driver, a talkative Christian Palestinian named Nackle.

"You are either brave or crazy," he says when picking me up at the Christmas Hotel. When the soldiers finally give us the O.K. to enter Bethlehem in the white Mercedes taxi, I am shocked by how quiet the town is. The crooked streets are empty. Stores are shuttered. The few locals who are sitting on steps or standing in doorways stare as we drive by. "They used to get at least 9,000 visitors a day," Nackle says. "Tourists are too afraid to come here now. It's very bad."

The famous Manger Square is also empty, except for three Palestinian security guards with guns, two pesky guys hocking cheap jewelry, and a couple of church guides hoping to give me a tour. The fortress-like Church of the Nativity, built over the birthplace of Jesus, is much smaller than I had imagined and sits directly across the square from a glittering mosque.

Originally designed to keep marauding horsemen out, the entrance to the church is aptly named the Door of Humility. As I duck through the sunken entrance, I reach up and stick my fingers into several rough, round holes. "Bullet holes," a guide with brown curly hair says to me. "Do you want to see where King Herod killed the children? There are bones there." I wonder what he takes me for.

Even though bright sunlight streams in from high, arched windows, it feels cold and damp inside the old church. I notice a few torn up floorboards. "During the hostage crisis there were about two hundred and forty people here in the church," the guide says while trailing me. "They were here for thirty-nine days. Eight people were killed." I walk away.

I confess my interest in Bethlehem is more historical than spiritual. After all, this is where it all started: the birthplace of one man who would have a profound influence on the world. I want to be left alone to absorb the essence of this powerful spot. I want to think about then.

I don't want to think about last April when Israeli soldiers stormed into the town searching for relatives of a suicide bomber. Several armed Palestinians, including some local policemen and the governor of Bethlehem, fearfully took refuge inside the church, creating a made-for-TV international incident.

While I feel sorry for the Palestinians who depend on tourism for their livelihood, I am secretly thrilled to have the church mostly to myself. Descending the narrow stone steps to the Grotto of the Nativity, I share the small white-marbled room with one other American tourist—a nice-looking guy from Nebraska named Dean, who has been traveling for several months. The cave, where it is said Mary gave birth to the baby Jesus, is softly lit by flickering candles and fifteen silver lamps. The walls are draped with shimmering tapestries. The curly-haired guide approaches: "People think Jesus was born in a stable, but it was actually in this cave." I struggle to feel something meaningful, have an epiphany perhaps, but all I feel is irritation. As I start back up the steps, he calls: "Do you want to see the bullet holes in the courtyard?"

Maybe some things never change: this is a church with a turbulent history. It has been one of the most fought over of holy places. The original structure was completely destroyed in the early sixth century. It has been seized and defended by a succession of armies, including Muslim and Crusader forces. Now it is run by three Christian denominations—Armenian, Roman Catholic, and Greek Orthodox—each with their own convent. To add to the confusion, the Palestinian Authority was given control of Bethlehem in 1995, and now a large color photo of Arafat hangs inside an office just off the main entrance.

I find myself standing in the hot afternoon sun, staring up at high terra-cotta colored walls pockmarked with white bullet holes. "They put a sniper crane in the square," the guide explains. "They could fire into the courtyards better that way. The Israelis claimed the Palestinians were holding the priests and monks hostage. But the church leaders just wanted to protect the church and help the wounded. They did not consider themselves hostages. You know, the Church of the Nativity is a place of refuge for everyone — that includes Palestinians and Israelis." He smiles at me proudly. His smile tugs at my heart.

A soft murmur fills the church. Several Armenian priests in long, black, hooded robes are conducting a prayer service. "Just give me some time alone, fifteen minutes," I beg the guide, feeling guilty for not wanting him around. Sitting alone on a step, I close my eyes, listen to the rhythmic chants, and imagine the ghost-voices of all those who ever uttered prayers in this ancient place. But the moment is shattered by two French tourists chatting loudly to each other while clicking at the priests with a fancy Nikon.

"Would you like to see where King Herod killed the children now?"

The guide has found me. I trail him down steep stone stairs. In another cave-like area, several small bones are displayed behind thick, yellowed glass. King Herod, the half-Jewish King of the Jews at the time Jesus was born, was never part of my family's Christmas program. Crazed with fear the newborn child would steal his kingdom, Herod ordered all male children under the age of two to be killed. If these 2,000-year-old baby bones are authentic, to me they represent the beginning of Bethlehem's disturbing history.

Needing some fresh air, I walk out into another courtyard and come across the small, unimpressive bell tower of the church. "The bell ringer was killed in the stand-off in April," the guide says. "The janitor was also killed," he says. I stare at him, expecting to hear more of the story, but he says instead: "Would you like to do some shopping after your visit? We have some very nice things in our gift store."

Suddenly I want out of this church, out of Bethlehem. I don't want the rest of the tour. I don't want to see any more or hear any more. I feel like I am digging for something I can't find. I keep trying to connect with my comforting illusion of the past only to be confronted with the violent, chaotic, and bloody present. It is then I realize the magical Christmas-card Bethlehem existed for only a brief shining moment, perhaps only as long as it took for the star to fade.

As I step out into the bright sunlight of Manger Square, I imagine Israeli tanks clattering across these worn cobblestones while an F-16 screams overhead. I imagine the sniper crane slowly turning in the very spot where I am standing. A man in a plaid shirt approaches me with a handful of beaded necklaces. "I have some very nice necklaces," he says. "Would you like to see them?" Hot and irritated, I wave him away, but will later wish I had bought all of his necklaces. He probably has a family to feed and there are no other tourists in sight.

Nackle is standing beside the Mercedes, waiting for me. "Let's go back to Jerusalem," I say. "I've seen enough." Air conditioning blasting, we snake back through the narrow streets and I reassure myself that I will go back to Bethlehem someday and finish the tour. I'll even get to Rachel's tomb. Only next time I will know what to expect. As we pull into the long line of cars and trucks waiting to get through the checkpoint, I can't seem to shake the haunting little melody I hear in my head.

Yet in the dark street shineth
the everlasting Light;
The hopes and fears of all the years
are met in thee tonight.

Pat Walker's businesses have taken her all over the world, and she has ended up in some strange, unruly places. Bethlehem, however, was by far the saddest trip she has ever taken. She is the founder of The Cultural Explorer, a cultural and philanthropic travel company featuring excursions into Southern Africa. She lives in San Francisco.

⋆ ⋆ ⋆

Without Cover

*Returning to war-ravaged Baghdad after two decades
of exile, this native finds dignity amidst adversity.*

"IF I HAD KNOWN YOU WERE UNVEILED, I WOULD HAVE
brought you a scarf to cover your head with," Abu Amin told
me as he got into the car that was to take us to Baghdad. Those
were his first words to me. It was 2 A.M. in Amman, Jordan.
Four of us were setting out for Iraq, and we faced a twelve-
hour ride east through the desert. We were all nervous.

I'd arrived in Amman a few hours earlier that day in May,
en route to see my native Baghdad for the first time in about
twenty years. An uncle long exiled in Jordan said he didn't
want me to travel alone—there were too many stories about
desert bandits and other dangers—so he arranged for me to
make the trip with a young driver and two older men. His wife
advised me that the older men were religious. She had prepared me to speak with them in a particular way, one virtually
required by the culture. The first of the men, Abu Haider, was
sweet. He asked me where I wished to sit. If I'd sat next to
either of the men, I might have accidentally brushed against
one of them during the long trip, ruining his ablutions and

making him impure, because I'm a woman. I didn't really want to ride in the front seat, but I did. As we were about to pick up the second man, the driver worried if he'd be bringing much luggage.

"No," Abu Haider said. "The man has a wife in Baghdad and one in Amman, so he doesn't need a suitcase."

That was my introduction to Abu Amin, who had started lecturing me even before he was in the car. My family, he said, "is a good family; they don't deserve a girl who is unveiled. God willing, you will veil. I should have brought a scarf for you."

"I have a scarf here, see?" I pointed to one around my neck that I'd brought along in case I needed to cover my head.

"The *hijab* represents…" I didn't hear the rest of what he said. I had heard such lectures from Muslim men before. I gave him my canned response. "Yes," I said, "it is beautiful when a woman becomes convinced that it is the right time for her to be veiled." I'm no wimp, but in my culture, it would show disrespect to my own family were I to reply harshly to an older man like Abu Amin. I remained polite.

"My daughter began veiling at fourteen," Abu Amin said. "She is a good girl. Not like so many women these days, disgracing the names of good families by going around uncovered."

"That's nice," I answered. "I hope she remains covered."

He looked surprised, so I told him of a family I know in the States that had forced their daughters to veil, only to find them with purple hair, tattoos, and body piercings as soon as they went off to college.

The wiry driver, Ali, averaged 85 mph, while keeping an eye out for cars coming toward us—in our lane—at the same speed. To keep himself alert, Ali picked a radio station that played Arabic pop songs. Abu Amin immediately ordered him to "put on the Koran." Ali said he had no Koran tapes, so Abu Amin told him which station plays Koran recitations around the clock. Ali found the station.

Koran recitation is beautiful and rhythmic, but hearing it while speeding through the desert night can be rather lulling. Abu Haider was the first to begin dozing, and I felt my own eyes closing as well. Ali started lighting one cigarette after the other just to stay awake. Nobody could say anything about the recitation because that would appear disrespectful to the religion. None of us could say "change the channel" without sounding like we didn't want to hear the word of God.

Rousing himself, Abu Haider asked me politely what I thought would happen next in Iraq. I said I thought it had to go well, because the Americans could not allow the situation to slip through their fingers. Democracy was not far away.

"May God not grant the Americans success!" declared Abu Amin. "A thousand curses on the Americans and their lackeys!"

"Do you think Saddam might return?" Abu Haider asked.

"By God," announced Abu Amin, "Saddam is a million times better than the Americans!"

I laughed. "Of course! Killing, imprisoning, and torture is good for Iraq!"

Dawn approached, and Abu Amin announced he had to pray. Ali asked him to wait until we got to the Jordan-Iraq border, where, for safety reasons, we would form a convoy with other cars, but Abu Amin said that would be too late because he would miss the exact time, sunrise, when he was supposed to pray. Islam permits travelers to delay prayer to help them reach their destinations promptly. Most travelers combine the five prayer times just before bed. But Abu Amin insisted we stop at a restaurant that had a room outfitted with prayer mats on the floor. As he stepped out of the car, he asked whether any of us wanted to join him. All three of us said no.

Back on the road, we were suddenly engulfed by a sand-storm. We could see almost nothing. Ali began driving very, very slowly, as did the other cars in the convoy we had joined at the border. The roads were narrow, most other cars were going fast, and we were all thinking of the bandits known to target nice cars like ours. Though it was daylight, it was as if we were driving through thick fog. Ali suddenly swerved because a small black car was stopped horizontally across the highway. It obviously had been hit by another car.

The convoy pulled over. Other drivers emerged, some wearing goggles, others with cloth tied over their faces. They were trying to determine if there were injured passengers in the car, but they were afraid to walk across the road. If a car was coming, you wouldn't see it in time. Had anyone seen any passengers in that car? No. We stood, a groggy group leaning forward in the sandstorm, while a man slowly recited Koranic verses on the radio. As we got back into the car, we were all repeating prayers under our breath. Sand had managed to get into everything, even inside a car with rolled-up windows. I had to tie my scarf on my face so I could breathe. If Abu Amin was pleased to see me veiled, he said nothing. Along with everyone else, he was coughing.

When we arrived on the outskirts of Baghdad, Abu Haider pointed out the notorious Abu Ghraib prison, where just about every Iraqi had had at least one relative imprisoned or executed. But I pointed to the elegant palms and bright bougainvillea that reminded me of my childhood in Baghdad. I was home again.

Many Iraqis are returning from exile, some briefly, some to stay and rebuild the country. They are coming to see family they haven't seen in decades and reestablish ties with siblings and cousins. Many are optimistic about a new Iraq. Business-men are excited about what they see as "a virgin market."

Many enter the way I did, surrounded by voices arguing over Iraq's future.

After living abroad for so many years, I had thought I would never see Iraq again. Although my childhood memories of Baghdad are happy ones, that is only because my parents shielded us from the city's dreadful realities. Thanks to my parents, I remember the city of my girlhood as if it were made up of gardens, like the one surrounding my family's house: filled with fragrant flowers, citrus trees, and unworried children at play.

It was actually a city filled with fear and secret police, as I later came to understand. But even as I grew older, my family tried to give my sister, my brother, and me a chance at a normal adolescence. They sent us to private schools with children whose parents had no ties to the Baath Party clique; we'd listen to foreign rock music and talk endlessly about our teenage ambitions and dreams. But eventually, the city's fear and its Baathist police penetrated our home.

My father got word that his colleagues from the import-export company he worked for suddenly were arrested, imprisoned, and in some cases executed. At the time, my father himself was out of the country on business, but he sent word for us to join him. Once out, Iraqi émigrés rarely visited home during the reign of Saddam Hussein. They had reason to fear they would be unable to leave again; there was even the chance of arrest. I was eighteen the last time I had seen Baghdad.

My family was certainly very pleased to see Hussein removed from power, but we were worried about the fate of our relatives in Baghdad. By the end of the major fighting, telephones were out and there was no way to reach my aunts, uncles, and cousins. I decided to go see them, to make sure that everyone had survived. And of course to see the city once again.

Ali dropped me off at the house of a cousin, whose wife,

Rana, a young mother dressed in tight stretch trousers and a tight t-shirt, came out to greet me. "Welcome home," she said, her hair sparkling in the bright Baghdad sunlight.

Baghdad turned out to be a city of surprises. Press reports had led me to expect a substantially bombed-out place, and although there was plenty of visible damage to government buildings, most homes were intact. On the other hand, many houses had gouged walls, and it seemed as if every window-pane in Baghdad had been smashed.

As soon as I arrived, Rana gave me a tour of the war damage in her own house. Her family lives in Mansour, a neighbor-hood that became well known to Americans when the Saa restaurant there was targeted in an effort to kill Hussein. Rana showed me a gaping hole in her garden wall—a result, she said, of the enormous explosion that night. Shrapnel had burst into the house and spattered the dining room. There was shrapnel melted into the fabric of the downstairs curtains.

Workers were still replacing the upstairs windows; all the glass in the house had shattered. Fortunately, Rana's family had fled the country during that part of the war. Though some were injured, all our uncles, aunts, and first cousins who remained in Iraq had survived. "It's O.K.," Rana assured me quietly. "This happened to everyone in Baghdad. At least the house is still standing." Some of Rana and her husband Yaser's neighbors were not so fortunate. A young woman and her children were among those killed in the Mansour bombing; her husband survived. At first, neighbors said, the husband just sat quietly in front of the house, refusing to move. Now, when people greeted him at the market he said, "The children are fine. Sana asks why you don't pass by anymore."

"Whatever bad thing you heard" about life under Hussein, Yaser told me soon after welcoming me, "multiply it by ten. Those of you who lived outside cannot possibly fathom what we went through living under his rule." Yaser, a lively and clever man of thirty-five, had supported his family through his tourism agency. Hussein's Iraq as a tourist destination was another surprise to me, but travelers came, if not from the United States, then from Italy, France, Spain, and elsewhere. Some came to see biblical Mesopotamia: Babylon, Nineveh, and Ur. Others wanted to hunt wild boar and deer. Some wanted to camp in the desert. Whatever they wanted, Yaser arranged it. Now, with Hussein gone, Yaser was optimistic about Iraq's future.

"Do you think," he once asked me, "that Americans would be interested in visiting Iraq?"

"Of course," I answered.

"I will welcome them myself." He smiled. "What's a fair price to charge for a package tour?"

In a sense, I was Yaser's first American tourist; Baghdad was busy and energetic—another surprise, given the lack of security and services, and the closed shops and offices. The streets were very congested, and in generally good shape despite the bombing. But some were pockmarked. That was the case in the Karrada district, where Hussein's main palace stood. When I was a child, my relatives would forbid me even to look at the palace when we passed it. They feared that a camera was taking photos of passersby, and they didn't want my face to be photographed by Baathist security police. Fear was endemic.

In any event, this day all the streets seemed packed with cars—many of them Volkswagens made in Brazil. There was also the occasional scrawny donkey pulling a cart, bicycles, and many, many Baghdadis on foot. Baghdad is a city on hold, and everyone was busy trying to find groceries for their families or to figure out a way to earn money.

Because there had been so much attention given to the unleashing of religious passions in Iraq, I had expected to see virtually all of the women wearing scarves as a sign of political Islam. While there were many scarved women, there were almost as many who went into public with their heads uncovered.

Indeed, I watched one day from Yaser's car as three attractive young women, dressed in traditional gowns, walked slowly through an upscale residential neighborhood. They had long, silky black hair and modest makeup. Two looked like they were in their twenties, the third probably a teenager.

"Check out the prostitutes," my cousin said.

Prostitutes? I had thought nothing of three young women making their way down the street. We had just passed the homes of some ambassadors and the headquarters of opposition leaders. Surely prostitutes would not walk these streets.

In the past, prostitutes were most often found at bus stops. They used to dress like everybody else, in knee-length skirts or dresses. They hung out at bus stops so as to have a reason to be standing in the street. Long before the Baathists came to power, there was a whole neighborhood of brothels near the Ministry of Defense. And there were the foreign women who hung out at nightclubs and commanded a higher rate than the local girls.

I rolled down the window and looked back. I actually thought they looked lovely. The only hint of their work was in their walk: You could see their hips swaying as they went down the street.

"Look at how they're dressed!" I said, looking at my own jeans and white cotton shirt.

"Many prostitutes cover up like conservative girls," said Rana. The subtle communication is necessary, of course, in a conservative culture. Their walk, their glances at the men in passing cars, their shy smiles may all have been signs to those in the know, but I had my doubts.

Yaser laughed. "You are ridiculously naïve," he said. "Just

watch them." Soon, a car slowed at the curb, and the men inside stopped at the top of the street. The young women continued to saunter along. I began to wonder if Yaser wasn't fooling with me after all. When the women reached the car, however, one of them leaned into the passenger side window to talk, and soon after, all three of the women hopped in.

In the wake of the war, most Baghdadis have been thrown deeper into family life. Family life is dear to all Arabs, but now there's little else in Iraq. Each morning, Rana's brothers appeared at her house at about 8:30. Like many Iraqis, the young men suddenly had no jobs to go to. Rana, smiling and gracious, dutifully prepared breakfast for them. Afterward, they started smoking and talking. With no power, there was no TV, no radio, nothing to do, and nowhere to go. Yaser joined them, as did other men from the neighborhood. Some of them said that they didn't care who ruled Iraq as long as that person could return their lives to normal. They wanted their work, and salaries, back.

Iraq, the men told one another, had become like "Texas of the movies." Everyone carries a gun. They said they didn't like having guns but felt a need to keep them in their homes. The American occupation authorities specifically permit Iraqis to keep AK-47s and pistols for protection. Most people didn't go out after the sunset, because it was too dangerous. There was gunfire in the streets every night during curfew (11:00 P.M. to 4:30 A.M.), and we would sit around and try to guess from which neighborhood the sound was coming.

It was difficult for Baghdadis to follow events around them. When there was electricity, people would sometimes tune in to al-Jazeera TV, or the BBC, or another satellite news service. (American authorities had set up a "local" news station, but I never met anyone who watched it.) However, TV reports intended for an international audience contained little practical information. For that, Iraqis would turn to the burgeoning local newspaper scene. There were dozens of new papers, most of them small dailies, and many of them ideological rather than newsy. That is, they often interpreted events rather than reporting on them, and much of their information was unreliable. The most respected of the new publications was *Azzaman*, edited by a prominent former Baathist named Saad Al-Bazzaz, who has long been pro-democracy. That was the paper Yaser read. I tried to follow the news through the websites of American and British papers, which I read at one of the newly opened Internet cafes in the city. A lot of Iraqis, though, seemed to get their news through gossip and rumor.

However people got their information, many of those I met who had initially welcomed the Americans with smiles now felt abandoned. When, they asked aloud, would the chaos end? A neighbor, Salwan, a shy accountant and father of a seven-year-old, hadn't worked in months because of the war. He often smiled quietly as we all discussed the troubled city.

Another neighbor, Mohamed, thirty-three, hadn't opened his jewelry shop in months because he was afraid of looters. The quiet young man said he had buried his gold in the garden of a relative's house. His small shop in Mansour, with its pretty calligraphy above the door, had a metal gate in front to keep the thieves away.

The heat was terrible, and because there was no power, there was no air conditioning. Rana's two-year-old daughter, Yasmine, was sometimes in tears because she was so hot. Yaser had somehow found a small, hand-held, battery-operated fan, and Rana and Yaser took turns fanning the baby with the gadget.

Rana tried to deal with the hardship by laughing at it. When discussing the absence of water and electricity, she said: "That's O.K., we're strong, we're going back to the era of the *jahiliya*"—the period of "ignorance" before the Koran.

Yaser's world revolved around his family. When a little nearby grocery sometimes opened, he would take Yasmine, put her on the counter, and tell her, "Go crazy!" The child would happily grab all kind of candies and smear herself with chocolates, and Yaser would laugh with delight.

One evening, Rana remained oddly quiet. If Yaser asked her anything, she'd answer in a word or two. He studied her behavior for a while, then suddenly changed expressions.

"What date is it?" he asked me. I told him. "Oh my God! It's our wedding anniversary!" He immediately walked over to Rana and gave her a kiss. She offered him a half-smile, then turned to me and asked, "Shouldn't he give me a gift that expresses his feelings?" I agreed: "Something that expresses his feelings on your earlobes, or on your wrist." Yaser looked at us as we laughed. Then he turned and left the house. "It's a war zone, Rana," I said. "He'll get you a belated gift when he can." Rana sighed. "I suppose," she said.

A little while later, Yaser walked in beaming and put a small gold ring on Rana's finger. "Happy anniversary!" he cried. Rana was pleased and gave her husband a real kiss. The ring was modest, but Yaser's love outshone it. I later asked him where in the world he got it. Mohamed the goldsmith; Mohamed, who had hidden his jewelry in the family garden. The war poisons every day, but on this one occasion it had rescued an evening.

Yasmine Bahrani was born in Baghdad and moved with her family to the United States when she was a teenager. She has worked at The Washington Post, Reuters, Knight-Ridder *and is now a features editor at* USA TODAY. *This story was excerpted from a piece that ran in* The Washington Post *on October 5, 2003.*

MAL KARMAN

✦ ✦ ✦

Gridlocked Tehran
at Gunpoint

Shrugging off stereotypes, this traveler is rewarded
time and again for his pluck.

MY GUIDE HASSAN URGES HIS PEYKAN SEDAN ONTO SHAHID
Sarafraz Street in the usual chaos of downtown Tehran traffic
when an Iranian soldier suddenly appears in front of the car,
brandishing a machine gun and spitting venom. I have just
grabbed a shot of the Canadian Embassy with my camcorder
and would love to immortalize his outburst on video, but in a
rare moment of common sense, I actually think better of it.

At most thirty years old, this stalwart Revolutionary Guard's
black eyes blaze with contempt, and his block-square jaw
shoots up unsettling images of Schwarzenegger gone berserk
in *Terminator*. He is tall, angularly muscular, with a smoldering
intensity that explodes out of its hearth with screams of
"*Bezan kenar! Bezan kenar!!*" Pull the car over! My guide, no
shrinking violet himself, fires back a furious barrage in Farsi,
and the more heated their exchange grows, the more promi-
nently the soldier proffers the machine gun. Then my heart
skips a pump as I watch him wrap two fingers around the
trigger. The fucking trigger!

243

"Hassan, pull the car over!" I squeal, surprised by the sudden soprano in my throat.

"He's an imbecile," Hassan says, seething.

An imbecile? Such a choice of words. I am impressed with my Iranian guide's English vocabulary. "He may be an imbecile," I howl, "but he's an imbecile with a machine gun!"

Hassan fumes. At the moment, he resembles a commuter who dashed up to the platform seconds after the 7:05 pulled out. His wry observation a day earlier that "two guys speaking Farsi sound like a pair of dogs beginning to fight" could not have been more apt. "He claims it's a serious crime to take pictures of the embassy," Hassan cries, scoffing. "I told him you are a visiting journalist. I told him there are no signs to forbid pictures. How are we supposed to know you can't film here?"

Following a second wave of pleas, he finally draws the car to the curb. "Trigger" stations himself at the left front wheel and summons the police on his walkie-talkie. Hassan, thirty-six, a crew cut, well-proportioned six-foot-two, sticks his head out the window and shouts at him again. He gets no response. In fact, the soldier is now glaring almost exclusively at me— the primary troublemaker—his coal-nugget eyes and his gun barrel a trio of black dots suspended in my line of vision. I blink hard and sit there, my hands consciously folded across my chest in plain view, not so much in defiance as in deference. "It is going to be a long wait for the cops, with all this traffic," Hassan mutters.

Before I left for Iran from the West Coast, more than a half dozen friends—in varying degrees of panic ranging from "quietly concerned" to "terrified about the uncertainties"— called to ask "Are you suicidal? Why not Madrid?" and "Whatssamatta with London?" They insisted I dash off a list of influential people I know "in case something should happen over there." I tried to shrug it off at the time without seeming cavalier, but then the closer I got to departure the more reasonable the idea seemed, and on this particular day in Tehran, in Rambo's gun sights, it felt positively insightful.

One friend attributed my decision to spend the Islamic holy month of Moharram in Iran to my "latest insanity," while referencing a litany of "past insanities"—a winter in northern Sweden, half a year alone on a sparsely populated island in western Canada, a solo trek to the Brazilian rainforest—in support of his diagnosis of my current mental condition.

But his perception, and what most of mainstream America has been brainwashed to believe, is that Iran is a nation made up of religious fanatics and nuclear-hungry evildoers who despise our freedoms and our chunky apple pie way of life.

Another childhood friend, a high school wrestling teammate who, after a career as a military police officer, became a professor of criminology at a college in Pennsylvania, tells me, "The only way I'd go to Iran is with the 82nd Airborne." God help us.

Many of those people my MP-turned-professor would bomb into oblivion look, talk, and think just like his neighbors in Scranton, Pennsylvania. They are educated. They are politically aware. They commute to work. They have kids at school. At home, they dress in jeans and sweatshirts and work in the yard. They enjoy sex. And, most surprising of all, they love America.

Having visited Behesht-e Zahra, a gargantuan cemetery outside Tehran where nearly 1 million Iranian youths are buried, killed in the Iran-Iraq War with the help of weapons supplied to Saddam Hussein by the United States, I'm not sure I understand the warmth. It is unnerving to stand before the vast rows of graves that vanish beyond the infinity of the horizon (it took a taxi fifteen minutes to drive the circumference of the cemetery) and be undressed by the photographs of the dead, many of them scrawny, fresh-faced kids as young as fourteen. When I ask Hassan about this affinity for America, he says, "Most of us can differentiate between the people of your country and your government."

Oh. If only we could do the same. While the Iranian press feeds bizarre untruths about the U.S. to its population, ours goes on doing the same about them. The difference is we fancy ourselves free thinkers and buy into it; they know they're repressed and don't.

"We can vote but we can't elect," Hassan says. "The *mullahs* decide who wins. That's why (Ali Akbar Hashemi) Rafsanjani is a big leader in the polls and then (Mahmoud) Ahmedinejad wins. You have 70 million people in the country and 70 percent are under the age of thirty. The age to vote is fifteen and young people are against this government. It doesn't matter because the *mullahs* decide everything. And after (former President Mohammed) Khatami, nobody believes, nobody votes. He said he would change things and he did nothing."

In my month-long exploration of this Shiite bastion, sandwiched nervously between Afghanistan and Iraq, I inhale the ether of history from one of the oldest civilizations on Earth — from the sweeping ruins of Persepolis, the Persian empire built on a plateau by the great Achaemenian king Darius I and later mutilated by Alexander the Great, to Esfahan, the Paris of Persia that Iranians call "half of the world," to the majestic Tower of Silence where Zoroastrians laid their dead to be picked clean by raptors before burial, to the beautiful blue-tiled mosaics of the Imam Mosque and the six-story Ali Qapu Palace, the site of horse races overseen by Safavid kings — but it is the people that make this visit so indelible.

During my first week in the south of Iran, suspicious of strangers glimpsing my camcorder, I turn on one who has followed me for blocks and snap, "I have no money for you!"

"No, no," he protests gently. "Practice my English."

I am completely disarmed by this hunger for human connection and contact with the Western world. Everywhere I go, I am greeted enthusiastically. At the ancient water mill in Shushtar, I even experience what it's like to be a rock star when dozens of shrieking teenage girls, their faces framed in black *burkas*, mob me for a glimpse of their first American.

In Yazd, two struggling working-class families throw open their doors and beckon me to visit. A merchant, from whom I bought nothing, bids me a warm farewell. A carpet *bazaari* invites me for tea—without trying to sell me a carpet. A film-maker and two colleagues serve me cream puffs in the street while excitedly pumping me for answers to their questions.

"What is it like in America?" "What do you think about George Bush?" "How do Americans feel about Iran?" "Will the U.S. Army try to invade Iran?" "Is it really possible to say what you want about people in government?"

Tehran is a suffocating, sprawling city in the manner of Los Angeles and Sao Paolo. No river runs through it to replenish the air, and the stretch of concrete is endless. It takes forty-five minutes to go anywhere because it is always rush hour, always bumper-to-bumper. Twelve million people live here and they all seem to be driving three cars at once. Streetlights are often ignored. One-way streets are only one way for most. Some feel they are exceptions. A left turn on a red light into oncoming traffic is not unheard of. Cars will mow anyone down, even in a crosswalk. The best way to venture to the other side of the road is to attach oneself to a cluster of pedestrians—drivers seem more reluctant to take out a herd.

They'll sound their horns when they speed up, when they pass, when they are about to force you off the road (some have yet to comprehend that two cars cannot occupy the same space at the same time), when they believe you have no business attempting to cross the street, when they see a woman whose *hejab* (head scarf) has revealed a little too much hair, when they are irritated, when they are happy, when they are late, when they just feel like it.

Only the stunningly beautiful Alborz Mountains to the north distinguish the capital and they are something to behold. When the hellish smog hangs over Tehran, the snowcapped Alborz loom above it, seemingly levitating. When the day is clear, which is unheard of any time of year other than winter, the view northward is mind-boggling. Mount Damavand is 18,700 feet high, more than 4,000 feet taller than Mount Whitney and just 1,600 feet shorter than Mount McKinley, the tallest peak in North America. If I could, I would select it for my current venue, out of the line of traffic and machine guns.

I apologize to Hassan for getting us in hot water. He says the fault is his, then adds, "But this soldier is a stupid person."

"All this for such an unimpressive building," I observe, referring to the squat, gray Canadian Embassy. My words hang in the air, laced with frustration. One moment I am thinking this is one of those ultra-vivid dreams, that this is not happening. Then another, I am conscious of my hunger, so I cannot be dreaming. I can taste the *fesenjun* (the chicken-walnut-pomegranate dish) of the previous night and smell the saffron and rosewater wafting through the air anywhere food is sold.

My mind drifts to other things I have filmed: the dusty bazaar in Minab, a village near the Persian Gulf, where two brown-skinned children follow me and burst apart with joy when I take a picture of them; Naqsh-e-Rostam, a massive, sheer cliff with hollowed out chambers where Persian kings

Darius I, Darius II, Xerxes, and Attaxerxes are buried; and the surreal Apadana mound, the world's largest existing ziggurat that looks as if it formed the base of a sphinx. Built around 700 B.C. as a house for the gods, it was presumably a bridge between heaven and Earth, so deities could be closer to the civilization at Chonga Zanbil in ancient Elam. There is even a large slab of preserved brick where human sacrifices were made.

In the hills near Ahwaz, the site of four terrorist bombings prior to the 2005 elections and not far from the ziggurat, I am thrilled to get a group of Bakhtiari nomads in front of my camera. Dressed in colorful rags, these handsome, weather-ravaged men and women appear to have been transported from a hearty eighteenth-century stock and plunked down 300 years later to cycle perpetually through the landscape of desert, hills, and mountains via camel, horse, and donkey. I am stunned by the simplicity of their lives and how they welcome this curiosity-seeker in their tents with tea, and a willingness to offer whatever few things they have. Through my country guide Farzaneh, I wonder aloud if they are as content as they seem and Ali, the nomad chief, replies, "I have three wives."

I laugh. "That means you are either quite happy—or quite miserable."

He assures me it is the former and invites me to return a year from now, when they will migrate to these same hills, to meet his fourth wife. Then, somewhat shyly, he asks where I am from. When I reply, "San Francisco," his brown, parched face looks bewildered for the first time.

"It's in the United States," I volunteer.

"Where is that?" Ali wants to know, and he is not putting me on.

"A long way off."

"How much?"

"Sixteen or eighteen hours away by plane," I reply.

By plane? He puzzles, deep in thought. "But how far," he asks, "by camel?"

Apparently the Tehran police have taken the call from the Revolutionary Guard very seriously and have phoned the Canadian Embassy to alert them to the "two terrorist suspects" apprehended in front of the building. Embassy workers come flooding onto the sidewalk for a glimpse of the plotters. They mill about, a beehive buzz in the air, until one rotund fortyish diplomat boldly ventures up to the car and looks in.

"You speak English?" he asks.

I nod.

"Where are you from?"

Very much in the mood to cooperate and hoping to enlist his help, I reply, "California. Can you do anything to short-circuit this mess?"

"You're American?" he asks, sounding astounded.

"Yes!"

Then he looks at me somewhat dubiously. "You have an American passport?"

"Well of course!" I say. "What kind of passport would an American have?"

"Yeah, O.K.—where else do you have passports from?"

"Nowhere. For God's sake, I don't collect them."

The man seems struck by my response and draws himself up. "Well," he says almost cheerily, "good luck!" and walks off.

Grim scenarios from Kafka receive an entree to my brain. So does the unsettling story of a Canadian photojournalist who was arrested in Tehran a few years ago for photographing Evin Prison and then died under mysterious circumstances while in custody. Reportedly from a brain hemorrhage.

Perhaps it's a sign of the times in which we live, perhaps it's a clear indication that Iran does not feel immune to the threat of terrorism, but the paranoia is palpable in the city. Airport check-ins include two pat-downs and are more rigorous than in the U.S. I am not allowed on the Tehran University campus without first being interviewed by someone from the administration. Filming there is out of the question. A hotel manager asks me not to use my camcorder on the grounds.

Realizing that if I am separated from Hassan, I will be unable to communicate with my jailers, my own paranoia is jacked up. I seize upon the idea of locating my Farsi phrasebook in the rear of the car, but then wonder if reaching back there might give Mr. Personality—already cocked like the bands on a mousetrap—enough of a tick to fire off a hundred rounds through the windshield. I try focusing on anything but my present reality: I'm in a teahouse in Shiraz sprawled across a mound of floor cushions smoking "double apple" tobacco through a hookah commonly known as a "hubble bubble," illegalized a short time ago as too hedonistic. I'm in an ice cream parlor in Shemiran, north of the capital, when a stranger spontaneously decides to treat fifteen or so of us in line, and then disappears before we can thank him. I'm in Esfahan, walking in pleasantly cool evening temperatures along the manicured park that follows the gentle bends of the Zayandeh River, feeling safe and surprised by how cosmopolitan it is in the midst of centuries-old mosques and palaces. Like the Seine in Paris, the Zayandeh flows through the middle of the city, traversed by a string of bridges illuminated like birthday candles in the night. Like the Rue de Rivoli, Chahar Bagh-e-Abbasi Avenue overflows with shops hawking the latest European fashions, none of which can be worn in public. And like Saint-Germain, the pavement is teeming with energy and life well into the late hours. Contradicting the paranoia in Tehran, merchants in Esfahan leave their shops and stalls unlocked after the noon call to prayer, from 1 to 4 P.M., without fear they'll be looted.

Near Nain, I'm crawling into a cave to meet two weavers, one seventy-seven, the other seventy-eight, men who have worked together for more than six decades in near darkness fashioning robes for *mullahs* on their looms. One of these elders asks if I am wearing black to honor Hossein, the prophet Mohammad's grandson, whose martyrdom is commemorated during this holy month of Moharram. I tell him yes and his eyes twinkle. "Americans and Iranians are not supposed to be friends," he says, "but obviously this is not true." When I start to climb out of the cave and thank him for the visit ("*Motar shekkerem*," I say in Farsi), he replies with something that translates to "Don't be tired." In other words, "Be well."

Hassan and I are growing increasingly restless now. We joke that we have been in the car long enough for a regime change. But the soldier has yet to find another career, much less take his eyes off us. "You have a small percent of the country like this man," my guide tells me. "The rest, everybody else, wants a new government."

Two days earlier, during Ashura, the culmination of the martyrdom holiday when Iranians offer free food, known as "*nazri*," on the street to anyone, we stop at a corner where a powerfully built man, perhaps fifty, with olive-brown flesh, fierce black eyes, and a black moustache lords over five massive cauldrons of bubbling hot food. His face is as round as the cooking drums and as steamy in its demeanor. Hassan tells him I am American and the man snaps to attention, pumps my hand vigorously and crows, "At your service!" He tells me through my guide that I am his guest and, therefore, do not

have to stand in the line curled around the block waiting for a
meal. I will be first to be served. He struts up and down, full of
self-importance, then rants about what a great country the U.S.
is and suddenly pronounces, "But the Jews will destroy it."

I look at him as if he's just offered us a plate of worms. "Ask
this jackass if he ever heard of the prophet Daniel," I tell
Hassan. My guide obliges and the man answers, "Of course—
he is an important prophet in Islam." Does he know there is a
special shrine for Daniel in Susa? Yes, he does. Does he know
the prophet Daniel was Jewish? As were several Islamic
prophets—the prophet Jonah? The prophet Isaac? The
prophet Joseph? The prophet Abraham? The prophet Moses?
Even the prophet Jesus? Does he know Esther and Mordecai
are buried with honors in Hamadan? Does he know Esfahan
was founded by King Yazdgerd's Jewish Queen Shushan Dukht?

The man looks stunned, as if I've just whacked him in the
stomach with a two-by-four. There is a dead silence while he
digests this, while his brain sputters, while it struggles to kick
in on all cylinders like a car engine trying to run on piss, until
suddenly his arm is waving feverishly through the air, swatting
away an invisible flurry of gnats. "But that was 5,000 years
ago," he says, dismissing it. "It doesn't count."

Later that day, Hassan brings me to the home of his in-laws
to meet his family. In these surroundings, there are no burkas,
no *hejabs*, no rules against touching. Everyone is dressed casually, in Western fashions. The women let their hair fall over
their shoulders and immediately regain the sexuality the shapeless tents they wear in public deny them. Invited friends bring
platters of *chelo kabab* (broiled lamb) and *khoresht e bademjun*
(meat-tomato-eggplant stew) to add to the holiday meal.
Liquor is illegal, but it is there nonetheless. Conversation runs
from business to investments to family matters to, curiously, the

Academy Awards. The TV is on. Kids are bouncing off the walls. It feels like Thanksgiving.

Many Westerners contend they don't understand this celebration of martyrdom, this fixation commemorating the death of a great prophet. They see it as peculiar—to use a kind word. But how it might differ vastly from the martyrdom celebrated during the Easter holiday truly escapes me.

Yet if we buy into the searing images fired at our deadened, commute-weary brains on American television news, we could believe that most Iranians—to memorialize this day— pour into the streets, slice open the tops of their skulls with a machete and let blood bubble down the sides of their faces. In a country of 70 million, there are a few who will go that far. What we do not see are the vastly more common parades and passion plays with live, soul-stirring music and men dressed in black shirts and slacks marching in cadence in symbolic self-flagellation. To see that would invite similarities with our own rituals—and, consequently, empathy for theirs.

When the police finally arrive at the Canadian Embassy, although I don't know what to expect, I am relieved to be out of the gun sights of Sergeant Intensity. Hassan tries to explain to them what happened, but nobody's listening. One officer climbs into the back seat of the car and we are ordered to follow the vehicle in front of us. A second car trails, as if anyone could entertain an escape in this molasses of wheels and metal.

At the station house, we are marched through a hall, into a courtyard where a group of lounging soldiers go silent as we pass, then up four flights of stairs to a spacious room painted a shade of green never seen in nature. It is furnished only with a desk and a few chairs. We are made to sit in front of the desk where a thin man—a sullen figure of perhaps thirty-five, with sunken cheeks, an untrimmed beard, and a black leather jacket—fires questions at us. He is expressionless as he writes down our responses, and I note privately that Larry King has nothing to fear. I'm told our interrogator is a police captain although he is physically indistinguishable from the guy selling pomegranates in the marketplace. But just as I begin to feel more favorably disposed to him because (a) he is calm and (b) he is not pointing a machine gun at me, he confiscates our passports and my video footage.

After half an hour of questioning, we are taken to another police station to see a higher-ranking official—through more maddening traffic: the usual forty-five minutes of it. There, we learn the official has gone home. It is now evening as we head to a third police station where we intercept a commanding officer in an overcoat, briefcase in hand, one foot out the door. He doesn't want to deal with us, he plainly makes it known, he is going home, and we should go to a fourth station house. The First All-Precinct Tour of Tehran, I'm thinking. The captain seems frustrated but keeps his cool.

As we hurtle through roundabouts, I am aware of murals, seen everywhere in the country, of Iran's supreme leader Ali Khamenei and the late Ayatollah Khomeini, of idealized portraits of Hossein, and—somewhat incongruously—of billboards for German cameras and Swedish shampoo. And while one might expect a government this anti-American to be just as anti-capitalist, I remind myself expectations here are rarely met. From the catacombs of stalls in the bazaars to the maze of shops on city streets, merchants and merchandizing are unmistakable. In fact, it is where the Islamic revolution gathered its steam in 1979.

   The fourth police station is hidden behind an eight-foot solid metal wall with a sliding metal door. We are admitted to the inner sanctum and held in a courtyard by two guards while the captain dashes inside. It is chilly and in stark contrast to the shirt-sleeve summery nights on the Persian Gulf.

The captain reappears forty minutes later, but nothing has been resolved. We return to the first police station and the room where the odyssey began. He tells us he is going to take matters into his own hands, that he will release us on the condition we report back in the morning at which time, if he receives approval from his superiors, I will erase the footage of the embassy, sign a statement, and have my passport returned. As we exit the station through the courtyard, the soldiers we saw earlier this time give us a big farewell. "Have a nice time," one says. "Hallo! Welcome!" says another.

You may not believe this, but after Hassan drops me at my hotel and I get to my door, I find someone from maid service has left a bath faucet on and the entire room is two inches deep in water. It's true, but that's another story.

Mal Karman wrote the political thriller The Foxbat Spiral, *the nonfiction book* The Poison River, *and is a co-author of the international bestselling satire* Naked Came the Stranger. *He won an Emmy, the Scott Newman Award, and a silver medal at the N.Y. International Film Festival for* Wasted: A True Story *and was a playwriting grant recipient for* The Bones of Simon Bottle.

PETER WORTSMAN

* * *

Holy Land Blues

*A wayward pilgrim finds the seamy and
the sublime in the promised land.*

THROUGHOUT THE THREE-HOUR-AND-FIFTEEN-MINUTE-
long flight from Vienna to Tel Aviv, following in Theodor
Herzl's tracks, I nursed the illusion of rebirth. It was 1975 and
the romance of Zion hadn't yet hardened into a grim reality of
tit for tat. Longing to escape from what, in my mythic take of
the moment, seemed like the great rubble heap of Europe to
the fragrant orange grove in the desert, I felt giddy with expec-
tation. This sentiment was further reinforced by the comport-
ment of some of my fellow passengers. A curtain separated the
plane's rear cabin from the rest, like the women's section in an
Orthodox synagogue. I heard muffled whispers and sighs and
was dying for a peek, when, at cruising altitude, the curtain was
pulled back and the stowaways, Russian emigrants hidden for
security reasons, let out delirious exclamations of rapture and
relief. Processed in the human clearinghouse Vienna had
become in the twilight of the Cold War era, the Russians were
on the last leg of their exodus.

I was on an exodus of my own. I'd spent the fall and winter

in Vienna researching my parents' severed European roots and the unhappy history that sent them packing, all of which I hoped to sandwich in between the covers of a book. The German woman I was seeing, a former child prodigy, took her cello to bed, which made for an oddly wooden *ménage à trois* in which I'm afraid the bulky instrument got the best of it. To make matters worse, the Viennese police paid me an unannounced visit one morning at 3 A.M. to investigate my activities, whereupon the neighbors stopped talking to me. The cellist took up with a conductor. And never being able to get my coal oven to work quite right, I slept alone with earmuffs and a ski cap and pecked at my work in progress on an Olivetti portable with fur-lined leather gloves. So much for the chilly charms of Herzl's Vienna.

We experienced some turbulence en route to Tel Aviv, but nothing compared to the hubbub that erupted when, to the rousing background notes of the Israeli national anthem, the captain announced that we were flying over Eretz Yisrael. The entire plane, the Russians and myself included, spilled to the right for a heart-thumping, tear-filled first glimpse of the Promised Land. Whereupon the aircraft tipped and the captain clamored for us to return to our seats, lest our lopsided enthusiasm send the plane into a tailspin. The ensuing panic detracted somewhat from the stirring effect. And though the landing was smooth enough, I nevertheless felt shaken off-balance, fighting off nausea, and foreboding.

Tel Aviv. My hotel was hardly a Hilton but the room was airy and the price was right. A mild sea breeze came as a welcome relief from the lonely chill of a Viennese winter, Israel already being well into a balmy Middle Eastern spring. On my very first night I was awakened in the dark by a distant rumble, and fearing a terrorist attack—an occasional disruption of daily life at the time—I leapt out of bed and, naked but for the bed sheet wrapped around me, Biblical style, bounded into the hallway. My neighbor's door was ajar and the light was on.

"Was that a bomb?" I cried out with dark misgivings.

"*Vot* bomb?" came the ironic, Central European accented reply. "*Sat vas chust* an Arab alarm clock!"

Stepping closer and peering in through the door, it took me a while to locate the speaker amidst the smoke and clutter. On the floor sat a man of indeterminate age with a sharp face and gray chin beard, a cigarette balanced precariously on his lower lip, surrounded by open trunks and suitcases, fingering their contents. "I'd ask you in for a cup of tea," he shrugged with what might best be described as a sneer spiked with a smile, "but I'm afraid there's no room and no tea."

"Loud noises make me jumpy," I said, "I just got here."

"*Velcome* to the Promised Land," he chuckled. "I've been in transit all my life, never bother to unpack. Let the bastards bury my remains in a steamer trunk," he shook his fist at the window, "it's cheaper than a casket."

Hakarmel Market, Tel Aviv. Like an abacus, the bobbing Adam's apple protruding from the long skinny neck of the *shoichet*—the ritual slaughterer—kept count of the kill. Deadpan, he grabbed pullet after pullet by the throat with his left hand, muttered a prayer, and passed a sharp knife quickly across with a rapid thrust of his right, efficiently dishing out death without a wasted gesture, though one of the headless carcasses squirmed on the ground before falling still.

The fruit vendor in the next stall, his face as rough and ruddy as the citrus he sold, sliced and crushed giant Jaffa oranges in a hand-operated press. It was Friday morning and business was brisk in preparation for the Sabbath. A spilt trickle of orange juice blended in the mud with a steady stream of chicken blood. A stray dog sniffed at this sea of an unsettling shade of red. The fruit vendor kicked the dog. The dog whimpered.

Later that day, Sabbath eve though it was, no milk and honey awaited me. Having neglected to make arrangements in advance for Friday night dinner, I risked going hungry. Rabbinic law, the law of the land in Israel, prohibits any form of transaction involving remuneration construed as work on the Day of Rest (which, according to Jewish custom, starts the night before). A couple of restaurants remained open all the same for tourists and agnostics, but cash was not accepted. The waiter at one such establishment, whose English was even more rudimentary than my Hebrew, pointed from my Timex to a calendar. It took me a while to catch on to the customary accommodation to the law: I could leave my watch in hock and pay up at sundown, Saturday, when the country reopened for business.

"Can I see the menu, please?"

"Chicken," muttered the man.

My stomach squirmed, a visceral replay of the dancing headless carcass—"Got any gefilte fish?"

"Chicken," he reiterated.

"Chicken," I nodded, my hunger more pressing than my disgust.

Patiently I waited, but no food was forthcoming. The waiter just sat there, fingering my watch, looking up every now and then to cast me a quizzical look. Then it dawned on me that I was supposed to fetch my own plate of cold chicken, potatoes, and peas that I only now noticed languishing in a halo of flies on the kitchen counter.

(Toward the end of his short life, dying of TB in Berlin, Franz Kafka fantasized spiritual rebirth in Palestine, where he dreamed of opening a little restaurant with his lover, Dora

Dymant. She would cook and he would serve, dreamed he—
a Sabbath waiter, no doubt, with ample time for reflection).

Jerusalem. Who can resist the magnetic lure of the Wailing
Wall? Every lane and alleyway in the noisy labyrinth of the Old
City inevitably leads to this sacred cul-de-sac where, on
adjoining plots, Solomon erected his temple and Mohammed
hiked up to heaven. Muslims flock to the Dome of the Rock,
the golden-roofed mosque built above, to mark the spot where
the Prophet ascended to heaven to meet his maker. Jews cling
to the cramped plateau below, where the lone western wall left
of their ruined sanctuary hugs the absence to the east, a wall
surrounding nothing. Every Jew reconstructs his own temple
from scratch.

The merciful shade of its ancient bricks proved a soothing
balm. Religiously unobservant though I be, my head felt light
and my legs went wobbly leaning against the symbolic parapet
of my people's dispersion. Home at last, I thought. Greatly
stirred, despite myself, I shut my tear-filled eyes and tried to
meld with the mortar of Zion, but I was disturbed by a tap on
the shoulder.

A bearded old man in black hat and long black coat held out
a *talis* (prayer shawl) and a set of *tephillim* (leather phylacteries),
urging me to put them on and pray.

"No, thank you," I gently shook my head, "I'd rather
mark the moment in my own way." Shutting my eyes again,
haunted by the eerie, high-pitched, tongue-trilled religious
rapture of Sephardic women in their roped-off cordon of
worshipers, I strained to reestablish contact with this sacred
rubble heap lovingly preserved in memory for millennia by my
scattered ancestors here on the World's Lower East Side. Can
a locale crystallized into a concept and dragged clear across
creation reacquire a physical reality? Surely we've shed enough

tears to irrigate the desert, I pondered, and sank to my knees, prepared for an epiphany.

But before I could resist, the old man had already flung a prayer shawl over my shoulders and begun to bind the leather thongs like manacles around my forehead and knuckles. He rocked and chanted, motioning for me to follow suit. Rising reluctantly, I moved and moaned in the requisite ritual manner, the spell of sanctity broken.

Holiness eluded me at Solomon's doorstep, but I found a glimmer of it in the squint of a sunburnt old kibbutznik in an orange grove in the Galilee, where I volunteered to help out with the harvest. "*Mah-ze?* What's this?" he asked by way of a riddle, plucking a grapefruit from an overhanging branch and crushing it in his powerful right fist. Perched on a ladder propped up against a tree he himself had planted in his youth, it might as well have been Jacob's ladder and he a patriarch. Smile lines criss-crossed his wizened face. A narrow-brimmed blue cap pulled down low over his bushy brow blocked out the sun. "That's no juice, my friend," he grinned with fierce pride, "that's my sweat!"

Perhaps it was my figurative predisposition primed by all those years of Hebrew School. Something biblical must have seeped in after all, though the moral was jumbled a bit. Everywhere I turned, parables and riddles hung ripe for the plucking. So, for instance, by some odd climactic fluke, the sunset split down the middle over the muddy waters of the Red Sea, at the Gulf of Aqaba where Israel and Jordan abut, blushing pink on one side of the border and glowing golden on the other (I can't remember which was which).

Eilat. We literally bumped into each other on a crowded bus. She was standing directly in front of me by an open window, a poster girl for Israel in a short, tight fitting khaki-colored skirt, whipping me in the face with her fluttering black mop of hair.

"Sorry," she smiled, making no attempt to tame and bind the savage mane.

"My pleasure," I smiled back, inhaling her scent.

The bus was headed for Nueba, a beachfront oasis of palm trees on the coastal strip of the Sinai in the territory Israel had captured from Egypt in the Six-Day War (and has since returned). At the time, Israeli youth flocked there to let it all hang out. Ophrah was going to meet her platoon-mate, Ziporah, and graciously invited me to join them.

An Iraqi Jew, Ophrah had dark coffee-colored skin and glistening onyx-colored hair, just as I imagine the Queen of Sheba. Her friend Ziporah, of Yemenite extraction, was no less alluring in an Afro that framed her deep brown face like the shade of a palm tree. Heads turned on the beach when the two shed their army uniforms, stripping down to scant bikinis. Is there any sight as sexy as a sun-baked Sabra straining the minuscule triangles of a bikini!

Meanwhile, lining the beach, the males of the species flexed their biceps and whistled catcalls, disconcerted at the effrontery of a foreigner consorting with not one, but two of their nubile fillies. Smiles flashed, winks fluttered, followed by a non-stop volley of lip-smacking come-ons, sassy put-downs, and swift repartees. Largely illiterate in Hebrew and hardly Mr. Universe material, I followed with awe and wonder.

Can this be the same people that languished, pale and anemic, in the dark ghettos of Eastern Europe and *mellahs* of the Middle East? What happened to the sallow-skinned, stooped *Yeshivah bochers*, the haggard yellow men who wiled away life-times in ill-lit prayer *Stibln*, pining for the metaphysical Sabbath bride to take their hand and lead them to a spiritual union in an imagined Jerusalem? What happened to the timid maidens and bewigged matrons cloistered behind shutters in Bialystok and velvet curtains in Fez?

Reborn like brash phoenixes out of the ashes of Auschwitz, having shed all Freudian inhibitions and the baggage of guilt, Herzl's pale brainchildren joined with their tanned Oriental cousins to once and for all times unleash the long sublimated Jewish libido. Once let out there was no zipping it back up. A little farther up the beach, naturists shed all and dallied in the dunes. Nueba was Eden minus the "don'ts." No skulking deity to chaperone the party. How I longed to go native and join the fun! I'd have gladly given all the book learning I'd amassed for a freewheeling spirit and a competitive physique.

Still, I could not help but notice the effect this unabashed spectacle had on the black-cloaked Bedouin who stood by, bemused, like shadows separated from their own bodies and the land that belonged to them and to which they belonged, eking out a subsistence living peddling trinkets and cold drinks to the interlopers, where they had once roamed freely.

Were we Jews not wandering desert nomads once, and are we not Bedouin in business suits still, dream-driven children of the wind? I thought of all the itinerant peddlers in my restless lineage, and of myself who feels most alive in transit. Was Herzl, the peripatetic prophet of Zionism, not the most compulsive nomad of them all!?

Having imprudently neglected to cover my head until it was too late, I contracted a pounding headache. A Bedouin woman draped in black from whom I bought a cap whispered something in Arabic to Ophrah and Ziporah that made all three of them giggle.

"What did she tell you?" I asked Ophrah.

A proud smile lit up the lovely Sabra's mahogany features. "She said, 'Black is beautiful!'"

The darkness and the absence of posted street names in

Ophrah's Eilat neighborhood and my deficient Hebrew made it difficult to pinpoint the address she'd scribbled on the inside flap of a book of matches soaked in sea water. Needless to say, I arrived late. The coffee was cold. So was Ophrah's welcome. The photograph of a soldier boyfriend, whose existence she had failed to mention, hung on the wall beside an army-issue Uzi.

"So tell me, Ophrah," I asked, feeling flustered, frustrated, ill at ease, far more *meta* than physical, "what does it mean to you to be Jewish?"

"There's my yardstick," she gestured with a proud grin at the firearm on the wall. "This is my land," she stamped her shapely sandaled foot, raising a cloud of red clay-colored dust. "That's the border," she pointed a finger out the window toward Aqaba, whose lights flickered in the distance, the condensation of a golden sunset. "Anybody crosses under my watch, I measure their grave in the crosshairs."

Back in Tel Aviv I fell ill, addled by the same ball of fire that the Egyptian Pharaoh Akhnaton recognized as the supreme deity, that swirling bundle of gases that kindled a loquacious shrub, etched the headlines into rock, and led a stuttering tour guide with a lousy sense of direction and his complaining entourage on an extended budget sightseeing tour of the Sinai—hotels and meals not included. I fathomed too late why Muslims and Jews cover their heads.

Feverish and semi-delirious with sunstroke, not wanting to return to my seedy Tel Aviv dive, I accepted the gracious invitation of paternal cousins thrice removed to convalesce at their apartment in a posh suburb. As I languished on a couch in the living room, Liuba, a still handsome woman in her late fifties, paused on my prompting from her housework to reflect on the fragments of a shattered old world left behind. She told me of the day she came home to her Warsaw apartment house, forewarned in the lobby by a well-intentioned neighbor not to mount the steps to the apartment, where her father had swallowed the cyanide capsule he kept close at hand in anticipation of his imminent arrest. Of going into hiding with forged Aryan identification papers. Of working as a nurse in a German military hospital and looking out one day to see the Ghetto in flames and burning women and children leaping out of windows. Of squelching her tears, lest she reveal too much, while the Poles pointed and laughed. She told me of the handsome young SS surgeon who one day out of the blue declared his love, proposing marriage, whereupon she fled in the night, never to return.

To the remembered ruins of Solomon's fallen temple Liuba added the rubble of her own incinerated youth. I never asked, though I was sorely tempted, if, given the hostility of neighbors on all sides, Israel did not sometimes feel like a gilded ghetto. Soothed by her chicken soup, vaccinated by her sadness, I soon recouped my strength and recommenced my exodus.

In Jaffa, I sat in an Arab café, sipping Turkish coffee, smoking an occasional cigarette for conversation's sake, while gnawing at green olives big as fists.

In the northern hill town of Safed, from whence, the true believers say, the Messiah will one day emerge, I too was dazzled by the ethereal blue light that sparked the wild reverie of the Kabbalists, though this time I made sure to wear a hat.

On a hilltop in Haifa, I sat cross-legged on a low stone parapet, peering down through the lush verdure of a public park, flirting with the blue eyes of the Mediterranean, reflecting on my hybrid Semitic and Teutonic roots transplanted in Anglo-Saxon soil stolen from the Manhattan Indians. But something distracted my eye. It took me a while to fathom that the fuzzy pink patch in the clearing was no cluster of desert fruit but a latter-day Adam and Eve actively engaged in the pursuit of knowledge. The leaves both framed and camouflaged this Holy Land peepshow upon which I gazed with a thoroughly unholy thrill. I was roused from my voyeuristic thrall by a high-pitched cough from the throat of a white-bearded gnome, round and red as a medicine ball, who walked up and declared: "From the cross of the young gentleman's legs, if I may make so bold, I can tell he is looking for love. The knees cry out your need. Permit me to introduce myself." Whereupon this Jewish Santa Claus plucked out a wrinkled, tea-stained business card, one side of which was inscribed in Hebrew, the other in English, *S.J. Friedlich, Matrimonial*. "I've got a long list of available brides, all of good family," he pandered, practically salivating, so eager was he to drum up business.

"I'll think about it, thanks," I said, taken aback, indeed stunned—had he not caught me with my pants down, so to speak, and bared the loneliness of my loins? About to pocket the card, I might well have called him the next day or the day thereafter had he not plucked the card back out of my grasp.

"If not now, when?!" he shrugged, replaced the card (no doubt the sole facsimile) in his vest pocket, and slunk away in a muttering huff, probably scaring off Adam and Eve, for when I looked back the clearing was clear.

The fresh water springs falling from the cliffs of the Judean Desert over the oasis of Ein Gedi on the western shore of the Dead Sea might just as well have been a mirage. This is the lowest populated place on earth and surely one of the hottest. A dip in the Dead Sea hardly helps. The bather emerges unrefreshed, body coated with oil slick and salt brine like a fugitive sardine. Parched and unforgiving though the surrounding desert is, humanity has been seeking out this fertile nook to refresh the spirit at least as far back as the fourth millennium B.C., as an unearthed sacrificial altar of a Chalcolithic temple attests. In caves nearby, John the Baptist's ascetic brethren, the locust-eating Essenes, fled civilization such as it was to submit to the elements and scratch their impressions on papyrus scrolls. Jesus could have strolled the oil slick of the Dead Sea without a spill, had he not perfected his act on the Sea of Galilee.

The youth hostel at Ein Gedi lacked most creature comforts. A lone ceiling fan in the lobby scattered flies and spread the heat thick as honey. Come nightfall, sleepless guests and staff spilled outdoors to mingle, soaking up a dark illusion of coolness.

It was here that I witnessed and participated in a sacrificial rite. Among the female lodgers was a German blonde who worked in the kitchen. She was big-boned and a bit ungainly, though not unattractive, and was surrounded every night by a swarm of admirers, other employees of the hostel. Taunts and teases with insinuating undertones were carelessly hurled and unskillfully rebuffed.

What began as seemingly playful flirting intensified little by little into something more serious. Like a storm cloud, the circle of lust shifted about from the brightly lit hostel entrance to an unlit corner of the patio, where paws grabbed and were slapped back. But just as things threatened to get out of control, the seemingly passive object of everyone's desire turned the tables on her aggressors, making clear with the flick of an imperious index finger that she—not they—was pulling the strings. With growls and groans of protest and a flutter of arms, those not chosen scattered like whimpering dogs in search of another bone.

"Why don't you try your luck?" Yossi, a dishwasher who slept in the bunk above mine, egged me on one night, as the circle dilated and contracted and I found myself sucked from its periphery ever closer to the center of attraction. "She's not my type," I shrugged, unaware that the German woman and I were standing back to back. Whereupon she whirled about. "*Komm, Liebchen!*" she commanded and I followed. Accompanied by a chorus of catcalls, we strode out into the Biblical Wilderness of Ein Gedi, where David hid out from the wrath of Saul and John the Baptist cleansed his soul through self-denial, in the pursuit of knowledge.

Though I only stayed a month or so, my visit to Israel actually wrapped itself up a year later at a belly dancing club on the south side of Chicago. The show had already started as I tiptoed past the tables and elbowed my way through the crowd. The sagging ceiling, the dense cloud of cigarette smoke, the press of bodies around me, and the remoteness of the exit door all served to multiply the claustrophobic feel of the place. As the dancer's hand cymbals clashed and the mustachioed oud player plucked and strummed his instrument, I tried to keep my cool.

Like every other member of the mostly male audience, my eyes were riveted to the ripple and roll of the dancer's rhythmic gyrations. The belly dance tames the libido, elevating teasing lust to an art form, just a twitch short of ejaculation.

At the end of the first dance, I followed the lead of the man to my immediate right, stuffing dollar bills into the elastic band of the dancer's skirt as she brushed by. Not stuffed in firmly enough, my tribute fluttered and fell.

"First time?" my dollar-dipping mentor inquired. "My brother's a bit shaky too, eh Sayeed," he grinned, motioning with the tip of his cigarette at the unsmiling man to my left, the latter as lean as the former was fat.

Sayeed said nothing, he just stared.

"Sayeed doesn't talk much," his brother explained, "ever since he stepped out of an Israeli jail."

I didn't ask what he'd done.

"Where are you from, my friend?" asked the garrulous one.

"New York," I coughed, the cigarette smoke aggravating my asthma and malaise.

"Jewish?" He practically spat out the question, the ash of his cigarette tumbling in an avalanche.

I nodded.

"Better leave now!" he advised, as silent Sayeed clenched his teeth.

I backed off slowly, grateful that the laws of guest-friendship precluded a knife in the back.

In Israel, meanwhile, the flaming sword of the cherubim stationed east of Eden has been replaced by tanks and suicide bombers wrestling for the deed to the tree of life. A new wall is going up to buttress the weeping stones of the old one, on both sides of which the earth opens her mouth daily to receive Abel's blood. Rebirth is on hold for the foreseeable future.

New York-born nomad Peter Wortsman has peddled his itinerant impressions to The Boston Globe, Los Angeles Times, *and* The Washington Post, *among other newspapers. He is the author of* A Modern Way to Die, *a book of short fiction; and two plays,* The Tattooed Man Tells All *and* Burning Words. *He also does translations from German to English, and his rendering of* Travel Pictures, *by Heinrich Heine, will be published by Archipelago Books in 2008.*

MICHEL MOUSHABECK

✦ ✦ ✦

The *Mukhtar* and I

An exile recalls his very last summer in the old city.

THE MORNING MY GRANDFATHER AND I TOOK A WALK
together—after feasting on a breakfast of *ka'ak* (oversized
sesame bagels) and *bayd hammeem* (oven-baked eggs) that my
grandmother bought from a street vendor by yelling and dropping a basket-on-a-rope from the dining room bay window
overlooking the market in the Christian Quarter—he turned
to me and said, "Today you get to spend the day with Sido
(grandfather); you are now old enough to come help me at the
qahwe (café)."

The year was 1966 and I was barely eleven years old. We
were living in Beirut. Often during the summertime my
mother would take me, together with my younger brother and
my sister, to visit Tata (grandmother) and Sido in the Old City
of Jerusalem. It was a summer holiday I often resisted and
fought against, for I preferred to spend my time on the beach
in Beirut with my best friends Mounir and Imad instead of
visiting my grandfather—a stern-looking, *tarboosh*-wearing
(fez), *za'oot*-sniffing (snuff), *nargileh*-puffing (water-pipe),

mustachioed man who to me looked more like an Ottoman Pasha than a grandfather, a man almost feared by everyone around him (at least that was my perception), someone who had never shown the slightest interest in me or any affection towards me.

I not only feared my grandfather, I was petrified by the sight of all the ugly, bearded monks who occupied the Greek Orthodox Convent where my grandparents lived after their forced exile from their home in the Katamon Quarter. The intoxicating smell of incense and burning candles, the spooky, narrow, cobble-stoned alleyways of the convent grounds, the robed priests roaming around in the dark (they gave me the creeps every time they looked me in the eye and whispered *kalimera* and *kalispera*, which I didn't know at the time meant good morning and good evening in Greek)—all contributed to a feeling of anxiety and discomfort I could do without.

My grandfather Issa Toubbeh, known to everyone as Abu Michel (father of Michael), was the *Mukhtar* (literally, the chosen), the head of the Eastern Orthodox Christian Arab community in Jerusalem, whom he dutifully served for more than fifty years, as his father had done before him and his eldest son after him. As *Mukhtar*, he was given a residence inside the Convent, which consisted of several large, high-ceilinged rooms abutting the walls of Mar Ya'coub (St. Jacob's Orthodox Church) and the Holy Sepulcher, located on the Convent grounds. Two rows of sweet-smelling potted plants and flowers, including gardenias and jasmine, lovingly tended to by my grandmother Tata Maria, graced the front entrance of the house and provided a welcome antidote to the unpleasant and overpowering (at least to a child) holy scents one encountered along the way. From the rooftop—the makeshift playground my cousins and I frequented—the view of the Mount of Olives, the Dome of the Rock, the al-Aqsa Mosque, and the

Church of the Holy Sepulcher overwhelmed my eleven-year-old eyes every time I gazed in the distance.

Everyone spoke highly of my grandfather, the *Mukhtar*, and his important role in Palestinian society. Abu Michel was quite erudite and always commanded people's attention and respect. He spoke fluent Arabic, Turkish, Greek, Armenian, and Russian. And he could even swear in English—with a posh British accent, nonetheless—something he picked up during his numerous dealings with the "cursed" British before their departure from Palestine in 1948. He survived the rule of the Ottomans, the English, Hashemite Transjordan, and the Jewish state, and was considered a shrewd and highly experienced problem-solver—a necessary prerequisite for the job of *Mukhtar*. His reputation as a successful mediator spread beyond his flock in the Eastern Orthodox Christian Arab community, and his services were highly sought after by people in the Muslim as well as Jewish communities in Jerusalem. "Abused women rushed to our house for protection while their abusers waited patiently outside for the arrival of my father, the mediator," my uncle Jamil once told me. It was also rumored that whenever my grandfather accompanied an entourage of men assembled for the purpose of asking for a girl's hand in marriage, it was guaranteed that their request would be granted.

Such was the importance of *my* grandfather, the *Mukhtar*. But no matter what people said about him, no matter how much praise was bestowed on his position in the society, it never really impressed me much. My older cousin Basima once came up to me and proudly told me that she saw Sido's picture in the newspaper walking next to the Greek Orthodox Patriarch of Jerusalem at the head of the procession on Easter Sunday. Big deal, I thought. My aunt Widad, the sweetest of my six aunts, bragged that no marriage in the community could take place without the official stamp of the *Mukhtar* on the marriage certificate; no birth could be legalized without his seal; no divorce approved without his counsel; no death authenticated without his presence. The more stories I heard about him the less affection I felt towards him. There is someone, I said to myself, who is doing good deeds all over town but has never said a kind word to me, let alone given me a grandfatherly hug. I was puzzled. How could a person have so much power over a community? Many more questions crossed my eleven-year-old mind: Do I really have to get his approval before I get married? Will he stand in my way if I choose to marry the belly dancer I saw in the Beirut restaurant a month ago? Must I steal the round, brass seal with Arabic calligraphy he keeps chained to his vest in order to do so?

The side I saw of Sido was in stark contrast to his reputation on the street. The verbal abuse he often unleashed on my aunts (mind you, never on my uncles) was shocking. The time he yelled at my mother for her disrespectful act of lighting a cigarette in his presence, and his refusal to speak to her for several days afterwards was quite upsetting to me. The way he treated my Tata (the world's kindest grandmother) was also painful to watch—especially the evening ritual of her taking off his shoes and socks and massaging his feet in a bowl of hot water for hours on end after his return from work. As if her days were easy when compared to his, I used to complain to my mother. I remember my mother scolding me one day for asking why he never massaged my grandmother's feet as payback or reward for taking her away from her family at age thirteen and impregnating her ten times (not counting the several miscarriages she had to go through) without a break in between.

Spending time at home with my grandmother and watching her slave away in the house all day made me very resentful of my grandfather's behavior. Maybe I felt this way because I grew up in cosmopolitan Beirut. Or maybe it was because I never saw my father treat my mother in this manner. I was too young to understand the role customs played on his behavior and attitudes, too naïve to fathom how deep-rooted in tradition some people can be.

But despite all this, I was not too young to understand that being "the grandson of the *Mukhtar*" had its benefits, too. And I shamefully admit that I exploited them to the maximum. I wasn't about to let these brief, unpleasant family episodes stand in the way of having fun on my summer vacation in Jerusalem. Everybody in the community knew the *Mukhtar* and, in very short time after my arrival, people everywhere would say: "Ah, you must be the *Mukhtar's* grandson." The local grocer would give me free sugar-covered chickpeas, the juice vendor, free lemonade. I got free ice cream, free falafel sandwiches, free bicycle rentals, free olive wood crosses (which I later sold to tourists a few blocks away), and—most important of all— free donkey rides. The *Mukhtar* connection opened so many doors for me that the Old City was soon transformed into one big amusement park. I would spend my days roaming the streets, going from quarter to quarter, hanging out with Hassan and Ahmad in the courtyard of the al-Aqsa Mosque while they waited for their father to come out of Friday prayer services, playing in and around the Church of the Holy Sepulcher with Charlie and George, sons of a souvenir store owner, and watching the mini-skirt clad *ajnabiyyat* (foreign women)—some pretty, I thought, but no match to the love of my life, the dark-haired belly dancer in the Beirut restaurant.

I had the freedom to go anywhere I wanted in the Old City—no worries there, since I was the *Mukhtar's* grandson and the *entire* community would look after me (be responsible for my safety is more like it). My only condition was that I return to the convent before the 8:00 P.M. closing time of the small, studded, metal door carved in the center-bottom of the monstrous iron door that sealed off and protected the fortress known as the Greek Orthodox Convent. I was constantly warned about the closing time by my mother and always allowed ample time for the walk back home—except once.

It was Sunday evening and I was having so much fun flying Salim's kite that I lost track of time. When I got to the Convent, the dreaded metal door was shut. And that was a lesson to remember. The street was almost deserted and the amplified sound of occasional hurried footsteps on the cobble-stoned sidewalk did little to ease my fears. Alone, I stood outside the Convent door sobbing for what seemed like eternity (it couldn't have been more than ten minutes) until a nice, elegantly-dressed lady came up to me and uttered the magic words: "You must be the *Mukhtar*'s grandson." She gently held my hand and let me rest my head on her chest (later I thought of marrying her, too) until someone sent a message to the monk inside who unhappily came and opened the door. After I thanked and bade my savior goodbye, the monk with the foot-long keys hanging from his belt slammed shut the squeaky metal door behind us, and I quickly ran to the house—totally ignoring the angry Greek words he spewed in my direction.

The "walk" with my grandfather took place the morning after this incident. And I dreaded it. My time of scolding has come, I said to myself, especially after his total silence on the matter the evening before. But to my surprise, there was no mention of it. Instead, he extended his hand to me and gave me a warm and loving look—something I was not accustomed to seeing. As we passed the frowning monk at the Convent entrance, the one whose prayer I disrupted the night before, Sido looked at me and gave me a wink and a smile. That was the start of a day I will remember and cherish for the rest of my life.

The first order of the day was a visit to the *Batrak*, the grand old Patriarch of the Greek Orthodox Church in Jerusalem—a real treat and a privilege very few people get, Sido told me. I was not only special but also the oldest son of his youngest daughter, he went on to say (a reason only a real smoothie would think about). Our audience with the *Batrak* was very brief. I remember feeling dazzled by the opulence of his quarters, but had little time to absorb any details except for the long baton with the round, golden head the *Batrak* held in his right hand. I was not thrilled at having to kiss the wrinkled old man's hand, and I had to do it twice—once at the beginning and another time after he placed around my neck a gold chain with a black-and-gold cross. This gift was special and would protect me from future evil, Sido quietly whispered in my ear, since the cross had inside it a wood splinter that came directly from the cross of Jesus Christ. (This valuable piece of information came in handy when I later sold the cross to my Lebanese Maronite schoolmate, who paid me the desperately needed Lebanese pounds to shower on the love of my life, the belly dancer, the next time I saw her.)

My memories of that day are as vivid and as bright as a silver coin in the sun. Sido and I, hand in hand, walked through the streets of Jerusalem, stopping every few paces to greet people he knew and those who knew of him. Along the way we passed the market, a bustling collection of colorful fruit and vegetable vendors. I instantly felt the flow of musical energy emanating from the place and its people. Music was simply all around: from the unforgettable melodic chanting of the muezzin's call to prayer—often juxtaposed against the ringing of church bells—to fruit and vegetable vendors in the market singing praises about pickling cucumbers (as small as babies' fingers) or prickly pears (so delicious they melt in your mouth); from the cheerful foot-thumping sounds of children practicing *dabke* dancing to the powerful emotional songs of Oum

Koulthoum blasting from transistor radios on window sills. To this day I am still able to close my eyes and transport myself back to the Jerusalem days. I am still able to smell the delicious food sold by street vendors, especially the wonderfully rich and evocative scent of roasted chestnuts and, of course, the sumptuous sweets drenched in *'ater* (sugar syrup) sold at Zalatimo's; I am still able to see the old street photographer with the wooden camera whose head often disappeared underneath a black cloth; still able to touch the olive oil soap stacked in the long cylindrical towers at the corner store.

But the one thing that intrigued me most of all, the one person who had a profound influence on me, was the juice vendor who walked with his body leaning forward and his Bordeaux fez with the black tassels tipped back. Not only did he carry a big tank filled with *sous, jellab*, and lemonade on his back as he traveled by foot from neighborhood to neighborhood, but he was a percussionist of the highest degree. I was fascinated by how he announced his arrival and mesmerized by how he played beautiful, intricate rhythmic patterns, using brass cups and saucers, to entertain customers and alert them of his presence — rhythms very similar to the ones the belly dancer in the Beirut restaurant moved her hips to. From that moment on I was hooked. I would sit on the sidewalk with my eyes fixed on the juice vendor's hands so I could learn his art. Back at the house later on, to my grandmother's horror, I would practice the same rhythms using her china, which produced disastrous results and, it goes without saying, a spanking. This marked the beginning of what was to become a life-long passion for Arabic music and rhythms.

Adjacent to Jaffa Gate was my grandfather's long-established café. Known to family and friends as al-Mahal (The Place) and to others as Qahwet Abu Michel (Father of Michael's Café) or Qahwet *al-Mukhtar*, the café was a renowned Jerusalem institution frequented in its heyday by the Palestinian literati, nicknamed *al-sa'aleek* (the vagabonds). According to my uncle Jamil, it was Palestinian author and educator Khalil Sakakini "who bestowed the title of *sa'aleek* on the group of intellectuals who met at al-Mahal. Members of the *sa'aleek* included Yusef el-Issa, publisher/editor of the daily *Alef Ba*, and Issa el Issa, publisher/editor of the daily *Filistine*, as well as Anistas Hanania, Adel Jaber, Ahmad Zaki Pasha, Khalil Mutran, Yacoub Farraj, and others." Poets, musicians, historians, storytellers, folks who wanted to be seen in their company, young Palestinians who aspired to be like them, or simply those who just wanted to listen to the exchange of ideas taking place, gathered at *al-Mukhtar's* café.

The café was buzzing with people when my grandfather and I arrived from the market. As we walked in the door, we were greeted by my uncle Mitri, who gave me a kiss on each cheek before going behind the counter to prepare an order of *mezze* for a customer. I was immediately put to work cutting cucumbers, chopping parsley, and preparing plates of olives and pickled turnips for the busy lunch crowd. *Arak* (a Lebanese alcoholic drink made of distilled grape juice flavored with anise) and *nargileh* were present at almost every table, which accounted for the lively, albeit smoky, atmosphere of the place. For the next hour or so Sido attended to the business of recording births, deaths, and marriages in his oversized leather book, giving advice in between, and stamping official documents that required his seal. When he was done, he signaled to me with his walking stick to follow him to the café backyard, a large paved area with rows of plants on each side, a round tiled fountain in the middle surrounded by tables and chairs, and a massive cage that housed chickens and over a hundred pigeons.

As we sat in the sun and snacked on watermelon and *Nabulsiyyeh* cheese, he told me funny stories and answered the many questions I had stored up over the years. His answers to silly questions like "Why do you wear a *tarboosh*?" and "What's that stuff you sniff and makes you sneeze all the time?" and more serious ones like "Why did you leave Katamon?" and "Why did you not fight the *Yahood* (the Jews) when they took your home?" kept me enthralled the whole afternoon. He told me about the bombing that demolished the Samiramis hotel down the road from their house in Katamon and how the blast that Menachem Begin masterminded at the King David Hotel, close to my uncle Michel's office, instilled fear in the community and was the catalyst that drove many Katamonians to flee their homes. I laughed when he described how one morning, on orders of Haj Amin Al-Husseini, the *mufti* of Palestine, he received a delivery of antiquated guns and ammunition loaded on five donkeys to be distributed to the men in the community at a time when the *Yahood* were parading the streets with tanks and cannons. I cried when he told me the story of the massacre that took place at the village of Deir Yassin. A quick change of subject to the art of pigeon flying restored my smile. And before we headed back home, he gave me an impressive demonstration by releasing all the pigeons and showing me how to fly them in a circle and then guide them back to their cage—all with only the help of a black piece of cloth tied to the end of a long stick. What he failed to tell me was that this exercise is done to attract other flying pigeons to the flock and ultimately back to the cage so that Uncle Mitri could later serve them to the customers.

Back at the house that evening, while my grandfather rested his feet on a chair in the living room, Tata asked me to run over to the neighbor's place to borrow a bowl of rice. Along the way, I met another neighbor who asked, "Where are you headed, son?" I told him about my mission to which he inquired, "Why? What's going down at *beit al-Mukhtar* (the *Mukhtar*'s house)?" I shrugged and kept on going. My guess was that he told another in the neighborhood, and another told another, and in no time more than twenty or so family and friends descended on my grandparents' house, which sent my grandmother—and a dozen or so female helpers—scrambling to the kitchen to prepare food for the guests. The feast and the festive atmosphere that ensued were like nothing I'd encountered before. Suddenly musical instruments appeared from nowhere, and poetry became the flavor of the day. While the men sang and played music in the living room, the women danced in the kitchen, and the children shuttled back and forth between the two. In between solo improvisations on the oud (a fretless lute), the *qanoun* (a zither-like plucked instrument), and the *nay* (a reed flute), that brought sighs of appreciation, the singer sang soulful *mawwals* (vocal improvisations in dialect) and made up new lyrics to familiar tunes. I recognized many of the rhythms the juice vendor played, and I was encouraged to join the musicians on the tambourine. The fun was interrupted when Tata ordered everyone to the dining room table. And what a table that was! There were *kefta*s and *kabab*s, *hashwet jaaj* (chicken with rice and pine nuts) and *koosa mahshi* (stuffed zucchini), and *mezze* plates as far as the eye could see: hummus (chickpea dip), *babghannouj* (eggplant dip), stuffed vine leaves, glistening black olives, braided white cheese, glossy vegetables, plump nuts, and lush juicy fruits. It was like magic: Where did it all come from? I wondered.

After stuffing ourselves to the chin (an Arabic expression often used by my mother), we all retired to the living room and the music resumed. This time the men and women danced together to the soothing and hypnotic compositions of Zakaria Ahmad and Sayyid Darweesh, Mohammad Abd el-Wahab and

Fareed el-Atrash. And I, naturally exhausted by the events of the day, fell asleep on my grandfather's lap.

Early the next morning, a crowd of family and friends lined up at the Convent entrance to bid us farewell. We got into the *service* (taxi) that drove us to Amman and from there back home to Beirut. From the car window I waved goodbye to my teary-eyed Tata and Sido and yelled *kalimera* to the bearded monk with foot-long keys.

That was the last time I saw my grandparents; the last time I saw Jerusalem.

Michel Moushabeck is an essayist, editor, publisher, and musician. He is the founder of Interlink Publishing, a Massachusetts-based independent publishing house. His books include Beyond the Storm: A Gulf Crisis Reader *(with Phyllis Bennis) and* Altered States: A Reader in the New World Order. *He is a founding member of the Layaali Arabic Music Ensemble. He plays riqq, tabla, and daff on the music soundtrack of an award-winning BBC/WGBH documentary on Islam, which aired as part of the series* The People's Century. *His recording credits include two albums:* Lost Songs of Palestine *and* Folk Songs and Dance Music from Turkey and the Arab World.

Recommended Reading

NON-FICTION:

Al-Rasheed, Madawi. *A History of Saudi Arabia*. Cambridge, UK;
  New York: Cambridge University Press, 2002.

Anderson, Jon Lee. *The Fall of Baghdad*. New York: Penguin Press, 2004.

Ashman, Anastasia M. and Jennifer Eaton Gökmen. *Tales from the
  Expat Harem: Foreign Women in Modern Turkey*. Emeryville, CA: Seal
  Press, 2006.

Baer, Robert. *See No Evil: The True Story of a Ground Soldier in the
  CIA's War on Terrorism*. New York: Crown Publishers, 2002.

Bradley, John R. *Saudi Arabia Exposed: Inside a Kingdom in Crisis*.
  New York: Palgrave Macmillan, 2005.

Bryant, Rebecca. *Imagining the Modern: The Cultures of Nationalism in
  Cyprus*. London: I.B. Tauris, 2004.

Campbell, Deborah. *This Heated Place: Encounters in the Promised
  Land*. Vancouver/Toronto: Douglas & McIntyre, 2002.

Carter, Jimmy. *Peace Not Apartheid*. New York: Simon & Schuster, 2006.

Dalrymple, William. *From the Holy Mountain: A Journey in the Shadow
  of Byzantium*. London: HarperCollins, 1997.

Davidson, Christopher M. *The United Arab Emirates: A Study in
  Survival*. Boulder, CO: Lynne Rienner Publishers, 2005.

Davis, Scott C. *The Road from Damascus: A Journey through Syria*.
  Seattle, WA: Cune Press, 2001.

De Bellaigue, Christopher. *In the Rose Garden of the Martyrs: A
  Memoir of Iran*. London: HarperCollins, 2004.

Dodge, Toby. *Inventing Iraq: The Failure of Nation Building and a
  History Denied*. New York; Chichester [England]: Columbia
  University Press, 2003.

Durrell, Lawrence. *Bitter Lemons*. (Cyprus memoir). New York:
  Dutton, 1957.

Ebadi, Shirin with Azadeh Moaveni. *Iran Awakening: A Memoir of Revolution and Hope*. New York: Random House, 2006.

Eck, Jeanne. *I Am Happier To Know You*. (Egypt memoir). Wheeling, WV: Angel Wings Publishing Partners, 2005.

Esposito, John L. *The Oxford Dictionary of Islam*. Oxford; New York: Oxford University Press, 2003.

Esposito, John L. *The Oxford History of Islam*. Oxford; New York: Oxford University Press, 1999.

Feiler, Bruce. *Walking the Bible: A Journey by Land Through the Five Books of Moses*. New York: William Morrow, 2001.

Fernea, Elizabeth Warnock. *In Search of Islamic Feminism: One Woman's Global Journey*. New York; London: Doubleday, 1998.

Fisk, Robert. *Pity the Nation: The Abduction of Lebanon*. New York: Thunder's Mouth Press/Nation Books, 2002.

Friedman, Thomas. *From Beirut to Jerusalem*. New York: Farrar, Straus and Giroux, 1989.

Halasa, Malu and Roseanne Saad Khalaf. *Transit Beirut: New Writing and Images*. London: Saqi Books, 2004.

Halliday, Fred. *100 Myths about the Middle East*. London: Saqi Books, 2005.

Hass, Amira. *Drinking the Sea at Gaza: Days and Nights in a Land Under Siege*. New York: Metropolitan Books/Henry Holt, 1999.

Hass, Amira. *Reporting from Ramallah: An Israeli Journalist in an Occupied Land*. Cambridge, MA; London: Semiotext(e), 2003.

Keddie, Nikki R. *Modern Iran: Roots and Results of Revolution*. New Haven, London: Yale University Press, 2003.

Kelsey, Tim. *Dervish: The Invention of Modern Turkey*. London: Hamish Hamilton, 1996.

Kinzer, Stephen. *All the Shah's Men: An American Coup and the Roots of Middle East Terror*. Hoboken, NJ: John Wiley and Sons, 2003.

Kinzer, Stephen. *Crescent and Star: Turkey Between Two Worlds*. New York: Farrar, Strauss and Giroux, 2001.

Leverett, Flynt. *Inheriting Syria: Bashar's Trial by Fire*. Washington, D.C.: The Brookings Institution, 2005.

Lewis, Reina. *Rethinking Orientalism: Women, Travel, and the Ottoman Harem*. New Brunswick, NJ: Rutgers University Press, 2004.

Maalouf, Amin. *The Crusades Through Arab Eyes*. New York: Schocken Books, 1984.

Mackintosh-Smith, Tim. *Yemen: An Unknown Arabia*. Woodstock, NY: Overlook Press, 2000.

Mamdani, Mahmood. *Good Muslim, Bad Muslim: America, the Cold War, and the Roots of Terror.* New York: Pantheon Books, 2004.

Mango, Andrew. *Atatürk: The Biography of the Founder of Modern Turkey.* Woodstock, NY: Overlook Press, 2002.

Moaveni, Azadeh. *Lipstick Jihad: A Memoir of Growing Up Iranian in America and American in Iran.* New York: Public Affairs, 2005.

Molavi, Afshin. *The Soul of Iran: A Nation's Journey to Freedom.* New York: W.W. Norton, 2002.

Navaro-Yashin, Yael. *Faces of the State: Secularism and Public Life in Turkey.* Princeton, NJ: Princeton University Press, 2002.

Owtram, Francis. *A Modern History of Oman: Formation of the State Since 1920.* London; New York: I.B. Tauris, 2004.

Packer, George. *The Assassins' Gate: America in Iraq.* New York: Farrar, Straus and Giroux, 2005.

Papadakis, Yiannis. *Echoes from the Dead Zone: Across the Cyprus Divide.* London; New York: I.B. Tauris, 2005.

Pappé, Ilan. *A History of Modern Palestine: One Land, Two Peoples.* Cambridge, UK; New York: Cambridge University Press, 2004.

Robins, Philip. *A History of Jordan.* Cambridge, UK; New York: Cambridge University Press, 2004.

Rodenbeck, Max. *Cairo: The City Victorious.* Cairo: The American University in Cairo Press, 1998.

Rodinson, Maxime. *Muhammad.* New York: Pantheon Books, 1971.

Ryan, Curtis R. *Jordan in Transition: From Hussein to Abdullah.* Boulder, CO; London: Lynne Rienner Publishers, 2002.

Said, Edward. *Orientalism.* New York: Pantheon Books, 1978.

Said, Edward. *Covering Islam: How the Media and the Experts Determine How We See the Rest of the World.* New York: Pantheon Books, 1981.

Salibi, Kamal S. *A House of Many Mansions: The History of Lebanon Reconsidered.* London: I.B. Tauris, 1988.

Saunders, David. *Dubai: The Arabian Dream.* London: I.B. Tauris, 2005.

Seal, Jeremy. *A Fez of the Heart: Travels around Turkey in Search of a Hat.* London: Picador, 1995.

Seale, Patrick. *Asad of Syria: The Struggle for the Middle East.* London: I.B. Tauris, 1988.

Segev, Tom. *One Palestine, Complete: Jews and Arabs Under the British Mandate.* New York: Henry Holt and Co., 1999.

Shadid, Anthony. *Night Draws Near: Iraq's People in the Shadow of America's War.* New York: Henry Holt and Co., 2005.

Shlaim, Avi. *The Iron Wall: Israel and the Arab World.* New York: W.W. Norton, 2000.

Stark, Freya. *Alexander's Path: From Caria to Cilicia.* New York: Harcourt Brace, 1958.

Stark, Freya. *The Southern Gates of Arabia: A Journey in the Hadhramaut.* New York: Dutton & Co., 1936.

Stark, Freya. *The Valleys of the Assassins and Other Persian Travels.* New York: Dutton & Co., 1934.

Tolan, Sandy. *The Lemon Tree: An Arab, a Jew and the Heart of the Middle East.* New York: Bloomsbury Publishing, 2006.

Tripp, Charles. *A History of Iraq.* Cambridge; New York: Cambridge University Press, 2002.

Villers, Jr., James. (ed). *Travelers' Tales Turkey: True Stories.* San Francisco: Travelers' Tales, 2002.

Watt, W. Montgomery. *Muhammad: Prophet and Statesman.* Oxford: Oxford University Press, 1961.

Wearing, Alison. *Honeymoon in Purdah: An Iranian Journey.* New York: Picador, 2000.

Wedeen, Lisa. *Ambiguities of Domination: Politics, Rhetoric, and Symbols in Contemporary Syria.* Chicago, IL: University of Chicago Press, 1999.

Weiland, Carsten. *Syria—Ballots or Bullets? Democracy, Islamism, and Secularism in the Levant.* Seattle, WA: Cune Press, 2005.

White, Jenny B. *Islamist Mobilization in Turkey: A Study in Vernacular Politics.* Seattle, WA: University of Washington Press, 2002.

Yelda, Rami. *A Persian Odyssey: Iran Revisited.* New York: A. Pankovich Publishers, 2005.

Zanganeh, Lila Azam. *My Sister, Guard Your Veil; My Brother, Guard Your Eyes: Uncensored Iranian Voices.* Boston: Beacon Press, 2006.

Zurcher, Erik J. *Turkey: A Modern History.* London: I.B. Tauris, 2004.

FICTION:

Barghouti, Mourid. *I Saw Ramallah.* Translated by Ahdaf Soueif. New York: Anchor Books, 2003.

Daneshvar, Simin. *Daneshvar's Playhouse: A Collection of Stories.*
  Translated by Maryam Mafi. Washington, D.C.: Mage Publishers, 1989.

Hedayat, Sadeq. *The Myth of Creation: A Puppet Show in Three Acts.*
  Translated by M.R. Ghanoonparvar. Costa Mesa, CA: Mazda
  Publishers, 1998.

Kanafani, Ghassan. *Men in the Sun and Other Palestinian Stories.*
  Translated by Hilary Kilpatrick. Washington, D.C.: Three
  Continents Press, 1978.

Kemal, Yashar. *Memed, My Hawk.* Translated by Edouard Roditi.
  London: Collins & Harvill, 1961.

Kemal, Yashar. *The Wind from the Plain.* Translated by Thilda Kemal.
  New York: Dodd, Mead & Company, 1960.

Khoury, Elias. *Gate of the Sun.* Translated by Humphrey Davies.
  Brooklyn, NY: Archipelago Books, 2005.

Mahfouz, Naguib. *Midaq Alley.* Translated by Trevor Le Gassick.
  Cairo: The American University in Cairo Press, 2002.

Mahfouz, Naguib. *The Cairo Trilogy: Palace Walk, Palace of Desire,
  Sugar Street.* New York: Everyman's Library, 2001.

Oz, Amos. *A Tale Of Love & Darkness.* Translated by Nicholas de
  Langes. Orlando, FL: Harcourt, 2005.

Pamuk, Orhan. *Snow.* Translated by Maureen Freely. New York:
  Alfred A. Knopf, 2004.

Pamuk, Orhan. *The Black Book.* Translated by Güneli Gün. New
  York: Farrar, Straus and Giroux, 1994.

Shafak, Elif. *The Bastard of Istanbul.* New York: Viking/Penguin, 2007.

Wiesel, Elie. *The Night Trilogy: Night, Dawn, The Accident.* New York:
  Hill and Wang, 1987.

POETRY:

Amichai, Yehuda. *The Selected Poetry of Yehuda Amichai.* Translated by
  Chana Bloch and Stephen Mitchell. Berkeley, CA.: University of
  California Press, 1996.

Darwish, Mahmoud. *Unfortunately, It Was Paradise: Selected Poems.*
  Translated by Munir Akash and Carolyn Forché, with Sinan
  Antoon and Amira El-Zein. Berkeley, CA; London: University of
  California Press, 2003.

Darwish, Mahmoud. *Why Did You Leave the Horse Alone?* Translated by Jeffrey Sacks. Brooklyn, NY: Archipelago Books; St. Paul, MN: Distributed by Consortium Book Sales and Distribution, 2006.

Gibran, Kahlil. *The Prophet*. Originally published: New York: Knopf, 1923.

Hafiz. *The Gift : Poems by the Great Sufi Master*. Translated by Daniel Ladinsky. New York; London: Penguin/Arkana, 1999.

Hikmet, Nazim. *Human Landscapes from My Country: An Epic Novel in Verse*. Translated by Randy Blasing and Mutlu Konuk Blasing. New York: Persea, 2002.

Rumi. *Rumi: In the Arms of the Beloved*. Translated by Jonathan Star. New York: Jeremy P. Tarcher/Putnam, 1997.

WEB SITES:

lonelyplanet.com

Middle East Report. The Middle East Research and Information Project. http://www.merip.org.

U.S. Department of State Bureau of Consular Affairs. Consular Information Sheets.
  http://travel.state.gov/travel/cis_pa_tw/cis/cis_1765.html.

travelerstales.com

FILMS:

Battle of Algiers. Director: Gillo Pontecorvo. 1966.

Being Osama. Directors: Mahmoud Kaabour, Tim Schwab. 2004.

Control Room. Director: Jehane Noujaim. 2004.

The Dupes. Director: Tawfik Saleh. 1972.

Distant. Director: Nuri Bilgi Ceylan. 2002.

Eflkiya. Director: Yavuz Tuğul. 1996.

Fifth Reaction. Director: Tahmineh Milani. 2003.

Good Kurds, Bad Kurds: No Friends But the Mountains. Director: Kevin McKiernan. 2000.

Lawrence of Arabia. Director: David Lean. 1962.

My Father and My Son. Director: Çağan Irmak. 2005.

Paradise Now. Director: Hany Abu-Assad. 2005.

Private. Director: Saverio Costanzo. 2004.

Promises. Directors: Carlos Bolado, B.Z. Goldberg. 2001.

Rana's Wedding. Director: Hany Abu-Assad. 2002.
Return to the Land of Wonders. Director: Maysoon Pachachi. 2004.
Steam: The Turkish Bath. Director: Ferhan Özpetek. 1997.
Syrian Bride, The. Director: Eran Riklis. 2005.
Ushpizin. Director: Giddi Dar. 2004.
West Beirut. Director: Ziad Doueiri. VHS. 2001.

Index

Acknowledgments

In the process of editing this collection, we have been fortunate to receive the kind of gracious support that would rival that extended by any Middle Eastern host. We would like to thank fellow traveler, writer, and editor Tom Miller, whose encouragement and faith helped our idea become a reality. Individuals in the Department of Near Eastern Studies, the Center for Middle Eastern Studies, and the Department of Journalism at the University of Arizona lent us guidance and resources during the initial stages of our project. The team at Travelers' Tales—James, Larry, Susan, Christy, and Sean—from the outset provided enthusiasm and counsel. Their confidence enabled us to develop the project in a way that allowed us to achieve our vision, and for that we are most grateful.

About the Editors

A Palestinian-American born in Kuwait and raised in the San Francisco Bay Area, Nesreen Khashan has for the past decade been a frequent traveler to the Middle East. Whether to the Palestinian territories and Israel, Lebanon, Syria, Jordan, Egypt or Morocco, each of her trips has been marked with special purpose and has carried with it one or more of her passions. She has ventured to the region as spiritual pilgrim, journalist, scholar, Arabic student, and serendipitous traveler. Currently a curriculum writer in Washington, D.C., Nesreen also teaches classes in the Department of Global Studies at Mission Community College near San Jose, CA. She holds a Master's degree in Near Eastern Studies from The University of Arizona and is proficient in Modern Standard Arabic and the Egyptian and Levantine dialects. Earlier in her career, she worked as a newspaper writer for six years, reporting for *The Salt Lake Tribune,* the *South-Florida Sun-Sentinel, The Boston Globe*, and *The Daily Star* of Lebanon, among others.

Jim Bowman has developed his understanding of the Middle East through years of living in Turkey, traveling through the region, and now studying about the Middle East from afar. He is currently at work on a doctoral dissertation about Turkey and travel writing. Though he would like to spend more time in the Middle East, he settles for annual returns to the region in order to lead cultural tours of Turkey and Cyprus, brush up on his ever-rusting Turkish, and visit old friends and beloved locales. His recent scholarly publications relating to the Middle East include essays about political memory in Cyprus and symbolic issues in the history of hookah smoking in Turkey. In addition to his interest in travel writing, he has also edited textbooks for composition students at the University of Arizona. He teaches and studies in the departments of English and Near Eastern Studies at the University of Arizona.